Left in the Pa

Left in the Past

Radicalism and the Politics of
Nostalgia

by
Alastair Bonnett

continuum

NEW YORK • LONDON

2010

The Continuum International Publishing Group
80 Maiden Lane, New York, NY 10038
The Tower Building, 11 York Road, London SE1 7NX

www.continuumbooks.com

Copyright © 2010 by Alastair Bonnett

ISBN: 978-0-8264-3006-9 (Hardback)
       978-0-8264-3007-6 (Paperback)

Library of Congress Cataloging-in-Publication Data
Bonnett, Alastair, 1964–
Left in the past : radicalism and the politics of nostalgia / by Alastair Bonnett.
  p. cm.
 Includes bibliographical references and index.
 ISBN-13: 978-0-8264-3006-9 (hardcover : alk. paper)
 ISBN-10: 0-8264-3006-6 (hardcover : alk. paper)
 ISBN-13: 978-0-8264-3007-6 (pbk. : alk. paper)
 ISBN-10: 0-8264-3007-4 (pbk. : alk. paper) 1. Nostalgia–Political aspects. 2. Radicalism–Social aspects. 3. Socialism–Social aspects. I. Title.
 BF575.N6B66 2010
 320.53–dc22

                                                                    2009051360

Typeset by Newgen Imaging Systems Pvt Ltd, Chennai, India
Printed in the United States of America

For Aphra

Contents

Acknowledgements

Many thanks to Marie-Claire Antoine at Continuum for her patience and support.

Chapter Five is a revised and adapted version of 'The nostalgias of situationist subversion', *Theory, Culture and Society*, 2006, 23(5), 23–48.

Chapter Six is a revised version and adapted version of 'The dilemmas of radical nostalgia in British pyschogeography', *Theory, Culture and Society*, 2009, 26(1), 47–72.

Introduction

This book argues that nostalgia has been an important but rarely acknowledged aspect of the radical imagination. Throughout the last century nostalgia was cast as the antithesis of radicalism. Emotions of yearning and loss were portrayed as embarrassing defects on the bright body of a movement associated with the celebration of the new and the youthful. Today this celebration is as lively as ever. But its link to the left is no longer clear. The left-radical project is in doubt, its meaning cloudy, its popular constituency scattered. Compared to 40 years ago, the status and influence of the left is diminished beyond recognition. It is not surprising, then, that many hark back to more reassuring times. There is a poignant but steadfast honesty in Svetlana Boym's summary of our condition:

> Survivors of the twentieth century, we are all nostalgic for a time when we were not nostalgic. But there seems no way back.[1]

In a post-communist era the pursuit of radicalism takes place in an atmosphere of freedom and doubt. It is a moment of adventure but also of bewilderment. It is also a moment of opportunity. For, in a period marked by the collapse of political certainties, awkward issues that were once side-lined may be approached with less trepidation. Throughout these pages I will be making the case that radicalism (a term identified throughout this book with the political left) emerged in and against modernity. This idea suggests another: that the contempt so often directed by radicals in the twentieth century towards nostalgia concealed a difficult and ambiguous relationship with the past.

I should declare straightaway that readers looking for an account of self-declared conservative socialists, or Tory radicals, will be disappointed. Such people do exist and their history deserves to be written but this is not it.[2] For the most part this book concerns itself with reading nostalgia against the grain of radical history. Thus it looks, less at people who think of themselves as yearning for the past, and more at those who think of themselves as fiercely forward-looking. It is the nostalgia that lies within and against the proponents of the modern that interests me. Even when I turn, in Chapter Two, to some of the usual suspects in any line-up of radical nostalgics – such as William Morris – my concern is with the difficulties and dilemmas of maintaining an increasingly *counter-orthodox* stance. The focus of this book is further refined by the fact that I approach these issues by exploring three particular arenas of radical left activity, namely early English socialism, anti-colonialism and post-colonialism and situationism and its aftermath. As this list suggests, it is upon the more radical voices of the left that I will concentrate. I make no claim to provide a representative survey of left opinion. Indeed, in its final chapters, *Left in the Past* explores ever wilder reaches of the avant-garde. In doing so my intention is to track down the awkward presence of nostalgia into the furthest redoubts of those who declare themselves 'partisans of forgetting'.[3]

This book is premised on the idea that we may learn more about the connections between nostalgia and radicalism from *difficult* encounters and *repressed* allegiances than we will do from less fraught situations. To identify and acknowledge such yearnings is revealing but also unsettling. It is no surprise that there are still many on the left who wish to portray themselves in more conventional terms, as part of a bold and marvellous project of tomorrow. In some quarters the recent crises of international capitalism have confirmed this traditional image. Even before the financial meltdown of 2008–2009, the election of a number of socialist governments in Latin America, as well as the emergence of transnational social movements, was being interpreted by some eager commentators as indicating *The Rise of the Global Left* (to cite one book title from 2006).[4] Although, after more than a century of similarly ringing declarations, this title has an anachronistic quality, the *desire* to narrate our times as an era of radical revolution, of the rising multitude, should not be underestimated. It also implies that the moment when the relationship between radicalism and nostalgia can be discussed in the kind of open-ended way I hope to achieve in this book may not last. To acknowledge ambiguity – the often clumsy juggling of attachments to the past and hopes for the future – is a far less inviting prospect than the heroic, transformational rhetoric that is the stuff of inspiring politics. It promises no cathartic resolution of our present woes and no warm glow of superiority over conservative enemies. Instead a compromised landscape comes into view; a terrain in which what is denied and suppressed is often as important as what is declared.

We should not underestimate how hard it is to rethink a topic that has, for so long, as Christopher Lasch notes, been a 'political offence of the first order'.[5] Any attempt to take nostalgia seriously, to see it as unavoidable, perhaps even an occasionally creative force, is likely to make us appear discontent with modernity. It rips us from some basic assumptions, not just about progress and change, but what it is to be a happy, optimistic and 'well-balanced' citizen.[6] Over the past ten years or so many writers have responded to the challenge of nostalgia. Yet for the most part they have maintained an attitude of deep suspicion. The idea that 'nostalgia can actually be radically critical' has been offered as a daring suggestion, to be hedged in with thickets of provisos.[7] The effort to recuperate selected and sanctioned aspects of nostalgia for radicalism, to make it safe by formulating hierarchies of acceptable forms (discussed in Chapter One), is testament, not just to the new interest the topic is provoking, but also to a continued nervousness in its presence.

Such hesitancy is understandable, for nostalgia is still routinely reviled as a lie, as the essence of reaction. For many years it has performed the function of a whipping post. Nostalgia brings people together in the act of enjoyably lashing out at something that everyone agrees is both pitiful and reprehensible. As an emotion it is accused of lacking accuracy. It is, says Peter Logan, 'a problem of memory'.[8] While other feelings are indulged, in all their complicated, sentimental, splendour, nostalgia is routinely taunted as disappointedly subjective. Representations of the politics of nostalgia swarm with expressions of disapproval. Susan Bennett is resolute that '*in all its manifestations* nostalgia is, in its praxis, conservative'.[9] In 1962 Eric Hobsbawm, after reminding us that 'human history was an ascent, rather than a decline or an undulating movement about a level trend', explained that,

> Compared to . . . relatively coherent ideologies of progress, those of resistance to progress hardly deserve the name of systems of thought. They were rather attitudes lacking a common intellectual method, and relying on the acuteness of their insights into the weaknesses of bourgeois society and the unshakeable conviction that there was more in life than liberalism allowed for. Consequently they require relatively little attention.[10]

Offering a similarly Olympian insight, Richard Sennett points out that,

> regret is a dangerous sentiment. Whilst it produces empathy for the past, and so a certain insight, regret induces resignation about the present, and so a certain acceptance of its evils.[11]

Hobsbawm and Sennett's interpretations of the political function of, respectively, 'resistance to progress' and 'regret' bare little scrutiny. They do not offer analysis but gestures of disdain; gestures that speak to and rely on a readership who are already firmly convinced that nostalgia is conservative and, hence, suspect.

Until recently one could say almost anything about nostalgia, as long as it was damning, and few would object. Sean Scanlan argues that nostalgia has long been imparted with the character of 'a sort of political crime causing well-intended leftists of several varieties to flee even the appearance of any connection'.[12] Another cultural theorist intrigued by this spectacle, Marcos Natali, suggests that it may, in part, be rooted in the way our ideas of left and right are mapped onto a language of past and future.

> The very word traditionally used to refer to the left in English and other European languages – variations of 'progressive' – emphasises commitment to the future, while the words that describe the left's adversaries – 'conservative' and 'reactionary' suggests devotion to the past.[13]

However, opposition to nostalgia is not peculiar of the left. Modern market driven societies surround us with messages that extol the future and warn of the dangers of stasis, the failure to change. From boardrooms to classrooms the 'miasma of nostalgia' is pitted against 'the fierce spirit of renewal'.[14] Despite the fact that, today, modernity is itself an object of nostalgia and the great utopian projects of the twentieth century have lost their bearings and most of their defenders (with the notable exception of capitalism), we remain addicted to the grand rhetoric of dismissing the past. It is a narrative that shapes and sorts good and bad political messages. But it is also a personal message. It helps us understand that when we are young we are 'the future', society's most precious resource. We also know that, as we age, our potential, our claim on the future and, therefore, our social value decreases. Perhaps the most effective dismissal of nostalgia is the simple claim that it is 'old people's talk'.

Cast in this way it is tempting to defend nostalgia; to tip into a perverse celebration of this politically mobile emotion. However, I shall try to keep my distance from this false trail. Nostalgia is too ubiquitous and too diverse to need or warrant it. This circumspect view will be extended to those recent re-evaluations of nostalgia that suggest that its critical and reflexive forms can be sifted out and welcomed as progressive. My emphasis is not on a prescriptive guide to nostalgia but on its constitutive and inescapable nature. I offer no check list of how to do nostalgia, or how to get it right. My aim is broader: to show that within the modern, ostensibly anti-nostalgic, left there exists a profound sense of loss. I will also show that such yearnings are not a cancerous or alien intrusion but integral to the radical imagination.

Anti-nostalgia is common place. Yet so, of course, is nostalgia. Indeed much of the recent debate the topic has inspired is premised on the assumption that there is more of it around than there used to be. Observing the prominence of fond yearnings in the arts, advertising and entertainment industries, Yiannis Gabriel finds that 'whole sectors of the economy are fuelled by nostalgia'.[15] The institutionalization of memory in heritage museums and urban gentrification programmes is a largely late twentieth-century phenomenon. In 2005 Glazer identified what he called a 'global epidemic of nostalgia'.[16] In 1989 Shaw and Chase noted that nostalgia had 'recently become . . . pervasive'.[17] A decade earlier Fred Davis observed that nostalgia is 'much in vogue these days'.[18] In fact, comparable remarks depicting the ubiquity of yearnings for the past can be found throughout the last century and even earlier. In 1831

John Stuart Mill challenged those who responded to the new 'spirit of the age' by carrying 'their eyes in the back of their heads'.[19] This litany of longing suggests not simply the prevalence of nostalgia but also that the identity and function of the modern social analyst is bound up with her or his ability to challenge this particular social 'problem'. Kimberly Smith goes so far as to argue that the idea of nostalgia is a creation of, and designed to serve, the progressive critic. Thus she identifies it as 'an addendum to progressive ideology', that both 'explains progressives' failure to persuade their opponents' and 'helps to silence the victims of modernisation'.[20]

However, it is also clear that, over the past 20 years or so, themes of yearning, loss and memory have become more important in the humanities and, to a lesser extent, the social sciences. The terrain of nostalgia is now well travelled by scholars. And while the presence of nostalgia within the left remains relatively unexplored, the role of romanticism within the radical imagination has provoked some important interventions. The genesis of *Left in the Past* may, in part, be found in the inspiration provided by such studies. Like many others, I have been impressed by Robert Sayre and Michael Löwy's ability to shed new light on the power and breadth of the revolutionary Romantic tradition.[21] Sayre and Löwy make an explicit connection to nostalgia, noting that 'it is precisely the *nostalgia* for what has been lost that is at the centre of the Romantic anti-capitalist tradition'.[22] They help secure this link by citing Arnold Hauser's opinion that a 'feeling of homelessness and loneliness became the fundamental experience' of the Romantics.[23] Many of Sayre and Löwy's depictions of the ambivalent role of romanticism could be applied to nostalgia. Romanticism, they argue has a,

> fabulously contradictory character . . . simultaneously (or alternately) revolutionary and counterrevolutionary, individualistic and communtarian, cosmopolitan and nationalistic, realist and fantastic, retrograde and utopian, rebellious and melancholic, democratic and aristocratic, activist and contemplative, republican and monarchist, red and white, mystical and sensual.[24]

Sayre and Löwy go on to defend and elaborate the utility of romanticism, probing the question of why we should 'revitalise the Romantic tradition for the left'.[25] However, it is with this question that a number of differences with nostalgia come into view: for nostalgia is not a distinct tradition that can be delimited and defended. It does not deserve or need *revitalization* but *acknowledgement*. These points of difference suggest a larger argument that identifies romanticism as a particular cultural articulation that overlaps with the more expansive and diffuse terrain of nostalgia (although it may also exceed and renounce it). Thus nostalgia appears as both more pervasive and less historically distinct than romanticism. It is conventional to assign romanticism to specific historical periods, the early nineteenth century, for example, or the 1960s. Nostalgia cannot be pinned down so easily. Nor does it have the subversive glamour of romanticism. Sayre and Löwy's depiction of romanticism as 'fabulously contradictory' does not sound quite right for nostalgia. This is not because nostalgia is not contradictory but because it is harder to imagine it as fabulous. Nostalgia is often a prosaic and slightly embarrassed sentiment. Its contradictions are more likely to appear gauche than sublime. And yet it is precisely the unloved quality of nostalgia that makes it so fascinating. It suggests a kind of resilience against the odds: an awkwardness and yearning for attachment that makes it deeply flawed, unlovable but human.

The Changing Meaning of Nostalgia

Nostalgia is a yearning for the past, a sense of loss in the face of change. This definition of the term is not much more than a century old but it is one that I will be applying much further back in time. My excuse for this anachronistic practice is that it helps more than it hinders; it allows us to explore and identify diverse attachments to the past.

The term 'nostalgia' was coined in 1688 by Johannes Hofer by combining the Greek *nostos* (home) and *algos* (pain).[26] It referred to what was considered to be a medical disorder, a disabling longing for home.[27] The course of the disease was described by Philippe Pinel, in 1761, as commencing with 'a sad, melancholy appearance, a bemused look . . . an indifference toward everything' and proceeding to 'the near impossibility of getting out of bed, an obstinate silence, the rejection of food and drink; emaciation, marasmus and death'.[28] The earliest English use of the term is from 1770 and derives from Joseph Banks, botanist on James Cook's *Endeavour*. 'The greatest part' of the crew, Banks wrote in his diary, are 'now pretty far gone in the longing for home which the Physicians have gone so far as to esteem a disease under the name of Nostalgia'.[29]

In the sense that these early associations tie nostalgia to the experience of mobility and isolation they also tie it to the experience of modernity. However, the pathological paradigm was giving way, by the end of the nineteenth century, to a broader conception of nostalgia's power. It became connected to the sentimentalization of the past, to common place feelings of loss, yearning and attachment.[30] In the first volume of *Remembrance of Thing's Past*, published in 1913, Marcel Proust is able to depict a form of nostalgia with which we remain even more familiar today. When his grandmother gives him 'the pastoral novels of George Sand' for his birthday, he describes them as,

> regular lumber-rooms of antique furniture, full of expressions that have fallen out of use and returned as imagery, such as one finds now only in country dialects. And my grandmother had bought them in preference to other books, just as she would have preferred to take a house that had a gothic dovecote, or some other such piece of antiquity as would have a pleasant effect on the mind, filling it with a nostalgic longing for impossible journeys through the realms of time.[31]

Yet nostalgia, having escaped from its medical origins, began to lead a double life. In the realm of cultural practice, of personal pleasures, of our flight to the comforts of home or holiday, it is ubiquitous and explicit. However, as we have already seen, within the realm of political rhetoric, of intellectual activity, of public life, nostalgia is routinely vilified. Indeed a willingness to scorn it remains a ready symbol of progressive inclinations and hard-headed vigour. This distinction also suggests that Fred Davis's insistence in *Yearning for Yesterday* (a book that offered one of the first appraisals of the sociology of nostalgia), that the topic must be defined as deriving 'from a personally experienced past', is too restrictive.[32] Davis admits that,

> in light of the word's great vogue in recent years, it is conceivable that in time [nostalgia will] acquire connotations that extend its meaning to *any* sort of positive feeling toward *anything* past, no matter how remote or historical.[33]

In fact, as Proust's use of the term shows, the yearning associated with nostalgia has been mapped widely for many years, taking in collective memories and a shared sense of social dislocation. Indeed, in 1957, the *Dictionary of Contemporary American Usage* spelled out the fact that the 'vogue word' nostalgia 'has come to mean any vague yearning, especially for the past'.[34] However, Davis's attempt to limit the application of the term does usefully highlight how nostalgia nearly always involves a claim to *attachment*. Such a claim implies that a sense of loss is more likely to concern the more recent and proximate past. Though nostalgia for the 'glory that was Rome', or the freedom of hunter gatherers, is common enough to show that distance can itself spur a kind of reverential regard, attachments are more readily and easily formed and maintained with more immediate times and places. Davis's approach is helpful in another way, for it reinforces the suggestion that, even though it is often publicly insulted, nostalgia is a ubiquitous facet of *personal* life. For Raymond Williams nostalgia 'is universal and persistent; only other men's nostalgias offend'.[35] There is a wry charm to William's observation but it misses and, hence, brings into relief, an important point. For while in the public realm nostalgia is rebuked, within the personal realm it tends to be tacitly indulged. We do not expect the treasured objects, the valued images, that we use to personalize our homes and 'work stations' to be sneered at. Indeed, modern etiquette demands that these tokens of attachment are beyond criticism. For, however sentimental they may appear to others, they speak not only of a shared humanity but also of a shared vulnerability, an emotional range that includes love, loss and loyalty. It is, conversely, the spaces that fail to convey nostalgia that 'offend': the blank wall, the empty desk, the absence of signs of depth and connection.

The disjunction between these two worlds of nostalgia – the public and the private – can sometime catch us out. A little while ago I bumped into an academic colleague in one of those publicly owned stately homes and gardens that draw in the weekend crowds across England. Our awkwardness was palpable and mutual. I think we both would have liked to find a loophole; to make a few disparaging remarks about the tweeness and the suspect nationalism of it all. Perhaps we could pretend we had been dragged along. Just observing the crowds. But some lies are too obvious to appear polite. So then what? Could we admit to have travelled miles from the brutal and noisy city to enjoy walking round the beautiful old gardens of a long departed gentry? Not that either. The shame would be too much. We were left with a mutually indulgent set of nods and smirks, registering not simply the humour that we could find in the situation but the fact, thankfully, that *off duty*, our nostalgia was forgivable.

What is Radicalism?

One of the consequences and indications of the decline of the left and the emergence of a post-socialist era is the fact that the meaning of radicalism has entered a period of considerable mobility. To many contemporary ears the word is more likely to evoke fundamentalist Islam or a new business plan as to suggest the left. As this implies, my use of the term as synonymous with those traditions of anti-capitalist egalitarianism, social emancipation and agitation which constitute the left, is in danger of appearing old-fashioned. It is, moreover, a usage that rolls together radicalism with socialism, communism and anarchism, in a way that obscures the fact that the earliest incarnations of these movements often sought to extricate themselves from radicalism. In the mid-late-nineteenth century, radicalism was often understood as a more combative form of liberalism. It was associated with a cross-class, populist and democratic agenda. British socialists of the period were often fierce critics of radicalism.[36] Adding further to the complex history of the term, in the late twentieth century it was reclaimed by some sections of the left as a marker of distinctly bold forms of political commitment. Hence the distinction between radical and socialist feminists was premised on the idea that the former offered a separatist politics of sexual difference while the latter viewed feminism as one part of a wider anti-capitalist struggle. 'Radicalism' came to evoke a range of anti-orthodox political forms, including anti-racism, queer politics and environmentalism, that were aligned to but also often critical of the 'traditional' left.

There are a lot of different claims upon the term 'radical'. Many of the objections that could be made to the employment of the term as a portmanteau for the left have merit. But the diversity of these claims also suggests that this is a word regularly deployed rather than owned by any one tradition. Moreover, while the link to the left is far weaker than it was, it retains enough purchase to be both defensible and comprehensible. Radicalism evokes a wider political landscape than the left and it is likely to outlast it. But the connections between the left and radicalism are so deep and run so powerfully through nearly all the material that I will be introducing over the next six chapters that I can claim, at least, a good excuse for collapsing the two.

The Dilemmas of Radical Nostalgia

Any study of the relationship between nostalgia and radicalism is a study of dilemmas. These dilemmas take different forms and each opens up questions that inform different chapters in this book. The paradox that is most fundamental to my enquires may be stated as follows: nostalgia is integral to radicalism; yet, radicalism has been offered as a narrative of anti-nostalgia. If nostalgia is not merely an error or lie perpetrated by reactionaries but an inherent aspect of modernity then the possibility of its complete suppression appears small. The fact that nostalgia is reviled does not necessarily mean that it has been banished. Instead we find it sustained in unrecognized and unidentified forms. It is a nostalgia that cannot be named, yet it fulfils an important role, guiding us back to authenticity, to solidarity, to the culture of the people.

The other dilemmas identified below suggest other areas where nostalgia appears as an uncomfortable moment or rupture within the left, an unacknowledged presence that produces anxiety but also sustains and coheres. A temptation when approaching this material is to organize it in terms of conflicting radical traditions. Sometimes these distinctions might be ideological (e.g. anarchists versus Marxists), sometimes they might be social (e.g. the middle class versus the working class). Yet the utility of separating out such constituencies is easily overestimated. They produce a misleadingly neat sense of discrete positions in a field characterized by precisely the opposite. In fact, the paradoxes identified below exist within and against a broad range of radicalisms. They are sites of dilemma found across the left.

Roots: Pulling Them Up or Letting Them Grow?

The word 'radical' derives from the Latin for root (*radix*). Used as a political term, radicalism refers to the desire to grasp and pull up the roots of an existing political arrangement, usually with the hope that an equally deeply planted but very different alternative can be nurtured in its place.

Yet radicalism has another, very different, relationship to roots. In this version radicalism grows from roots: it emerges from authentic social experience; it is the voice from below, the cry of the people against an uprooted elite. This narrative identifies the enemies of radicalism with those who seek to dig away at memory, to grub up organic identities and reduce communities to malleable individuals without ties of loyalty or attachment.

The desire to preserve or change the landscape provides a prominent example of the interplay and clash of these different ideals. The radical eye is often represented as looking beyond 'backward villages' and 'dirty old towns' to the gleaming modern vistas of tomorrow. Yet it is within the old places, the real places, the streets and the living communities, that narratives of popular identity, as well as class and community solidarity, are found and admired. This potentially fraught combination of aspirations creates ample opportunity for paradoxical responses: for *regret* that it is *necessary* to replace living communities with soulless housing blocks; for the uncertain hope that the destruction of so much will prove, in the end, to have been worth the pain.

This unstable terrain maps onto the uncertain status and role of *the people* in radicalism. Radicalism is often presented as a popular tradition; indeed as inherently and by definition the politics of the people. It is an association that suggests that the memories and traditions of the people should not only be cast as the fertile earth of radicalism but be respected, collected, preserved, revered. Allied to this association are many others, such as the connection between radicalism and patriotism (a connection central to early European radicalism and still widespread in the global South) and the assumption that radicalism is, or should be, 'from below', 'street-level', ordinary not posh. Yet as soon as these links are made doubts rush in, both about the authenticity of the popular claim and the advisability of handing political power to the masses. Populism is an object of intense suspicion within left-wing thought, often because it is associated with demagogy. Such scepticism is sustained by the belief that the unreformed culture of ordinary people is conservative and backward-looking. This perspective identifies the authentic locus of radicalism as the militant, a revolutionary agent who stands with, for, but in front of the people. However, the constant claims of engagement, of *returns* to the people, of populist symbolism, that we find across vanguardist radicalisms in the last century, also suggest that this is another arena, not of discrete political choices, but of dilemma. The radical is nothing without the people. She wishes to be rooted in the people. Yet the peoples' 'rootedness' makes her suspicious and uncomfortable.

Towards Authenticity or towards Alienation?

The desire to overcome alienation and return humanity to authenticity is an important radical motif. Thus radical visions of the future often suggest visions of the past, more especially a time before class, before power, before hierarchy, before money. This paradoxical historical sensibility has been cohered within Marxism through a dialectical understanding of the interplay of revolution and alienation. The communist insurrection which will abolish alienation is made possible by proletarianization; that is, by the formation of an alienated and, hence, rebellious class identity. In this way past and future come together into an image of reintegrated, authentic existence being created out of the maelstrom of revolution.

Yet alienation is not easily tamed. How can communist authenticity be rendered out of the impersonal bureaucracies and mass society of modernity? Even among those radicals for whom alienation appears to have a clear value, the desire to valorize authenticity often comes into view as a form of yearning. An obvious way out of this dilemma is to condemn the quest for authenticity as a sham and celebrate deracination as providing its own kind of liberation. Yet, as we shall see in Chapters Three and Four, although this possibility seems to appeal to some radical 'anti-essentialist' theorists, it is itself stalked by a sense of loss.

Towards Nature or Escaping Nature?

The dilemmas of authenticity evoke a closely related set of concerns about the idea of nature. The concept of nature is one of the foundations of the radical tradition. It has been offered many times as a source of rights and freedoms. It has also been central to the extension of radicalism beyond purely political worries and into a larger, romantic, sensibility that grasps the wonder and fragility of life on earth. Indeed, environmentalism is often represented as a form of radicalism, especially when it is portrayed as a critique of consumerism and of lives alienated from the earth.

Yet radicalism can just as easily be identified as a tradition that is premised on and encourages an escape from nature. It seeks the politicization of social choices and an affirmation of people's capacity to shape the world to their will. The twentieth century saw radicals, especially those who had won power, embrace technology and industry so enthusiastically that electricity plants and tractors became icons of communism. The left became associated with the subjugation and, in many countries, the ruination of the environment. Those sceptical of technocracy became marginalized into a green counter-culture. This counter-movement is now mainstream. But its relationship to the left is contested and uncertain.

Solidarity beyond Politics?

Solidarity is a central word in the radical lexicon. It is associated with others: struggle, comradeship, co-operation. Radicalism is an ideology of fellowship, of the power of union and alliance. Within these emotional and organizational bonds lies a conviction that human beings are meant to act and work together. It is a conviction that inevitably evokes a sense of authentic community (even of 'primitive communism') and of the strength of close, intimate associations (the ties that bind 'the people', 'brothers', 'sisters' and 'comrades').

However, the nature of this solidarity is ambivalent. It is offered by many socialists as something forged, not natural but created in conflict. Thus it is cast as distinct from 'conservative', organic, solidarities. Unlike them it is not passive, backward-looking and insular but politically conscious and oriented to the future, towards change and action. Yet the lines of distinction between these types of solidarity are hard to maintain. The idea of solidarity always contains a hope of human togetherness that cannot be reduced to political utility, to mere strategic value. Hence, the ideal of solidarity exceeds politics, it calls on and looks for something more. And by doing so it inserts a potentially troubling sense of loss into the radical project.

Acknowledging Nostalgia: Four Provocations

Paradoxes are rarely enough. On its own the recognition of ambiguity is too bloodless an ambition. And it fails to convey the danger and the excitement that must be part of any rethinking of the relationship between nostalgia and the left. To get us thinking critically about nostalgia we also need provocations. Below I offer four.

Against Reducing Nostalgia to a Tool of Resistance

The power of the past is often domesticated within radical history into a resource, a set of useful tools, to apply to the present. Memories and loyalties are valued but only in as much as they may be cast as weapons of the oppressed. Thus, for example, Peter Glazer's study on Spanish civil war veterans in the United States, *Radical Nostalgia*, is structured around the question 'can nostalgia serve the needs of a progressive community?'[37] Glazer's answer is yes. But what if our relationship to the past cannot be scissored up into such dutiful patterns?

The yearnings that I trace in this book certainly sometimes take the form of 'radical traditions'. But they also evoke a far more unkempt, and generous, acceptance of forms of attachment whose importance, and persistence, cannot be reduced to their political productiveness. Indeed, they quietly rebel against the politicization of life, against the idea that things are only of value if we can find a place for them in a political ideology. At a time when the meaning of radicalism is in crisis – when all that was once solid in socialism has melted into air – the relationship between nostalgia and the left can and should be investigated in ways that question instrumental logic. The *a priori* expectation that the only forms of nostalgia that should interest us are those that conserve today's (or is it yesterday's?) 'progressive community' is no longer tenable.

Nostalgia Can be a Site of Creativity, Danger and Transgression

Within modernity nostalgia is marginalized. It is treated as a failure to adapt. In modern stereotype, nostalgia is cast as merely a 'paralysing structure of historical reflection'.[38] Yet modernity is the condition of nostalgia, it provokes and shapes it. Around nostalgia accrue many of the discordant and creative practices that excite and disturb modern audiences. Nostalgia disturbs modern life. The most self-consciously troubling spirits of the modern age – the avant-garde – shocked the West by working through and against nostalgia. Their characteristic tropes of spontaneity and organic, free creation are imbued with a counter-modernity that easily slipped into a yearning for the pre-modern. In an era of mass production for mass societies, the avant-garde's strange, hand-crafted acts of adventure are troubling and disorientating precisely because they simultaneously evoke a refusal of the present age, while demanding to be understood as presaging a new one.

The argument goes further: if modernity is a time of alienation then all attempts to speak of human sympathy and solidarity are likely to offer a politics of transgression in the form of a sense of loss. We are used to imagining nostalgic longing as akin to reverie, a moment of drooping repose. But it seems it is also a moment of creativity, of discord and danger.

Looking to the Past Can be Less Sentimental than Looking to the Future

The notion that nostalgia is a set of misty-eyed myths found among the old and the weak minded is common place. One can hardly dispute that nostalgia distorts, that it offers a rose-tinted view of the past. But the idea that its tendency towards sentiment is notably more developed or egregious than comparable emotions is less convincing. Is nostalgia really more sentimental than wishful visions of the future, those hazy images of tomorrow's bright new world that are so prominent within progressive politics? Why are the backward-looking called 'misty-eyed' but not the forward-looking? The point is reinforced by the simple fact that nostalgia is often based on acquired information, on memory. Thus its relationship to myth is frequently cross-cut and sustained by experience. Ian Dyck notes of radical rural labourers in early nineteenth-century England that 'they remembered a better life and they wanted it back'.[39] There is a hard-headed quality to such acts of recall. It seems that, while nostalgia is sentimental, its connection to experience means that it may be less purely wishful than other forms of emotional transference.

Nostalgia in and against Politics: Politics in and against Modernity

Modernity is the era of industrialization and bureaucracy but also of alienation, of revolution and of rapid social change. Does it follow that modern politics is the justification and celebration of these projects? It seems not. Indeed, modern politics is better represented as being organized around claims to solidarity (whether in terms of nationality, class, party or ethnicity). The politician holds out his or her hands to the assembled and makes a case for action in the name of tradition, of identity, of 'our values'. In this way politics can seem akin to a declaration against modernity: a protest against the receding possibility of connection. Another way of representing this ambivalent relationship is to emphasize the way politics has sought to tame modernity and to respond to its consequences. Modernity may be the time of politics but a great deal of modern life is not experienced as a political choice. It does not feel like a political choice to not have time to see one's family, or know one's neighbours, or have incessant traffic noise grinding in our ears. Politics can appear ineffective, even meaningless, when pitted against these remorseless features of modern existence. If we also accept that nostalgia is itself a kind of rebellion in and against the instrumental rationalities associated with purely political judgement, we are left with a view of politics as a site of anxiety and disappointment. Perhaps though these characteristics are also a testament to its necessity. Politics gestures towards a redemption from modernity at the same time as it offers us bigger and better modernities. It is a troubling combination but it is one that we moderns seem to need.

Six Windows onto Radical Nostalgia

Left in the Past has three parts and six chapters, six windows onto the place of nostalgia in and against the left. In each the unsettling presence and persistence of nostalgia within a different aspect of radicalism is explored. My approach does not aim to be all-inclusive. Its eclectic quality reflects my personal fascination with three particular areas of radical thought, notably early English socialism, anti-colonialism and anti-racism and the avant-garde (more specifically, the situationists). Chapters Two to Six are grouped around these three themes.

Chapter One sets the political and academic scene, exploring the dismissals as well as the reassessment of this insistent but disquieting topic. This chapter provides theoretical and historical arguments about the political nature of nostalgia, developing and exemplifying the idea that nostalgia exists within and against modernity and is integral to the radical imagination. It also further supports the argument that the margnalization of nostalgia created the conditions for it to become a sphere of transgression and excitement for the counter-cultural movements of the last century. These movements adopted and adapted the past as a sphere of challenge and release. The current academic reassessments of nostalgia which are also introduced in this chapter are, in part, a testament to the ability of these counter-currents to create the cultural space for the critique of modernity.

After Chapter One, *Left in the Past* offers a number of more specific studies of the relationship between nostalgia and radicalism. *Drawing on English examples, Chapter Two addresses nostalgia in early socialism.* I argue that, in the late nineteenth century, the uses of the past seen in earlier forms of radicalism were filtered through an increasingly anti-nostalgic worldview. This thesis is developed around a discussion of the political appropriation of Thomas Spence. This portrait is followed by two others, of William Morris and Robert Blatchford. These backward-looking socialists are used to explore different ways that radical nostalgia became an increasingly self-conscious and unorthodox political trajectory.

Chapters Three and Four explore the connections between anti-colonialism, post-colonialism and nostalgia. Chapter Three addresses two interconnected forms of radical nostalgia. First, the nostalgia of anti-colonialism and, second, the nostalgia of post-colonial critical scholarship. It is argued that anti-colonial nostalgia provided a challenge to monolithic visions of modernity (both Western and communist). The portrait of post-colonialism that I offer, by contrast, suggests that its concern with essentialism has created a new lexicon of suspicion towards attachments to the past. At the same time, post-colonialism displays powerful nostalgic commitments. Some of these echo anti-colonial claims about the nature of indigenous knowledge. However, a more distinct and characteristic nostalgic theme is identified in the post-colonial yearning for the political drama and moral clarity of the era of anti-colonial struggle. Chapter Four looks at how multicultural and anti-racist forms of radicalism emerged in Britain and how their hostility to nostalgia has shaped the representation of metropolitan culture. In this new metrocentric multiverse, nostalgia is routinely reduced to a racist grunt, an ugly noise made by place-bound primitives. But it has also become an awkward and disruptive presence, a discordant sigh of regret; an embarrassing lapse in the up-beat sound track for a tirelessly celebratory urban radicalism. These ideas are approached with the help of a specific example: Paul Gilroy's resolutely anti-nostalgic *After Empire: Melancholia or Convivial Culture?* (published in the United States as *Postcolonial Melancholia*).

Chapters Five and Six form another connected pair. Both address the relationship between nostalgia and the situationists and those influenced by them. Chapter Five offers a close reading of the place of nostalgia within the ideology and practice of this small band of postwar avant-garde Marxist revolutionaries. By doing so it provides a case-study of the intimate yet contradictory relationship between, on the one hand, an attachment to the past and, on the other, an ultra-radical desire to commence a new society. I argue that nostalgia had both a productive and disruptive role in situationist thought; that it enabled some of their key insights yet also introduced incoherence and tensions into their political project (in part, because it was unacknowledged). This productive and disruptive relationship is explored through two central situationist themes: the idea of the spectacle and the critique of urbanism. These two examples also allow me to show how the form and object of nostalgia can be identified in two distinct (if connected) ways within situationism. The idea of the spectacle contains what I describe as an 'unrooted' nostalgia: a free-floating sense of loss that presents permanent marginality and 'the alienated life' as a political identity. The Situationist International's concern for the demise of the city in the wake of modernizing bulldozers suggests a different tendency of nostalgic form and object, a tendency that evokes specific places and particular experiences and memories. Chapter Six follows the development of the situationist's psychogeographical agenda in British avant-garde culture over the past 20 years. It explores two forms of British psychogeography. The first and most well known of these forms is the travel narratives of Iain Sinclair. The second form is often wilfully obscure but is shown to be an original response to the crises of the left. Revolutionary psychogeographical groups sprang up in a number of British cities in the mid-1990s. These groups shared with Sinclair a quixotic, love-hate relationship with the past. Like Sinclair, they emphasized historical re-readings of the everyday landscape and exhibited an uneasy combination of deracinating modernism and folksy localism. Within Sinclair's travel books, the modern landscape becomes a site of creative purgatory, a necessary violence that simultaneously anchors the writer in modernity while establishing marginal spaces and histories discovered on foot as expressions of a profound cultural and social loss. This double mapping of modernity and nostalgia is then used to imagine a community of creative and other cultural workers who have found a way of being 'at home' and finding friendship in and against an alienating landscape.

Notes

1. Svetlana Boym, *The Future of Nostalgia*, (New York: Basic Books, 2001), 355.
2. If focused upon Britain such an account could chart the lineage from Tory radicals, such as Richard Oastler (Cecil Driver, *Tory Radical: The Life of Richard Oastler*, Oxford: Oxford University Press, 1946) to guild and anti-industrial socialists (such as Arthur Penty, *Old Worlds for New: A Study of the Post-Industrial State*, London: George Allen and Unwin, 1917) and many points beyond and in-between (e.g. Y. Knott, *Conservative Socialism or Politics for the Middle Classes*, London: Swan Sonnenschein, 1909).
3. Situationist International, 'Les souvenirs au-dessous de tout', *Internationale Situationniste*, 2, (1958), 4.
4. Boaventura de Sousa Santos, *The Rise of the Global Left: The World Social Forum and Beyond*, (London: Zed Books, 2006).
5. Christopher Lasch, *The True and Only Heaven: Progress and Its Critics*, (New York: W. W. Norton, 1991), 113.
6. The pathologization of sorrow is discussed by A. Horwitz and J. Wakefield, *The Loss of Sadness: How Psychiatry Transformed Normal Sorrow into Despressive Disorder*, (New York: Oxford University Press, 2007).
7. Stephen Legg, 'Contesting and surviving memory: space, nation and nostalgia in *Les Lieux de mémoire*', *Environment and Planning D: Society and Space*, 23, (2005), 488.
8. Paul Logan, 'Nostalgia without nostalgia: review of Linda M. Austin, *Nostalgia in Transition: 1780–1917*', *Novel*, 42, 1, (2009), 141.
9. Emphasis added. Cited in Paul Glazer, *Radical Nostalgia: Spanish Civil War Commemoration in America*, (Rochester, NY: University of Rochester Press, 2005), 7.
10. Eric Hobsbawm, *The Age of Revolution, 1789–1848*, (New York: New American Library, 1962), 290.
11. Richard Sennett, *The Fall of the Public Man*, (New York: Alfred Knopf, 1977), 259.
12. Sean Scanlan, 'Introduction: nostalgia', *Iowa Journal of Cultural Studies*, 5, (2005), http://www.uiowa.edu/~ijcs/nostalgia/nostfe1.htm, accessed 07.09.2009.
13. Marcos Piason Natali, 'History and politics of nostalgia', *Iowa Journal of Cultural Studies*, 5, (2005), http://www.uiowa.edu/~ijcs/nostalgia/nostfe1.htm, accessed 07.09.2009.
14. Robert Hewison, *The Heritage Industry: Britain in a Climate of Decline*, (London: Methuen, 1987), 146.
15. Y. Gabriel, 'Organizational nostalgia – reflections of "The Golden Age"', in S. Fineman (Ed.), *Emotion in Organisations* (London: Sage, 1993), 119.
16. Glazer, *Radical Nostalgia*, 35.
17. Christopher Shaw and Malcolm Chase, 'The dimensions of nostalgia', in Christopher Shaw and Malcolm Chase (Eds), *The Imagined Past: History and Nostalgia*, (Manchester: Manchester University Press, 1989), 3.
18. Fred Davis, *Yearning for Yesterday: A Sociology of Nostalgia*, (New York: Free Press, 1979), viii.
19. John Stuart Mill, 'The spirit of the age', *Examiner*, 9 January (1831).

20. Kimberly Smith, 'Mere nostalgia: notes of a progressive paratheory', *Rhetoric & Public Affairs*, 3, 4, (2000), 507, 506. David Lowenthal makes a similarly provocative point: 'Perhaps our epoch is awash not with nostalgia but in a "widespread *preoccupation* with nostalgia" amongst intellectuals and the mass media'. David Lowenthal, 'Nostalgia tells it like it wasn't', in Christopher Shaw and Malcolm Chase (Eds), *The Imagined Past: History and Nostalgia*, (Manchester: Manchester University Press, 1989), 29.

21. Michael Löwy and Robert Sayre, *Romanticism against the Tide of Modernity*, (Durham, NC: Duke University Press, 2001); Michael Löwy, 'The revolutionary romanticism of May 1968', *Thesis Eleven*, 68, (2002). Robert Sayre and Michael Löwy, 'Figures of romantic anti-capitalism', *New German Critique*, 32 (1984).

22. Sayre and Löwy, 'Figures of romantic anti-capitalism', 56.

23. Löwy and Sayre, *Romanticism against the Tide of Modernity*, 21.

24. Ibid., 1.

25. Ibid., 240.

26. Johannes Hofer, 'Medical dissertation on nostalgia by Johannes Hofer, 1688', *Bulletin of the History of Medicine*, 2 (1934). Translated and introduced by Carolyn Kiser Anspach. Naqvi notes that,

> There is also some confusion in the literature about the date for Hofer's own dissertation – 1685 and, especially, 1678, being two dates cited with some frequency. I take Anspach's date to be definitive, both because it makes more sense given Hofer's year of birth (i.e., 1669), and given the corroborating evidence of the date on the incunabulum's title-page that Anspach has reproduced in her translation.

> Nauman Naqvi, *The Nostalgic Subject. A Genealogy of the 'Critique of Nostalgia'*, Working Paper 23, (University of Messina: Centro Interuniversitario per le ricerche sulla Sociologia del Diritto e delle Istituzioni Giuridiche, undated), http://www.cirsdig.it/ Pubblicazioni/naqvi.pdf, accessed 09.09.2009.

27. Hofer notes existing terms 'das Heimweh' – which 'the gifted Helvetians have introduced not long since into their vernacular language, chosen from the grief for the lost charm of the Native Land' – and 'la Maladie du Pays' – found among 'the Helvetians in Gaul'. However he offers 'nostalgia' as a more medical and scientific category:

> Nor in truth, deliberating on a name, did a more suitable one occur to me, defining the thing to be explained, more concisely than the word Nostalgias, Greek in origin and indeed composed of two sounds, the one of which is Nosos, return to the native land; the other, Algos, signifies suffering or grief; so that thus far it is possible from the force of the sound Nostalgia to define the sad mood originating from the desire for the return to one's native land. (Hofer, 'Medical dissertation on nostalgia', 380–1)

28. Cited by David Lowenthal, *The Past is a Foreign Country*, (Cambridge: Cambridge University Press, 1985), 10.

29. *Oxford English Dictionary* (1989).

30. For discussion see Linda M. Austin, *Nostalgia in Transition: 1780–1917*, (Charlottesville: University of Virginia Press, 2007). Lasch notes that 'the new of broader usage was firmly established by the 1920s', Lasch, *The True and Only Heaven*, 106.

31. Marcel Proust, *Swann's Way*, (Newton Abbot: David and Charles, 2002), 34. The French
     text is as follows:

     Or, justement, les romans champêtres de George Sand qu'elle me donnait pour ma fête,
     étaient pleins ainsi qu'un mobilier ancien, d'expressions tombées en désuétude et redev-
     enues imagées, comme on n'en trouve plus qu'à la campagne. Et ma grand'mère les avait
     achetés de préférence à d'autres comme elle eût loué plus volontiers une propriété où il
     y aurait eu un pigeonnier gothique ou quelqu'une de ces vieilles choses qui exercent sur
     l'esprit une heureuse influence en lui donnant la nostalgie d'impossibles voyages dans le
     temps.

32. Davis, *Yearning for Yesterday*, 9.
33. Ibid., 8.
34. Bergen Evans and Cornelia Evans, *A Dictionary of Contemporary American Usage*,
     (New York: Random House, 1957), 322.
35. Raymond Williams, *The Country and the City*, (Oxford: Oxford University Press,
     1975), 12.
36. In nineteenth-century Britain the radicals formed a wing of the Liberal Party which
     'united middle-class manufacturers with the favoured sections of the workers, who
     seldom dreamed of setting up in complete independence of their middle-class allies
     [and] . . . shared with middle-class Radicals certain political aims: the fight against aris-
     tocratic privilege and for the extension of parliamentary democracy' (Eric Hobsbawm,
     'Introduction', in Eric Hobsbawm (Ed.), *Labour's Turning Point 1880–1900: Second
     Edition*, Hassocks: Harvester Press, 1974, xv). However, a shift towards more 'socialistic
     measures' in later radicalism was signalled by *The Radical Programme* introduced by
     Joseph Chamberlain in 1885 (Joseph Chamberlain, *The Radical Programme*, London:
     Chapman and Hall, 1885, 13).
37. Glazer, *Radical Nostalgia*, 9.
38. John Frow, 'Tourism and the semiotics of nostalgia', *October*, 57, (1991), 135.
39. Ian Dyck, *William Cobbett and Rural Popular Culture*, (Cambridge: Cambridge University
     Press, 1992), 147.

PART ONE

CHAPTER ONE

Nostalgia and the Left: Denial, Danger and Doubt

To make the past irrelevant to the present and to the future is the task of modernity.
Dipankar Gupta[1]

The ability to forget . . . is the mental faculty which sustains submissiveness and renunciation.
Herbert Marcuse[2]

Introduction

This chapter offers an overview of the role of nostalgia within the radical imagination. It is wide-ranging and exploratory. First, it sets out in some detail the argument that nostalgia is produced within modernity. Nostalgia is shown to emerge from an awareness of new eras and lost pasts; from a new historical consciousness that is a distinctive component of post-traditional societies. This familiar insight is developed and tested in the remainder of the chapter by way of both an introduction to, and an analysis of, three of the main currents in the story of the relationship between the left and nostalgia. These are as follows: the left's antagonism towards nostalgia; the marginal and, hence, transgressive role of nostalgia; and, finally, the critical reassessment of nostalgia.

Nostalgia as the Modern Dilemma

The idea of a better past appears to be as old as recorded civilization. When Raymond Williams tried to locate a point, a moment of restful origin, for England's own fables of a happier time, he found only an ever rumbling 'escalator' of remembrance. '[W]e could find no place, no period', he writes, 'in which we could seriously rest'.[3] Psychologists have also claimed nostalgia as 'universal and ubiquitous'; as 'always latent in the human imagination'.[4] Anthony Smith agrees that 'Nostalgia for the past, especially the ethnic past of "one's own" people has indeed been a feature of society in all ages and continents.'[5] He provides an existential explanation:

> people have always sought to overcome death and the futility with which death threatens mortals. By linking oneself to a 'community of history and destiny', the individual hopes to achieve a measure of immortality which will preserve his or her person and achievements from oblivion.[6]

However, while certain underlying aspects of the nostalgic imagination may be universal, nostalgia is routinely presented as a product of modernity, a direct response to a historically specific condition. These two, apparently contradictory, perspectives suggest, that not all expressions of loss are, to use William's phrase, 'in the same mode'.[7] Ancient nostalgia typically took the form of myths of a distant Golden Age or Eden. A time, Hesiod tells us, that was,

> remote and free from evil and grief . . . (mortal men) had all good things, for the fruitful earth unforced bare them fruit abundantly and without stint.[8]

Hesiod's narrative offers an origin story. It does not concern an immediate or experienced loss – or any sense of trauma – but provides a beguiling tale from long ago. It appears that such mythic nostalgia is a diffuse and relatively minor facet of all 'traditional communities'. Smith points out that,

> in a 'traditional' society, one was expected to fashion one's life-style and ambitions in terms of collective traditions, so that there was little need to yearn for a past that was being continued.[9]

By contrast, the modern era is characterized by change and a far more intense and urgent relationship with loss. Concerns about the uprooting of the past, and the disappearance of certainties of faith and attachment, may be discerned emerging from the early modern period and gathering strength and visibility in rough proportion to the increased pace of upheaval. In the wake of traditional society, concludes Smith, 'All that is left is memory and hope, history and destiny.'[10]

We may conclude that the difficulty of dealing with sudden and massive social change is the condition, not of all nostalgia, but of its distinctly modern form. Peter Fritzsche has recently explored this predicament in a monograph with the suitably plaintive title *Stranded in the Present: Modern Time and the Melancholy of History*. Fritzsche quotes a young European aristocrat, Alexander von der Marwitz, writing in 1812, in the midst of revolutionary turmoil, about the *new time* in which he lives:

> Lightning strikes the soul, omens reveal themselves, and ideas drift through time and like the mysterious appearances of ghosts point to a deeper meaning, the revolution of all things, in which *everything* Old disappears like the ground pulled under by an earthquake, while underneath the ruins volcanoes heave up a new and fresh ground.[11]

To find in the world around one that '*everything* Old disappears' is to inhabit a state of a profound disorientation. It is to suggest, moreover, that the past is emerging as a site of shared and continuous rupture, in a society that has come to be characterized by uncertainty.

'The *sense of history* is completely new in our world' wrote Flaubert in 1859.[12] John Stuart Mill offered the same thought nearly 30 years earlier, with an additional and important rider. The 'idea of comparing one's own age with former ages', he tells us in *The Spirit of the Age* (published in 1831), is something novel. For the 'spirit of the age' is 'a new expression, no more that fifty years old'.[13] Today, Mill continues, 'Old bonds no longer unite, nor ancient boundaries confine.'[14] This transformation was viewed by some with optimism – as it was by Mill and by Richard Horne in *A New Sprit of the Age* (1844) – by others with melancholy – for example, by Carlyle in *Signs of the Times* (1829).[15] In both reactions, however, we find a shared sense of time as an arena of mobility and unpredictability.

While the name for the new era was much debated, Carlyle's suggestion has an unpretentious appeal: 'Were we required to characterize this age of ours by any single epithet, we should be tempted to call it . . . the Mechanical Age.'[16] The title of one of the most influential Victorian journals of political commentary, *The Nineteenth Century* (founded in 1873 by James Knowles), encapsulates the new historical sensibility in even plainer language. With its energetic and diverse content (including Marxists, anarchists, mystics, liberals, imperialists and conservatives) the journal offered the present age as both an object and a time of critique. Its omnivorously critical perspective was premised on the inevitability, but also the disputed nature, of upheaval and progress.[17]

The emergence of mass circulation political journals, like *The Nineteenth Century*, also suggests another aspect of the new temporal consciousness, its broad social base. The 'new age' applied to all and concerned all. This is a point later emphasized by György Lukács in his discussion of the birth of the novel. The idea of historical change, Lukács argued, had become a mass experience.

> It was the French revolution, the revolutionary wars and the rise and fall of Napoleon, which for the first time made history a mass experience, and moreover on a European scale. During the decades between 1789 and 1814 each nation of Europe underwent more upheavals than they had previously experienced in centuries. And the quick succession of these upheavals gives them a qualitatively distinct character, it makes their historical character far more visible than would be the case in isolated, individual instances: the masses no longer have the impression of a 'natural occurrence'.[18]

The denaturalization of time and society may be said to have created the conditions not only for history but also for the social sciences. Max Weber's sociological theory of bureaucratization, along with Ferdinand Tönnies's conception of a shift from organic community to fragmented and superficial 'association', offer both an account and a reflection of the new sensibility. Their theories are acts of both analysis and political unease. The 'rationalization, intellectualization and, above all, disenchantment of the world', identified by Weber, placed melancholy at the heart of sociology.[19] It also implied that how we 'preserve a remnant of humanity from this parceling out of the soul' became, a 'central question'.[20]

The nostalgic content of these founding narratives of social science has not been lost on contemporary critics who, eager to identify the old masters as old-fashioned, have turned this insight into an accusation of conservatism. Thus, for example, Georg Stauth and Bryan Turner narrate the birth of sociology as 'a nostalgic analysis of communal relations'. They go on to claim that a broad range of 'melancholic intellectual[s]' have been drawn to nostalgia in order to defend an 'elitist' aversion to popular culture.[21] Christopher Shaw and Malcolm Chase offer an even more damning version of the same thesis. They suggest that the dewy-eyed founders of classical sociology were full of resentment against change and, hence, failed to develop a rigorous and balanced analysis:

> [T]he paradoxically utopian nostalgia of much grand social theory [represents] a recognition, and at the same time an elision, of the fact that all that is solid has melted into air. The temptation was to conjure up a past defined not by painstaking investigation of the historical record but by positing a series of absences, of negatives. If we now have *Gemeinschaft*, there must have been *Gesellschaft* [*sic*]; if our consciousness is fragmented, there must have been a time when it was integrated; if society is now bureaucratised and impersonal, it

must previously have been personal and particular. The syntax and structure of these ideas makes them superficially attractive but this appeal is no warrant for their veracity.[22]

Yet, Chase and Shaw's confident dismissal of the basic works of modern sociology as 'conjure[d] up' and wanting in 'veracity' exhibits an iconoclasm that may itself be accused of being only 'superficially attractive'. The transitions depicted by Weber and Tönnies, along with Durkheim and Marx, cannot be dismissed without calling into question the transformation to modernity itself. The fact that the major theorizations of this transition are nostalgic is a reflection of their attempt to depict the denaturalization of time, society and nature. Chase and Shaw assume that, in rooting out this nostalgic trait, they have identified something rotten at the core of the social sciences. They would cast aside such backward-looking perspectives and replace them with a celebration of uncertainty. Thus they argue that people should not 'cling to the alleged certainties of the past' but embrace the fact that in the modern world the 'only certainty is uncertainty'.[23] Yet this advice relies on the reality of the transitions described by Weber and Tönnies. The difference is not one of analysis but of conclusion. Whereas the 'classical' social theorists are suspicious of the consequences of modernity, Chase and Shaw have a ultra-modernist (or post-modernist) relish for making themselves 'somehow at home in the maelstrom'.[24] Yet this unlikely ideal is surely even less plausible than the 'utopian nostalgia' of Weber and Tönnies. Chaos and disorientation are rarely relished by those who have direct experience of them. Moreover, the idea of finding a 'home' in a 'maelstrom' already concedes, not only the basic thesis of the classical sociologists, but the hope of finding *sanctuary* in world drained of meaning, stability and solidarity. As we shall see in later chapters (especially Chapter Five on the situationists and Chapter Four on radical multiculturalism), endless deracination is difficult to sustain either as an aspiration or a reality. When one seeks a 'home' in uncertainty, nostalgia is never far from one's door.

The 'ruthless criticism of all that exists'

'Making a new world' is a central claim of the radical imagination. Indeed, radical politics can be represented as having a literal Year One, inaugurated by the French National Convention in 1792. Over the next two centuries – from Owen's New Lanark to the 'New Civilization' of the Soviet Union and Mao's 'New Democracy' – a desire to abolish the old and build an entirely different kind of society has provided a core belief for socialists and others on the revolutionary left.

The most influential modern revolutionary is Karl Marx. Central to Marx's project was an explicit challenge to all that had gone before.

[I]f constructing the future and settling everything for all times are not our affair, it is all the more clear what we have to accomplish at present: I am referring to ruthless criticism of all that exists, ruthless both in the sense of not being afraid of the results it arrives at and in the sense of being just a little afraid of conflict with the powers that be.[25]

Marx returned repeatedly to the need to escape the past.

The social revolution of the nineteenth century can only create its poetry from the future, not from the past. It cannot begin its own work until it has sloughed off all its superstitious regard for the past. Earlier revolutions have needed world-historical reminiscences to deaden their awareness of their own content. In order to arrive at its own content the revolution of the nineteenth century must let the dead bury their dead.[26]

By the late nineteenth century, the damning of the past had became an expected facet of revolutionary rhetoric. Yet this rhetoric was also often notable for its evocation of the 'Spirit' of history. In 1842, ten years before Marx instructed his followers to 'let the dead bury their dead', his bitter rival for influence within the working-class movement, Mikhail Bakunin, had made use of the same biblical phrase.[27] Bakunin joins the command with an anarchist affirmation of the creative power of destruction.

> Open the eyes of your mind; let the dead bury the dead, and convince yourselves at last that the Spirit, ever young, ever newborn, is not to be sought in fallen ruins! . . . Let us therefore trust the eternal Spirit which destroys and annihilates only because it is the unfathomable and eternal source of all life. The passion for destruction is a creative passion, too![28]

Marx and Bakunin were both advocates of class struggle. Both identified a new uprooted class of labourers who would perform the necessary work of overturning the past. This new class was alienated from tradition and unsentimental and vigorous in its disregard for authority. Marx explained the social formation of this novel historical force but it is Bakunin that provided the most passionate evocation of the sense of release occasioned by its power. He offers a feverish representation of the coming redemption:

> Everywhere, especially in France and England, social and religious societies are being formed which are wholly alien to the world of present-day politics, societies that derive their life from new sources quite unknown to us and that grow and diffuse themselves without fanfare. The people, the poor class, which without doubt constitutes the greatest part of humanity; the class whose rights have already been recognized in theory but which is nevertheless still despised for its birth, for its ties with poverty and ignorance, as well as indeed with actual slavery – this class, which constitutes the true people, is everywhere assuming a threatening attitude and is beginning to count the ranks of its enemy, far weaker in numbers than itself, and to demand the actualization of the right already conceded to it by everyone. All people and all men are filled with a kind of premonition, and everyone whose vital organs are not paralyzed faces with shuddering expectation the approaching future which will utter the redeeming word. Even in Russia, the boundless snow-covered kingdom so little known, and which perhaps also has a great future in store, even in Russia dark clouds are gathering, heralding storm. Oh, the air is sultry and pregnant with lightning. And therefore we call to our deluded brothers: Repent, repent, the Kingdom of the Lord is at hand![29]

For Bakunin, the revolutionary class is an agent of deliverance and the act of revolution a moment of moral cleansing. His excited prose has the hyperbolic quality of ecstatic preaching. However, the supposedly fiery masses often exhibited a deep scepticism about the value of such clarions. The anti-nostalgic fervour of both Bakunin and Marx can also be read as reflecting a *frustration* with the way that existing popular struggles usually combined anti-capitalism with a deep sense of loss.

Although the persistent tendency of working-class movements to look to the past for models of social freedom was challenged by revolutionary authors in a variety of ways, the commonest and most indicative response was to represent nostalgia as a form of political immaturity. The nostalgia of the masses was met head-on by Marx:

> We say to the workers and the petty bourgeois: It is better to suffer in modern bourgeois society, which by its industry creates the means for the foundation of a new society that will liberate you, than revert to a bygone form of society which, on the pretext of saving your classes, thrusts the entire nation back into medieval barbarism.[30]

Marx's hostility to nostalgia emerged in an antagonistic relationship, not merely with the backward-looking workers, but with a related and, often, overlapping group, backward-looking nationalists. The forging of nationalist movements across Europe relied on various forms of nostalgic longing. Marx was unimpressed by 'this worldwide necromancy' which he rooted in the 'unheroic' bourgeois's need to appropriate the heroic narratives of the past.[31] Thus he saw in the revolutionary episodes that swept across France a cynical deployment of history:

> [T]he Revolution of 1789 to 1814 draped itself alternately as the Roman Republic and the Roman Empire; and the revolution of 1848 knew no better than to parody at some points 1789 and at others the revolutionary traditions of 1793–5. . . . unheroic as bourgeois society is, it still required heroism, self-sacrifice, terror, civil war, and battles in which whole nations were engaged, to bring it to the world . . . In these revolutions, then the resurrection of the dead served to exalt the new struggles, rather than to parody the old, to exaggerate the given task in the imagination, rather than to flee from solving it in reality, and to recover the spirit of the revolution, rather than to set its ghost walking again.[32]

In summary, for internationalists and revolutionaries, such as Marx and Bakunin, yearning for the past was doubly suspect and doubly deluded. Not only did it lead the revolutionary classes away from the task of creating a new society but also, where it did provoke people to action, it diverted their energies into the bourgeois delusion of nationalism.

However, to properly understand the disdain of the anti-nostalgic creed, we must place it in the wider context of nineteenth-century progressivism. Aspirations towards political revolution emerged from within societies growing accustomed to revolutionary ideas and practices in many different spheres. The muscular energy of the socialist challenge reflected a distinctly mid-late-nineteenth-century iconoclasm. The 'mighty movement' spoken of by Herbert Spencer was '[a]lways towards perfection . . . towards a complete development and a more unmixed good'.[33] In 1902, another Social Darwinist, Benjamin Kidd, extended Spencer's idea into a transcendental conception of the future guiding the present:

> It is, we see, the meaning, not of the relation of the present to the past but of the relation of the present to the future, to which all other meanings are subordinate, and which controls all the ultimate tendencies of the process of progress in which we are living.[34]

Kidd's manifesto for the future was also a statement of faith in the superiority of Western civilization. While all the other cultures of the earth were stuck in the past, the unique ability of the West to rid itself of nostalgia marked it out as 'destined to hold the future of the world'.[35] When woven with the medical connotations of nostalgia, which remained prevalent into the late nineteenth century, the 'backwardness' of non-European races could thus be pathologized as 'backward-lookingness'. For the French medic, V. Widal, writing in 1879, 'nostalgia is the opposite of civilization and arises in harsh country. The wild, primitive and simple tribes are the most prone to the evil of nostalgia.'[36] The identification of nostalgia with non-Europeans reflected an assumption, found across the political spectrum in Europe, that progress within the static and moribund societies of Asia and Africa was only possible through colonization and Westernization. Despite his hostility to British cruelty, Marx regarded colonial conquest by the West as desirable. Only the destruction of 'traditional' societies and their replacement with new, modern, social processes and forces, he argued, would enable people to achieve class consciousness and the material conditions required for communist revolution. Marx explained,

> England has to fulfil a double mission in India: one destructive, the other regenerating – the annihilation of old Asiatic society, and the laying of the material foundations of Western society in Asia.[37]

The 'idyllic village communities' characteristic of the East, Marx claimed, 'restrain the human mind within the smallest possible compass . . . enslaving it beneath traditional rules, depriving it of all grandeur and historical energies'.[38] In order for history to dawn within Asia, and other non-Western societies, they must be subject to the revolution that is modernity.

> England, it is true, in casing a social revolution in Hindustan was actuated only by the vilest interest, and was stupid in her manner of enforcing them. But that is not the question. The question is, can mankind fulfil its destiny without a fundamental revolution in the social state of Asia? If not, whatever may have been the crimes of England she was the unconscious tool of history in bringing about that revolution.[39]

In similar vein, Engels, writing to Marx in 1851, explained that,

> Germany take Schleswig with the right of civilization over barbarism, of progress against stability . . . this right carries more weight than all the agreements for it is the right of historical evolution.[40]

Such opinions indicate that, far from being an anti-conservative challenge to a conservative society, communism is better understood as a revolutionary current within revolutionary times. Indeed, Marxism is premised on this contention. The 'destructive power' of capitalism was consistently identified by Marx as at the centre of the revolutionary process. The 'British bourgeoisie' he wrote in 1852,

> cannot avoid fulfilling their mission, battering to pieces Old England, the England of the past and the very moment when they have conquered . . . will date the *social revolution of England*.[41]

In the late nineteenth century and the first decades of the twentieth century, a very different stereotype of the bourgeoisie was to become prominent. They became associated by revolutionary critics with decline and fear of change. In large part, this shift was due to the successes of the communist movement, and what Lenin called the 'parasitism and decay of capitalism' associated with imperialism.[42] Nevertheless, the notion that the left needed to both understand the revolutionary potential of capitalism and keep up with its innovations remained potent. This viewpoint could be heard particularly clearly within the early years of the Soviet Union. Soviet ideologists looked around for models of rapid growth and found them in capitalist America. The following auto-dialogue by Trotsky, from 1934, exhibits his determination to turn this emulative trend into both a defence of anti-nostalgic politics and a rebuff to the suggestion that the Soviet system was unusually ruthless. Trotsky poses himself the question: 'Does the Soviet State turn men into robots?'

> Why I ask? The ideologists of the patriarchal system, like Tolstoy or Ruskin, object that machine civilization turns the free peasant and craftsman into joyless automatons. In the last decades this charge has mostly been leveled against the industrial system of America (Taylorism, Fordism). Shall we now, perhaps, hear from Chicago and Detroit the outcry against the soul-destroying machine? Why not return to stone hatchets and pile dwellings, why not go back to sheepskin coverings? No; we refuse to do that. In the field of mechanization the Soviet Republic is so far only a disciple of the United States – and has no inclination of stopping halfway.[43]

The question was framed by Trotsky for an easy rebuttal and is easily batted away with a few semi-serious remarks. This glib response reflects the negligible intellectual prestige of nostalgia. But it also means that his answer rather too smoothly side-steps the importance of the concerns glimpsed in the question.

The communist 'total state' was an integrated project that relied upon a vision, not simply of a new economy, or a 'new civilization', but of a new type of 'man'. 'Soviet Man' was a creature of progress; a product of a political ascent towards earthly perfection. In a rapturous passage in *Literature and Revolution* Trotsky explained that,

> The human species, the sluggish *Homo sapiens*, will once again enter the stage of radical reconstruction and become in his own hands the object of the most complex methods of artificial selection and psychophysical training . . . Man will make it his goal . . . to create a higher sociobiological type, a superman, if you will.[44]

The interweaving of authoritarianism and a bold political claim on the future was a characteristic of nearly all the communist regimes that emerged in the twentieth century. The 'Great Leap Forward' launched by the Chinese Communist Party in 1957, followed by the 'Great Proletarian Cultural Revolution', initiated in 1966, provide two of the most dramatic illustrations of this combination of power and vision. The Cultural Revolution rallied the young into Red Guards to combat the so-called four olds: Old Customs, Old Culture, Old Habits and Old Ideas. One Government newspaper explained, in September 1966, that,

> During the past week . . . Red Guards have scored victory after victory as they pressed home their attack against the decadent customs and habits of the exploiting classes. Beating drums and singing revolutionary songs detachments of Red Guards are out in the streets doing propaganda work, holding aloft big portraits of Chairman Mao, extracts from Chairman Mao's works, and great banners with the words: 'We are the critics of the old world'; 'we are the builders of the new world'. They have held street meetings, put up big-character posters and distributed leaflets in their attack against all the old ideas and habits of the exploiting classes. As a result of the proposals of the Red Guards and with

the support of the revolutionary masses, shop signs which spread odious feudal and bour-geois ideas have been removed, and the names of many streets, lanes, parks, buildings and schools tainted with feudalism, capitalism or revisionism or which had no revolutionary significance have been replaced by revolutionary names.[45]

The ruthlessness of the young in dealing with 'Olds' was celebrated and encouraged by Mao. 'The more people you kill', he advised, 'the more revolutionary you are'.[46]

The unleashing of the revolutionary spirit in the Chinese Cultural Revolution was designed to pull apart non-political social bonds and family ties. Over recent years it has been offered as an instance of the way deracination can create a more malleable and vulner-able population.[47] Such perspectives contrast with the excited reaction among many left-wing students and scholars in the West at the time. Positive opinion ranged from vicarious glee at Maoism's new anarchic edge – for Edward Hyams the Maoists do not lead the people but move among them like a radical spark, a 'detonator of the revolutionary bomb' – to more tempered discussion of the need for 'the management of change' in the face of conservative resistance.[48] The latter perspective may be represented by the major sociological and international sur-vey compiled by Peter Marris, *Loss and Change*, published in 1974.[49] Marris was concerned with ensuring that populations are educated to understand the inevitability of radical change and, hence, come to welcome the eradication of their traditional way of life. Discussing the Chinese Cultural Revolution, Marris roots what he calls its 'degeneration' into violence in the frustration caused by conservatives. He goes on to characterize the most effective form of revolutionary activity as a 'patient process of re-education and reconstruction':[50]

The revolution becomes a great teacher, and every class of society with an acknowledged place in its future is absorbed in the process of learning its new identity. If the teaching is too clumsy and authoritarian, it will reactivate the sense of loss.[51]

As Marris's words imply, displays of nostalgia have often been countered by a managerial discourse which presupposes that opposition to 'progress' is temporary and removable.

The idea that resistance to change is a poorly thought-out, somewhat pathetic, clinging to the past by the old and the frightened was not unique to communist regimes. However, what was unique to communism was the militancy with which this conviction was translated into action.[52] The process of deracination was carried out on a number of fronts, including through political education, warfare, 'ethnic cleansing' and rural and urban development programmes. The eradication of old buildings, old place names and old monuments, and the construction of new places, new names and new monuments, became a leitmotif of com-munism. This eagerness to build anew was never simply a mere concretization of radical ideology. It was also an assertion of authority over the past. Thus acts of devastation were as important as acts of construction. In *The Destruction of Memory*, Robert Bevan chronicles the almost fetishistic desire for demolition that accompanied the creation and maintenance of state communism.[53] Thus, for example, he explains the failure of attempts 'to persuade Mao that the new Beijing should be built adjacent to the ancient, sacred city', by pointing out that,

[T]he obliteration of the past was as much a consideration as the building of the new. The desire to create a socialist man and a socialist city . . . has built within it a desire to bring about that change through the very act of destruction and rebuilding – the violent *process* of change.[54]

In fact, the extreme forms of discrimination, that emerged from Mao's struggle against all things old, had the paradoxical effect of making his particular brand of communist revolution appear like a form of regression. Despite the rhetoric of 'leaping forward', the emphasis on revolutionary purity unleashed a seemingly primal thirst for redemption. One of the nadirs of the last century's many violent revolutionary episodes commenced with the 'Super Great Leap Forward' of 'Year Zero', announced by the Maoist influenced Khmer Rouge regime in Cambodia in 1975 (the idea of Year Zero emulated Year One of the French Revolution). The regime's leader, Pol Pot, instructed: 'Don't use money: don't let the people live in cities.'[55] With the cities emptied and money forbidden it was hoped that a truly communist, purely peasant, Khmer society could begin (the Khmer are the largest ethnic group in Cambodia). Despite the fact that, as Christie notes, 'the intellectual influences' on the Khmer Rouge were 'primarily Chinese and French', leftists in the West soon began to dismiss them as an aberration, an 'anti-Marxist' deviation.[56] The Khmer Rouge was represented as mere atavism. However, in one respect at least, the Khmer Rouge government was comparable with other communist states. For it offered a familiar combination of militant transformational practice with a critique of the alienating, inauthentic nature of life under capitalism. In this sense it was not an aberration but a distillation of the paradoxical nature of the revolutionary imagination: a leap into the future that was also a step into the past.

Radical Nostalgia

The introduction of historical time suggests the possibility of progress; an avenue for what Hegel called humanity's 'impulse of perfectibility'.[57] Yet the introduction of history is also the introduction of the past and of resistance to the present in the name of the past. Thus modernity and anti-modernity are related and intertwined. For Bruno Latour,

[T]he modern time of progress and the anti-modern time of 'tradition' are twins who failed to recognise one another: The idea of an identical repetition of the past and that of a radical rupture with the past are two symmetrical results of a single conception of time.[58]

Peter Fritzsche provides us with a similar image:

Nostalgia stalks modernity as an unwelcome double, a familiar symptom of unease in the face of political and economic transformation . . . it takes the measure of the distance people have fallen short in their efforts to make themselves 'at home in a constantly changing world'.[59]

In this book I pursue this sense of 'unease' in the company of the radical left. I also argue that nostalgia is always in and against the left (and, hence, the left is in and against modernity). It is reasonable to ask how I can make this claim when, as we have just seen, the left has been the mortal enemy of nostalgia? If we accept, with Latour, that progress and tradition 'are twins', then radicals' anti-nostalgic self-image may start to come into doubt. Yet Latour's pleasingly symmetrical birth plan does not tell us enough, especially about the role and nature of radical nostalgia in the 'time of progress'. To investigate this phenomenon further it will be useful to break down radical nostalgia thematically. In the rest of this section I address three nostalgic currents within the left: the historicization of solidarity and alienation; the left 'left behind' by modernity and the deployment of nostalgia as transgression. I will briefly sketch the first two of these before turning to focus on the third.

The Historicization of Solidarity and Alienation

In the time of modernity, solidarity and authenticity become idealized and identified with the past. Thus the hope of regaining community and the reintegration of life and labour constantly threatens to offer, or resort to, the pre-capitalist and organic past as a source of socialism's most basic hopes. This process is also visible within the practice of left activism. The ethos of comradely struggle posits the possibility and need for honest and authentic human relationships and looks forward to the creation of a new world that displays a similar integrity.

The idea that communism 'knows itself', as Marx expressed it, 'as the reintegration or return of man into himself', is a persistent theme in his work.[60] Although sometimes associated with the romanticism of his early years, it was also at the fore in his interest, in later life, in the discovery that pre-modern societies practised common ownership and, hence, 'primitive communism'. Influenced by the work of Georg Maurer and Lewis Morgan, Marx wrote to Engels in 1868 claiming that 'the primitive age of every people . . . corresponds to the socialist tendency' and concluded that one could find 'what is newest in what is oldest'.[61] The task of revolution thus becomes, in the words of Bloch, 'the synthetic-dialectic restoration, accepted by Marx, of the state of liberty, equality, fraternity, as it reigned among the old communist *Gens*'.[62]

The hope of unified 'man' emerges from a theory of alienation. 'To subdivide a man is to execute him', Marx argued, '[t]he subdivision of labour is the assassination of a people'.[63] 'What requires explanation', said Marx, 'is not the unity of living and active human beings with the natural', but the loss of this desired and regainable condition.

> What we must explain is the separation of these inorganic conditions of human existence from this active existence, a separation which is only fully completed in the relation between wage-labour and capital.[64]

Bertell Ollman explains the political conclusion of Marx's argument:

> If alienation is the splintering of human nature into a number of misbegotten parts, we would expect communism to be presented as a kind of reunification. And this is just what we find . . . In communism the breach is healed, and all elements which constitute a human being for Marx are reunited. Many of the characteristics ascribed to full communism, such as the end of the division of labor and the erasure of social classes, are clear instances of this reunification process at work.[65]

The argument that Marxism is a secularization of Christian millenarianism also draws heavily on Marx's use of themes of return and reintegration.[66] Igal Halfin has provided a sophisticated development of this thesis based on a close reading of 'Marxist eschatology' in the Soviet Union.[67] Halfin argues that the pursuit of communism was premised on the notion that a reintegrated humanity could achieve 'the end of history' and, hence, salvation from 'historical time'. However, the implication that Marxist nostalgia is a by-product of an unacknowledged religious sensibility should be resisted. As we have seen, modernity produces the past as a site of yearning. The desire for human wholeness bares the imprint of this secular context. It is modernity not God that wracks the revolutionary soul.

Overtaken by Modernity

The left and modernity are not identical. They are better understood as an unequal pairing; the left being just one project within modernity, a project that has, at times, appeared as its leading edge. But at other times radicalism faces modernity with concern and bewilderment. Modernity is a politically mutable and plural set of practices. Its most ubiquitous forms – notably bureaucracy, industrialization, rationalization and capitalism – have far exceeded the influence of the revolutionary left. The success of these projects within modernity and the failure of the left to eradicate capitalism creates the conditions for a sense of resentment to come to the fore and, hence, for political radicalism to appear as a nostalgic response to change. Indeed, there arises the possibility that radicals do not recognize themselves in modernity. A reactive and conservative role was one occupied by many radicals in the struggle against capitalism in the eighteenth and early nineteenth centuries. However, it remains a persistent possibility and can be identified in many different contexts over the past 200 years.

One group who are especially likely to feel 'left behind' by modernity are the old. Two of the distinctive aspects of the modern era are (a) youth becomes privileged over age; and (b) during the course of their lives people are likely to see the transformation of familiar landscapes and communities. Hence biographies become bound up with the experience, both of a loss of individual value and profound social change. If we accept that many of the deepest emotional attachments are formed in early life and that a sense of loss for one's younger days is a common human trait, it also follows that older radicals – the group often entrusted with narrating 'the story of the movement' – may have a particularly difficult relationship with the paradoxes of left nostalgia. This argument also implies that the 'old radical' is a contradictory figure: a symbol of commitment, yet liable to be treated with suspicion.

The Danger of Loss: How Nostalgia Became Counter-Cultural

One of the most intriguing aspects of radical culture in the twentieth century was that, despite the lowly and contaminated status of nostalgia, the desire to return to the organic, the local and the authentic were central to a succession of radical avant-gardes and 'alternative' cultures.

From the late nineteenth century, nostalgic attachments became marginalized and, hence, available to an emergent avant-garde as a forbidden and alluring, resource for cultural transgression. In other words, one of the consequences of the opprobrium that came to surround the topic was that the past acquired an aura of danger (especially when cast in the form of the 'primitive' and pre-civilized) that attracted a new group of creative and anti-orthodox intellectuals. Among Dadaists, surrealists, expressionists and cubists, the peasant and non-Western past were routinely employed and deployed to represent rebellious, spontaneous and irrational forces. The conservative associations which were, by the early twentieth century, firmly attached to nostalgia, were thus bypassed by a desire to rebel against civilization and celebrate the non-bourgeois and the primal.

The avant-garde's paradoxical relationship to modernity was reflected in its paradoxical categories. For example, the 'neo-primitivism' of the Russian avant-garde and the expressionist 'savages of Germany', introduced by Franz Marc as creating 'fiery signs of a new era'.[68]

Tristan Tzara in his 'Lecture on Dada', delivered in 1922, claimed that: 'Dada is not at all modern. It is more in the nature of a return to an almost Buddhist religion of indifference.'[69]

We want to continue the tradition of the Negro, Egyptian, Byzantine and gothic art and destroy the atavistic sensitivity bequeathed to us by the detestable era that followed the quattrocentro.[70]

However, Tzara's rejection of modernity acted to disturb time rather than provide a coherent alternative to progressive time:

Dada: *abolition of memory*; Dada: *abolition of archeology*; Dada: *abolition of prophets*; Dada: *abolition of the future*; Dada: *absolute and unquestionable faith in every god that is the product of spontaneity.*[71]

Thus the desire to 'proclaim', in the words of the Louis Aragon in 1925, a 'total detachment from, in a sense our uncontamination by, the ideas at the basis of a still-real European civilisation', established stereotypes of the pre-modern as a central repository of avant-garde sedition.[72] The avant-garde's desire to 'rupture the continuity of time' created intentionally disconcerting anti-modern gestures.[73] This process also established a characteristically haughty image for the avant-garde. They were transgressive yet anachronistic; protean yet disdainful. As this implies, the relationship between avant-gardism and nostalgia is necessarily uneasy. It is always in danger of going 'too far', of resulting in pomposity and snobbishness. It also meant that the radical identity of the avant-garde was an object of suspicion and bemusement within the orthodox left.

Within avant-garde praxis, it was at the level of everyday space, especially of the changing urban scene, that we find nostalgia most forcefully asserted. The 'gothic' revolutionary spirit of the surrealists and later the situationists, cast the street as a terrain of intimacy and creativity, a space hidden from and threatened by the suppression of the street augured by modern traffic and modern planning. Thus the avant-garde were involved in an attempt to defend popular or ordinary space from the technocentric and exclusionary landscapes of modernity. The dilemmas negotiated within this body of work remain topical. There are many recent examples from around the world of the critical deployment of nostalgia by avant-garde groups.[74] Indeed, as we shall see in Chapter Six (in the company of contemporary British psychogeography), released from the suspicious and censorious gaze of a wider socialist movement, these diverse currents exhibit a desire to take the openness to the past exhibited by earlier avant-garde engagements further and into new territory.

An explanation of this aspect of twentieth-century radical culture might refer to a wide variety of theorizations. Walter Benjamin argued that the surrealists were 'the first to perceive the revolutionary energies that appear in the "outmoded"'. He maintained that deploying the 'immense forces of "atmosphere" concealed in these things' was part of the surrealist's 'particular task' of harnessing 'the energies of intoxication for the revolution'.[75] However, although Benjamin's approach helps us grasp the nature of the surrealists' interest in the 'outmoded', it does not help us understand why the past has been deployed across a wide range of avant-garde activity. A broader explanation is also needed. We might, for example, look to the thesis that all artists have an investment in nostalgia as a moment of displacement and, hence, creativity.[76] Or, perhaps, to Adorno's belief in difficulty and dislocation as the hallmarks of properly revolutionary art.[77] Another contender may be found in the idea that the avant-garde is the cultural translation of anarchism.[78] This argument implies, in turn, that anarchism is the nostalgic counter-culture of orthodox radicalism. Utopian aspirations centred round themes of organic community, localism and pastoralism have certainly played a continuous and major part in anarchism, since its first explicit defence by Proudhon in *What is Property?* (published in 1840).[79] The accusation made by other revolutionaries, especially Marxists, that anarchists are conservative and backward-looking has been almost as constant. However, while the connections between anarchism and avant-garde (and counter-cultural) movements have sometimes been important, any attempt to conflate these currents should be resisted. Although the anti-authoritarianism that they share may be loosely termed 'anarchistic', the counter-cultures of modernity are too various and eclectic in their commitments to be corralled under the label of anarchism. We should also recall that anarchism is a movement which has had a relatively tiny band of serious activists or supporters.

A more fruitful approach is to acknowledge that, by the early twentieth century, the admission of loss, of emotions of regret and yearning, had emerged as a site of provocation and transgression within and against the wider revolutionary movement. It tended to be the least conventional thinkers on the left who pursued this trajectory.[80] There is tremendous political diversity within this group. Indeed, it sprawls well beyond the confines of the avant-garde. In the next chapter we meet one such unconventional thinker, the socialist patriot Robert Blatchford. However, the far more introspective and reflexive figure of Siegfried Kracauer will help us link the avant-garde, counter-cultural and critical components of this marginal history. Kracauer's attitude of 'hesitant openness' encouraged him to consider how the loss of historical memory unpicks social solidarity. Writing in the 1920s and 1930s, Kracauer found the 'unhistorical nature' and 'the formless disquiet' of modern Berlin disturbing.[81] In 'Streets without Memory' he depicts the Kurfurstendamm as 'empty flowing time in which nothing is allowed to last'.[82] In 'Screams of the Street', the ebb and flow of the modern street is associated with a barely concealed violence:

[B]uses roar through them, whose occupants during the journey to their distant destinations look down so indifferently upon the landscape of pavements, shop windows and balconies as if upon a river valley or a town in which they would never think of getting off; that a countless human crowd moves in them, constantly new people with unknown aims that intersect like the linear maze of a pattern sheet. In any case it sometimes seems to me as if an explosive lies ready in all possible hidden places that, in the very next moment, can indeed blow up.[83]

The 'new community' Kracauer depicts is an unsettled, pliable agglomeration of solipsistic individuals; a social form that concedes not merely ultimate but daily and intimate power to the dominant political order. In this way Kracauer's seemingly simple evocations of the street conjure a much wider landscape of powerlessness and displacement.

A suspicion of instrumentalism and technocracy characterizes German critical theory. One of the finest achievements of this body of work, Theodor Adorno and Max Horkheimer's *Dialectic of Enlightenment* (first published 1944), is premised on the idea that,

Men pay for the increase of their power with alienation from that which they exercise their power. Enlightenment behaves toward things as a dictator toward men. He knows them in so far as he can manipulate them.[84]

Adorno and Horkheimer assert the need and possibility 'not for the conservation of the past, but the redemption of the hopes of the past'.[85] This aspiration was also central to many of the counter-cultural movements of the late twentieth century. It was echoed in the key texts of the hippie and '68' generation, such as Herbert Marcuse's *One-Dimensional Man* and *Eros and Civilization*.[86] For Marcuse,

> As a technological universe, advanced industrial society is . . . the latest stage in the reali-zation of a specific historical project – namely, the experience, transformation, and organ-ization of nature as the mere *stuff* of domination.[87]

The enemy were identified as 'technocrats', a group described by Henri Lefebvre, in *Contre les technocrats*, as having replaced human authenticity with a fractured sense of identity based around mere 'things'.[88] And among these things there is one fetishized above all,

> In this society in which things are more important than people, there is a king-object, a pilot-object: the automobile. . . . The car is an incomparable and perhaps irremediable instrument, in neocapitalist countries, of deculturation, of the destruction from within of the civilized world.[89]

In the 1960s, counter-cultural radicalism blossomed. It was green-tinged, often intensely localist, and deeply suspicious of 'technocrats'.[90] For Melville the counter-cultural 'vision of the good life identifies the good with that which is natural, completely unencumbered by civilization'.[91] What Theodore Roszak categorized as the 'magical vision' of the counter-culture, and what Löwy labels as the 'revolutionary romanticism' of the 'spirit of May 1968', were both pitted against the damage 'technocratic society' had inflicted on human creativity and wholeness.[92]

As with Weber and Tönnies, nostalgia came to be identified as the Achilles heel of critical theory and its counter-cultural inheritors. Adorno and Horkheimer's critique of the erosion of 'real life' was represented as aristocratic, indulgent, melancholia. For Lukács, the German critical theorists occupied the 'Grand Hotel Abyss',

> [A] beautiful hotel, equipped with every comfort, on the edge of an abyss, of nothingness, of absurdity. And the daily contemplation of the abyss between excellent meals or artistic entertainments, can only heighten the enjoyment of the subtle comforts offered.[93]

Both conservatives and orthodox Marxist commentators found themselves united in a hostility towards the counter-culture's 'reactionary revulsion against modernity' (to cite the conservative critic, Irving Kristol).[94] Yet the nostalgia of critical theory and, more broadly, of the counter-culture, was always ambivalent. It cannot be adequately summarized as either elitist or populist. Indeed, it often acts to confound and confuse such designations and, by extension, the ability of radicals to ever be entirely 'at home' with either modernity or anti-modernity. Moreover, the challenge to modernity was already emerging as much more than a marginal, or residual, current.

'We have lost something': The End of Utopia

In *The Rise and Influence of Rationalism in Europe*, first published in 1865, William Lecky offered a portrait of 'one of the great triumphs of civilization'; a dazzling rise and a 'brilliant picture'.[95] Yet considering the decay of the 'unclouded assurance' of former, more faithful, years he concludes his book with the words 'it is impossible to deny we have lost something in our progress'.[96] Lecky's remark illustrates how the idea of loss can emerge from a narrative of ascent. To be forward-facing is to make what lies behind a site of fascination and uncertainty.

The grand narrative of progress is, in part, vulnerable simply because so much is expected from it. The idea is crowded with so many aspirations that disappointment and disillusionment are inevitable. However, it is not merely high hopes that have cast a shadow over progress. In 1932 Lewis Mumford wrote of progress as 'the one notion that has been thoroughly blasted by the facts of twentieth-century experience'.[97] In 1948 Richard Hofstader directly tied the rise of nostalgia to a widespread sense of fear and disillusionment.

> [W]hat underlies the overpowering nostalgia of the last fifteen years is a keen feeling of insecurity. The two world wars, unstable booms, and the abysmal depression of our time have profoundly shaken confidence in our future.[98]

A 'climate of decline' has been used to explain the power of nostalgia on many occasions.[99] Sometimes it has been supplemented by the notion that a 'nation under siege' experiences 'moral panic' in the face of change.[100] However, Hofstader's argument has a more despairing tone, for it suggests that the collapse of belief in bright new tomorrows is based on experience and evidence. It was in the context of the hard lessons of both colonialism and the Second World War, that Simone Weil offered what remains the century's clearest European statement of *The Need for Roots* (the French title is *L'Enracinement*, published in 1949).

> The future brings us nothing, gives us nothing; it is we who in order to build it have to give it everything, our very life. But to be able to give, one has to possess; and we possess no other life, no other sap, than the treasures stored up from the past and digested, assimilated and created afresh by us. Of all the human soul's needs, none is more vital than this one for the past . . . For several centuries now, men of the white race have everywhere destroyed the past, stupidly, blindly, both at home and abroad . . . Today the preservation of what little of it remains ought to become almost an obsession. We must put an end to the terrible uprootedness which European colonial methods always produce.[101]

Weil's dramatic affirmation of the need for cultural preservation remains difficult to digest for modern intellectuals. Yet her anger and disappointment were increasingly understood and shared.[102] For, although a pessimistic representation of progress can be found at any point over the past 200 years, it was to become more prominent during the course of the second half of the twentieth century. A growing disillusionment with modernity, including its communist variants, and a developing sense of the damage of industrialization, began to shape and challenge mainstream politics. Two themes are particularly important in understanding this process: the rise of the green critique and the brutal nature of communism in power.

The Green Critique

In the late twentieth century, the green critique of industrial modernity began to be both more widely urged and heard. Pollution, the decline of biodiversity and soil and climate change, were identified as consequences of unchecked economic growth and human expansion. In calling for a new relationship between the economy and the planet, environmentalists were also calling for a *return* to earlier, more sustainable, more natural, conditions and social practices. In *Silent Spring*, Rachel Carson evoked the past to condemn the present. The turn to industrial agriculture was a turn away from a more natural way of using the earth.

> There was once a town in the heart of America where all life seemed to live in harmony with its surroundings . . . Then a strange blight crept over the area and everything began to change.[103]

Fritz Schumacher provided an economist's perspective on the same problem. The 'modern industrial system', he observed in *Small is Beautiful*, 'consumes the very basis on which it has been erected . . . it lives on irreplaceable capital which it cheerfully treats as income'.[104] By the 1970s environmentalism was entering the centre ground of politics and providing a series of challenges to technocratic models of growth. The warnings offered by the environmental and demographic modellers who wrote *The Limits of Growth* were stark:

> If the present growth trends in world population, industrialization, pollution, food production, and resource depletion continues unchanged, the limits of growth on this planet will be reached sometime within the next one hundred years.

Donella Meadows and her team also noted that 'it is possible to alter these growth trends and to establish a condition of ecological and economic stability that is sustainable.'[105] The new paradigm of sustainability was premised on the idea that natural resources are finite and require careful conservation. It is a sobering vision, a cold shock designed to dispel the authority of less holistic and more technocratic visions of the future.

Communism in Power

Many different forms of left-wing government came to power in the twentieth century. However, it is the experience of, specifically, Marxist revolutionary government that drained the socialist project of legitimacy. It is a savage irony that the achievements of the democratic left in creating more humane and fair societies in many different countries should be overshadowed by totalitarian communism. Yet the communist experiment was not merely a large part of the experience of the left in power. It offered itself and was widely accepted as its leading edge, the most left, the least compromised by capitalism.

Our language at this point must be stark. Communism left a trail of death that dwarfs anything else seen in the most bloody century in human history. Estimates round off the number to the nearest million, or even tens of million. Unreliable totals reach 94 million; 110,000,000 million; 149,469,610.[106] Yet it is the fact that the final figure is guesswork, that millions died but were not countered, that provides the most telling indictment of communism in practice.

In many ways the reaction to this record, outside the former communist states and right-wing commentary in the United States, remains oddly muted. The cruelties of Nazism are studied and taught. They are part of our everyday cultural landscape. The injustices and terror of European imperialism are also familiar. These 'isms' are more likely to be approached as historical experiences than as theories. The same cannot be said for Marxism or anti-capitalism. In the West, especially in the English speaking West, these currents are routinely debated as if they were intellectual projects, challenging and untried.

The importance of acknowledging the tragic dimensions of the communist experiment in the twentieth century is a matter of morality rather than of political strategy. However, it also provides a profound challenge to how we think about systems of authority and power. In the West, critical intellectuals tend to think about power and authority in terms of capitalism, gender, sexuality and race. But many of the greatest atrocities of the last century were occasioned by *political* distinctions, more specifically the division of society into class enemies and class allies. To be rendered disposable people were first assigned a *political* label (such as class traitor, conservative or counter-revolutionary). In this way the twentieth century witnessed the emergence of politicization as a process of disempowerment and removal.

These melancholic lessons remain unpalatable. But the dead, acknowledged or not, have eaten away at the credibility, not simply of communism, but of the whole radical tradition. By the start of the present century, the fact that, despite the appalling and chaotic record of capitalism, there are few in Europe, Asia and Europe (i.e. the continents with widespread experience of communism and socialism) who appear to want to 'go back' to communism and socialism, is not simply a function of the fact that state socialism 'fell apart' or that it 'didn't work'. There is also the horror of that experience. Today, somewhere within any discussion of radicalism, of utopianism, of bold new societies, lie the dead, in uncountable numbers.

'Therefore one plays'?

Perceiving the shift away from the industrial models of yesteryear and registering the calamity of Nazism and Soviet communism, the avant-garde Co-Ritus group announced, in 1962, that: 'Now the utopian epoch is over. No more utopias can be produced. Time has run out.'[107] In the last few decades of the century the failure of utopia and the end of progress began to be theorized as part of a transition towards post-modernity. The German post-modern dramatist, Heiner Müller, explained that,

> There are no more utopias, there is no point to anything any more . . . One doesn't know where one is going in this empty space, one doesn't know how to move, which direction makes sense. Therefore one plays.[108]

Müller offers us a provocative chain of association between the collapse of progress and a refusal to take the world seriously. It is an association that acknowledges the importance of the past only to suggest that it signifies nothing. However, the relationship between history and memory has attracted less extreme forms of revision. We can explore this emergent field further in the company of the literary critic Andreas Huyssen. Huyssen agrees that the promise of history – notably the onward march of progress – can no longer be believed. He depicts 'a fundamental disturbance . . . of history itself and its promises'. It is not only 'a disturbance of our notions of the past, but a fundamental crisis in our imagination of alternative futures'.[109] We are left, Huyssen argues, with a transitory and intimate relationship to the past which we call memory. Trying to explain what he calls 'the explosion of memory discourses at the end of the twentieth century',[110] Huyssen writes,

> For about two centuries, history in the West was quite successful in its project to anchor the ever more transitory present of modernity and the national in a multifaceted but strong narrative of historical time. Memory, on the other hand, was a topic for poets and

their visions of a golden age or, conversely, for their tales about the hauntings of a restless past. . . . This model no longer works.[111]

Linda Hutcheon has offered another, more prosaic, reason why the past might have become more available as an object of constant yet distant contemplation. 'The more memory we store on data banks', she suggests, 'the more the past is sucked into the orbit of the present, ready to be called up on the screen.'[112] For others, the sentimental comforts of memory explain its allure. When Wendy Wheeler writes of nostalgia as, 'a central feature of post-modernism', she has in mind the idea that 'the nostalgic image arises in postmodernity as an almost unbearably intense and uncanny yearning for the homely comforts of a settled way of life.'[113] It is a small step to the association of post-modern nostalgia with the comforts of commodification. In her study, *Discourses of the Vanishing*, Marilyn Ivy makes this link explicit, noting post-modern capitalism's creation of 'a nostalgia . . . that is kept on the verge of vanishing, stable yet endangered (and thus open for commodifiable desire)'.[114] The link between neo-liberalism and nostalgia has been made on several occasions and usefully highlights how a 'retreat' into private space can be accompanied by the 'consumerization' of memory.[115] However, the idea of capitalism, post-modernism and nostalgia as a unified programme is difficult to sustain. In many ways nostalgia is the mortal enemy of superficial consumer culture. Post-modernism offers the past as pastiche and, hence, empty of significance. As this suggests, the yearning for authenticity and meaning that is so important within nostalgia is blatantly traduced within post-modern 'play'.

In the most provocative and critical expressions of post-modern culture (which have had a notable presence in the theatre, including through the work of Müller and companies that have taken a similar path, such as Forced Entertainment) the inadequacy of 'play' takes on a tragicomic character. A longing for unobtainable meaning is registered against a background of disturbance and sudden violence. The power of the performance relies on the inadequacy of simulacra and, hence, the failure of post-modernism to adequately prescribe or describe.[116]

In fact, nostalgia did not achieve a consistent role within post-modern discourse. Advocates of post-modernism were often somewhat embarrassed by its links to nostalgia and sort to deny or displace them. Thus, for example, Stauth and Turner contrast 'post-modern cultural pluralism' with the 'backward-looking' and 'nostalgic' inclinations of 'critical theory'.[117] Perhaps even more telling is the irony of late twentieth-century Marxist critiques of post-modernism as, in Jameson's terms, a 'nostalgic film', a 'desperate attempt to appropriate a missing past'.[118] The accusation relies on post-modernists' discomfort with nostalgia in order to hit home. The post-modern theorist, Linda Hutcheon, bats the charge back with the obvious question:

Is Jameson's implicit mythologising and idealising of a more stable, pre-late-capitalist (that is, modernist) world not in itself perhaps part of an aesthetics (or even politics) of nostalgia?[119]

It seems that neither Marxists nor post-modernists want to be labelled as nostalgic. Hence, each accuses the other of being precisely that. Today post-modernism, like Marxism, appears before us a vanguard of yesteryear (although, as we shall see later in this book, some of it concerns have been carried on within multiculturalism and post-colonialism). Its transition into a historical object makes it easier to identify as a site of struggle over the past. It is a site where discourses of loss and progress were cohered and rescripted into an alluring and malleable ideal of play and fragmentation. Yet, it is a narrative whose attraction quickly soured, as its proclaimed superficiality came to symbolize a failure to take seriously the consequences of living in an era of rapid and enforced change.

Nostalgia's Uncertain Return

The struggle of man against power is the struggle of memory against forgetting.

Milan Kundera[120]

Nostalgia has returned. It is being increasingly acknowledged as a neglected component of the modern imagination. However, as we shall see, this reassessment is often hesitant and uneasy. This awkwardness is reflected in the desire to cut nostalgia up into good and bad bits, to reassemble it in a more familiar shape, such as a tool, or resource, whose worth is to be measured by its utility for the progressive project.

However, I will begin this exploration of nostalgia's uncertain return with a famous yet disconcerting statement: 'The tradition of the dead generations weighs like a nightmare on the minds of the living.'[121] It is one of the most quoted lines from 'The Eighteenth Brumaire of Louis Bonaparte', Marx's treatise against the misuse of history. The line is arresting because it is so agonized and because it demands of us a heroic and straightforward response. Let us throw off the weight of 'the dead' and become free! In one of the texts that opened the door for the critical reassessment of nostalgia, *Spectres of Marx*, Derrida homes in on this line in order to deconstruct Marx's efforts to find the spirit of the revolution while repressing the spirits of the past.[122] For Derrida this is a doomed project; one that articulates a yearning for transcendence yet also a haunted fleeing.[123] The two types of spirit (of the revolution and of the past), he argues,

contaminate each other sometimes in such a troubling manner, since the simulacrum consists precisely in miming the phantom or in simulating the phantasm of the other, that the 'striking' difference strikes, precisely, at the origin, and leaps into view only in order to jump up and down before your eyes. To disappear by appearing, in the phenomenon of its phantasm.[124]

Derrida seeks to reveal Marx's relationship to the past as haunted and anxious. Marx becomes someone who 'loved the figure of the ghost' and 'he detested it . . . Like all obsessives, he harassed the obsession.'[125] By following this paradox, *Spectres of Marx* takes familiar ideas and sentences lodged within radical thought and makes them strange to us. However, Derrida is also protective of Marx. He is careful to offer the ambivalances he explores as integral to the creativity and political importance of Marx.

A similarly care may be seen at work within Sayre and Löwy's reassessments of the place of romanticism in the Marxist tradition. In 1984, Sayre and Löwy, perhaps sensing a new openness towards themes of loss, sought to cast the repression of the past as one of the deviations of 'vulgar' Marxists.[126] Marxism's difficulty in admitting the possibility of affinities between nostalgia and radicalism was coming to connote, not intellectual focus and strength but rigidity. For Löwy and Sayre, 'Romanticism is one of Marx's and Engels's neglected sources', a current that, far from being restricted to an early, pre-scientific, phase, is of foundational importance for communist anti-capitalism.[127] It is only 'official Marxism' that denies the

'Romantic element that is unquestionably present in the works of Marx and Engels'.[128] Sayre and Löwy's argument reflected a wider trend towards the sympathetic engagement with those unorthodox Marxists who combined their radicalism with romanticism. In particular, they create intellectual space for a romantic interpretation of Marx by turning to Ernst Bloch, the most nostalgic of Marxist historians. Bloch's *The Spirit of Utopia* offered a long history of apocalyptic creativity, desires and disruptions.[129] His later work, *The Principle of Hope*, pulls in myriad utopian moments from the past to provide a portrait of previously maginalized emancipatory moments.[130]

In their 1984 article, Sayre and Löwy also commence an analysis of the social basis of romanticism. In what sounds initially like a reversion to standard Marxist sociology, they claim that 'it is clear that the *producers* of the Romantic anti-capitalist worldview are *certain traditional sectors of the intelligentsia*, whose culture and way of life are hostile to bourgeois industrial civilization.'[131] With this remark we seem, abruptly, to be thrown back to the days when nostalgia was a reactionary ailment that requires class diagnosis. Indeed, Sayre and Löwy's analysis closely echoes Marx's own opinion of the class roots of reactionary radicalism:

> The lower middle class, the small manufacturer, the shopkeeper, the artisan, the peasant, all these fight against the bourgeoisie, to save from extinction their existence as fractions of the middle classes. They are there not revolutionary, but conservative. Nay more, they are reactionary, for they try to roll back the wheel of history.[132]

Yet the spectacle of Marx's remorselessly rolling wheels of history appears to unnerve Sayre and Löwy. For having broached this mode of analysis they then pull back from it. Having argued that the 'producers' of a romantic world-view can be easily identified, they decide that the 'audience' for this perspective cannot be so neatly located: for 'the *audience* of the worldview, its *social base* in the full sense, is far more vast'.[133] It is an awkward manoeuvre, since it implies that there are whole, unnamed, sectors of society that hungrily but passively consume an ideology that originates elsewhere. Nevertheless, this argument allows Sayre and Löwy to acknowledge, not only the ubiquity of romanticism, but also its seemingly vital and creative power in contemporary forms of social opposition. Thus they conclude by challenging the neutralization of nostalgia by those critics who assign it to frustrated class factions. Indeed, Sayre and Löwy portray the idea that we can 'reduce the audience of Romantic anti-capitalism – its social public – to certain archaic, pre-capitalist "pockets of resistance"', as absurd.[134] Not only is it deeply and broadly present in popular culture, but 'several of the most important recent social movements – ecology, feminism, pacifism, the theology of liberation – express feeling and aspirations strongly colored by Romantic anti-capitalism'.[135]

Nostalgia's uncertain return may also be registered by reference to the way radicals of the = '1960s generation' have discovered the pleasures of wistful remembrance. The collapse of socialism has meant that activists can cast themselves as representatives of 'lost worlds' of political militancy. The 'lost worlds' tag, employed by Samuel to narrate the story of British communism, was also used by Lynne Segal to title two articles in *Radical Philosophy* on the 'memoirs of the left in Britain'.[136] Although Segal seeks to place her interest in radical memoir as part of a 'new psychosocial approach to history', it is also, unmistakably and more straightforwardly, a reflection of a contemporary sense of loss among left intellectuals.[137] In one recent symposium debate on socialist feminist memoir, one contributor asked a question that would have once been unthinkable: 'how can the feeling of radicalism – the linked feelings of newness, excitement and belief in change – be freed from a location of always in the past?'[138] The answers offered to this question revolved around the idea of distinguishing *useful* forms of nostalgia. It is towards the premises and problems of this increasingly influential aspiration that I now turn.

Useful Nostalgia and Its Limits

Over the past two decades we have seen nostalgia gain its revenge on Marx's attempts to banish and deny it. In what is widely announced to be our post-communist epoch, the left's hostility to nostalgia has begun to look hollow and self-defeating.

Sean Scanlan argues that 'nostalgia is no longer the programmatic equivalent of bad memory.'[139] Yet this is a topic still freighted with suspicion. To argue that nostalgia is a chronic dilemma is to suggest that radicalism is both backward- and forward-looking. It is also to imply that, when nostalgia is reconsidered by 'progressive' intellectuals, the resulting reassessment is likely to sustain many existing assumptions.

However, before considering more recent work, it is important to acknowledge that the concept of a useful past has always had a profound attraction. Henri Bergson scolded that,

> he who lives in the past for the mere pleasure of living there, and in whom recollections emerge into the light of consciousness without any advantage for the present situation, is hardly better fitted for action: here we have no man of impulse, but a *dreamer*.[140]

One of the most prominent narratives found within radical movements is the attempt to apply the movement's past to the movement's present. Thus, for example, histories of English socialism provide one the oldest and most continuous forms of documentation associated with English socialism. These histories have often sought to turn socialism into something about which English people may feel a sense of connection and ownership. From Hyndman's patriotic message in *The Historical Basis of Socialism in England* (published in 1883) – 'We islanders have been revolutionists' – to the solace Tony Benn finds in recollection of the Diggers – 'it is ... deeply encouraging to know that the democratic and socialist traditions are so deeply rooted in our own national experience' – English socialism has been characterized by the desire to use the past in the service of the present.[141] Drawing out its claims on the past, Paul Ward has suggested that, between the 1880s and 1920s, British socialism may be cast as a 'new form of historical politics'.

> As socialism emerged in the 1880s and 1890s it was invested with an ethical and moral quality, much of which was based on a socialist historiography of the English past. This was used to pre-figure a future socialist society. Across a range of activities, history for socialists became not so much a guide to the present, but to the future. This reading of the past provided not only an explanation for the fundamental shortcomings of capitalism, but also a vision of a new society in which social equilibrium would be restored. British socialism therefore sought to combine both class and national identities in a new form of historical politics.[142]

Another argument that locates a useful past is the claim that, within the nostalgic and romantic protests of earlier generations, one can find half-formed, embryonic signs of the mature radical consciousness of later years. In post-Second World War Britain, the rediscovery of the popular roots of class consciousness by radical historians, reflected this belief. The related emphasis on 'history from below', associated with the History Workshop movement, offered a similar set of concerns. As well as reflecting the acute need to offer a local, democratic history of socialism, in an era of when the Soviet Union was a communist superpower, these historical agendas challenged many of the tenets of British Marxism: for they showed that militancy arose from a wide cast of political actors and traditions. Thompson explained,

> I am seeking to rescue the poor stockinger, the Luddite cropper, the 'obsolete' hand-loom weaver, the 'utopian' artisan, and even the follower of Joanna Southcott, from the enormous condescension of posterity.[143]

As Jackson Lears argues, in 'a society where even conservatives are besotted with progress', such acts of 'rescue' have a political value.

> Social and cultural historians introduced a whole new cast of heroic figures: the leatherapron boys, artisans who subordinated entrepreneurship to communal solidarity; traditionalist textile workers keeping St. Monday, which drove their bosses crazy . . . Thompson, Raymond Williams and other inspired by them found more than 'the idiocy of rural life' in the English countryside, they found the sources of political radicalism. Their work showed how loving memories of the past could spark rebellion against the present in the service of future generations.[144]

The re-evaluation of the politics of memory and custom has been developed and amplified well beyond the discipline of history. Over the past two decades, this reassessment can be found taking place across the humanities and social sciences. The nettle of nostalgia is finally being grasped. Thompson, like other radical historians who pitted themselves on the side of the 'Luddite cropper', was careful not to upset this, most ingrained, of radical taboos. However, more recently, social and cultural theorists have been lining up to do precisely that. Thus, for example, in a study of the recent privatization of the railways in Britain, the sociologist, Tim Strangleman, argues that nostalgia remains one of the most powerful discourses of resistance. He suggests that nostalgic memories may 'be positive in that they create an increasingly historically-aware popular culture, one therefore that is *less* open to manipulation'.[145] He also points out that in 'breaking the link between experience and emotion the possibilities for manipulation and falsification increase'.[146] In similar vein, Peter Glazer finds that 'the performance of radical nostalgia can serve valuable ends, reinfusing lost histories with credibility, substance, and emotional resonance.'[147] These depictions evoke a vast and global cultural history that connects servitude and vulnerability with the loss of memory. For Hayden White,

> The breakdown of narrativity in a culture, group, or social class is a symptom of its having entered into a state of crisis. For with any weakening of narrativizing capacity, the group loses its power to locate itself in history, to come to grips with the Necessity that its past represents for it, and to imagine a creative, if only provisional, transcendence of its 'fate'.[148]

One of the more novel aspects of the new wave of work on nostalgia lies in the attempt to depict the role of nostalgia among communities subject to ethnic violence and removal. The Native American story-tellers discussed by Jennifer Ladino have long remained marginal to radical representations of those who are to give voice to Marx's 'poetry from the future'.[149] As viewed through Ladino's research, they articulate a sense of loss and remembrance that reflects their experience of modernity as a racialized condition which has shown little interest in their future. An attention to the way such 'counter-nostalgia' can be employed to resist dominant images of the past and, more generally, Westernization and racialized modernity, provides Ladino's work with a politicized sense of the value of an attachment to 'the dead'.

> Counter-nostalgic narratives complicate simplistic narratives, invert oppressive ones . . . . Against the widespread negative characterizations that dismiss or limit nostalgia, it is essential to draw attention to the range of ways in which nostalgia functions in order to recover more productive uses of this powerful and prevalent cultural narrative.[150]

'Counter-nostalgic narratives', Ladino concludes, 'create the potential for new formulations of social justice that utilise the unlikely ally of nostalgia as a catalyst for action.' Ladino's concept of 'counter-nostalgia' echoes Foucault's 'counter-memory' and, hence, can be seen to overlap with the insurgent counter-memory Stephen Legg identifies in colonial India; the 'strategic nostalgia' Tina Steiner portrays in post-colonial fiction; or the 'counter-narratives' of melancholic longing Linda Tabar finds in Jenin refugee camp.[151]

Nostalgia is being re-evaluated and revalued in these accounts. But it is still eyed warily. A 'radical, progressive nostalgia', Glazer warns, 'can become available and advantageous under specific social, historical, cultural, and performative circumstances.'[152] Nostalgia is found to be acceptable only when it can be shown to be 'a catalyst for action', a resource for progressives and insurgents. Hence, contemporary reassessments of nostalgia are marked by the effort to differentiate good forms of nostalgia from bad forms of nostalgia. Such attempts at political and moral classification introduce a hierarchy of nostalgic forms, a division that implies that nostalgia is a subtle art which the ignorant can easily get wrong. Fred Davis set the terms of much of the subsequent debate by introducing the following scale: 'simple' nostalgia; 'reflexive' nostalgia; and 'interpreted' nostalgia (what he also called First, Second and Third Order forms).[153] The evolution from 'simple' to 'interpreted' is an ascent from unquestioning yearning to critical distance. The clear implication is that the more removed one's relationship is to the past the better. Svetlana Boym provides a similarly loaded contrast between 'restorative' and 'reflective' nostalgia. The former is 'an attempt to conquer and stabilise time', to imaginatively reconstruct a lost home, while the latter is 'ironic, inclusive and fragmentary',[154] or in Legg's terms, 'nomadic, evasive'.[155] These comparisons ask us to ironize the past in order to make it safe for political consumption. In her influential discussion of the relationship between post-modernism, irony and nostalgia, Linda Hutcheon makes the same suggestion, concluding that,

> Our contemporary culture is indeed nostalgic; some parts of it – postmodern parts – are aware of the risks and lures of nostalgia, and seek to expose them through irony.[156]

The historical sensibility that animates many of these recent attempts to distinguish and privilege ironic forms of nostalgia is intriguing. Although rarely acknowledged, it is clear that they are defining this form of nostalgia against a particular set of images of non-ironic nostalgia. Enough nods and winks are supplied to suggest that the model, the ur-type, of non-ironic nostalgia that is being offered, is fascism. It would be useful briefly to draw this example out in the open. For when we do we find that irony, far from being incompatible with fascism, was often freely incorporated within it. The 'aestheticized politics' of European fascism created an authoritarian performativity, a grandiose and willed spectacularization of the classical and ancient past that was both totalitarian and historically self-aware. Fascism, concludes Andrew Hewitt, 'results from the application of a specific form of aesthetic, ironic subjectivity to the political realm'.[157] In *Heritage of Our Times* (first published in 1934) Bloch opened out the contradictions of the Nazis's deployment of the past. He makes it clear that these 'shabbily cunning plagiarists' deploy intoxicating spectacle and 'dazzling illusion' to evoke 'non-contemporaneity'.[158] The performance of fascism/Nazism was premised on a play of 'appearances'. It is reasonable to conclude that the politics of irony are not pre-determined. Irony can and has been adopted and adapted by a variety of political traditions.

Moreover, Hutcheon's illustrations of ironic nostalgia do little to further convince us that this form can be separated out and claimed for progressive politics. Her two examples are the 'histriographic metafictions of Salman Rushdie' and the 'parodic architectural ideas of Charles Moore's once splendid Piazza d'Italia'.[159] As soon as these concrete cases are evoked the purpose and possibility of the demarcation of ironic and non-ironic nostalgia becomes even more doubtful. Today, the very quickly 'once splendid' Piazza d'Italia is little more than a minor illustration of the ephemerality and social failure of post-modernism. It has also become clearer that Rushdie's historical novels are not odes to deracination but rely on the creative tension between, and meshing of, the dualism that Hutcheon wishes to set him on one side of. Indeed, it is with a sense of the importance of acknowledging unresolvable longings that, in *The Ground Beneath Her Feet*, Rushdie explains that,

> Among the great struggles of man – good/evil, reason/unreason, etc. – there is also this mighty conflict between the fantasy of Home and the fantasy of Away, the dream of roots and the mirage of the journey.[160]

The attempt to separate out progressive ironic nostalgia from reactionary non-ironic nostalgia appears designed to neutralize the accusations of conservatism that still surround the topic. In this way it recreates the politics and pleasures of scorning the truly backward-looking. As this implies, and despite the emphasis on the value of the 'nomadic' and 'evasive', such hierarchies rely on a characteristically modern sense of discomfort with the past.

This argument also brings critical attention to another, more ubiquitous, way of separating out a progressive way of looking backward. I am referring to the idea that *memory* is superior to and distinct from nostalgia. The separation of the two has often relied on the claim that, in contrast to memory, nostalgia is irrational, inaccurate and incapable of drawing lessons from the past to apply to the present. Thus Christopher Lasch argues that nostalgia is 'the abdication of memory'; it wallows in the past while 'memory draws hope and comforts from the past in order to enrich the present'.[161] Gayle Green has made a similar point:

> [N]ostalgia and remembering are in some ways antithetical, since nostalgia is a forgetting, merely regressive, whereas memory may look back in order to move forward and transform disabling fictions to enabling fictions.[162]

Yet, while the epistemological intent of these demarcations is clear, their plausibility or practicality is not. If memory, in Lasch's terms, 'draws hope and comfort from the past', then it is nostalgic. Conversely if memory is stripped of its yearnings and attachments, then much of the moral and social strength of Lasch's defence of it (and his critique of the ideology of progress) is drained away. If memory is merely a strategic application of the past to the present then it becomes another, typically modern, technique for burying the awkward presence of nostalgia.

A broader problem with all these attempts to valorize reflexive distance over 'simple' or 'restorative' nostalgia, is that they underestimate the intrinsic complexity of nostalgia. To be nostalgic *is* to be dislocated, alienated, homeless and, hence, removed from one's object of desire. As this implies, nostalgia is inherently reflexive: it presupposes a self-conscious relationship with history.[163] Recall Peter Fritzsche's depiction of nostalgia as 'a familiar symptom of unease' ('the measure of the distance people have fallen short in their efforts to make themselves "at home in a constantly changing world"').[164] Rather than identify nostalgics as lacking 'reflection' and 'interpretation', it would be more plausible to argue that these mental faculties are likely to be absent from people who live purely in and for the present and/or for the future. Nostalgia's blatant vulnerability, its pathos, are premised on the *impossibility* of its struggle against time, its wistful *realization* that the past is out of reach.

The attempt to dissect nostalgia and stitch together its ironic bits so that they 'serve the needs of the progressive community' is premised on the hope that this fantastic new creature will leap into the future with a self-questioning roar.[165] Such clumsy surgery ignores the fact that the concept of nostalgia denotes the existence of a complex and interconnected set of emotional relationships with the past. Moreover, this set of relationships appear to be an indelible feature of modern life. They are intellectually graspable: the typically paradoxical relationship we have to nostalgia can be acknowledged and understood. But the idea that it can be made politically safe by being neutered of its transgressive sense of loss and abandonment is a delusion.

Any attempt to fashion nostalgia to our political needs is also complicated by the way memory and affiliation are culturally cross-cutting. Nostalgic transference often proceeds through the identification of a romanticized object of affection that evokes or has retained some pre- or anti-modern virtue that 'we' have lost.[166] The idealization of working-class pasts by middle-class radicals is one example of this process and is highly pertinent to the discussion of the situationists provided in Chapter Five. As we shall see, the situationists displayed a telling mixture of anthropological distance and fond attachment to the proletarian places and communities of Paris. Such processes of nostalgic transfer further question the plausibility of demarcating and privileging ironic over non-ironic forms of nostalgia. The middle-class romanticization of working-class pasts is deeply freighted with irony; so too the urban evocation of pastoral Edens; or the Western exoticization of distant natives. Does it follow that these estranged attachments should be valued over and above the nostalgia of those with more direct and authentic connections to these valued sites of memory? Is the reflexive pastiching of tribal and indigenous pasts by colonial Westerners of more value and more critical, than the 'restorative' nostalgic recreations of 'the natives' themselves?

It seems that the attempt to value irony and evasion in nostalgia, and/or create hierarchies within nostalgia and memory, is beset with difficulties. These difficulties point to the wider problem of taking an instrumental approach to nostalgia. The insistence that nostalgia is to be taken seriously only when it can be presented as a useful political tool, a weapon of resistance, fails to meet the challenge posed by this chronic response to the modern condition. The deployment of oppositional pasts demands that these histories be reduced to cogs in the engine of progress. Thus notions of counter-nostalgia and counter-memory, although important in other ways, do not necessarily represent a break with an ingrained hostility towards attachments to the past. And why do we need to break from such hostility? Not because nostalgia is a fine and noble thing. Very often it is quite the opposite. It is because nostalgia is a part what we are. It is not something we can opt in and out of. It is an inescapable aspect of the radical project. To flee it is to run towards it.

To Begin Differently?

Between the simple backward look and the simple progressive thrust there is room for long argument but none for enlightenment. We must begin differently.

Raymond Williams[167]

We need to acknowledge nostalgia. This is the modest argument found throughout this book. It does not so much suggest a direction but a process of opening up. Rather than closing up paradoxes, we should be trying to allow them to become visible. This idea is exemplified in the photography of one of the principle theorists and artists of nostalgia, Svetlana Boym. Boym has returned time and again to the uncomfortable yet necessary relationship we all have (perhaps especially ex-Soviet citizens and those on the political left) with abandoned aspirations and mouldering assumptions. The photos of decayed buildings and things 'not working' that dominate her work evoke an open-ended sense of loss, but also a set of aspirations towards modernity and community, towards the future and the past. Boym offers what she calls an 'Off-modern Manifesto'. 'Art's new technology', we are told, 'is a broken technology. Or shall we call it dysfunctional, erratic, nostalgic?' Perhaps sensing she has gone too far, Boym reassures us that her 'Broken-tech art is not Luddite but ludic'.[168]

The potential for an open-ended exploration of nostalgia can also be found in the reminisces of many on the left, if only as a series of hints, or as an tantalizing awkwardness in an otherwise polished performance. One of the places I find such awkwardness is in one of the major statements of British cultural Marxism, *The Country and the City* by Raymond Williams.[169] Perhaps the book's most difficult moment came after publication. In his review of *The Country and the City* Terry Eagleton, writing from a more insurgent tradition, and eschewing the kind of fond remembrances he finds in Williams, damned him with the label 'left-Leavisite'.[170] William's response was disconcertingly tart: 'What I want to ask is who Terry Eagleton is?'[171] This unnerving question arose from Williams's belief that Eagleton's analytical radicalism is disingenuous; that it is only through attachment and experience that radicalism emerges and can be understood. Thus,

> [The] basic fault of the kind of formalist Marxism which Eagleton is now in is that it assumes that by an act of intellectual abstraction you can place yourself above the lived contradictions both of your society and of any individual you choose to analyse, and that you are not yourself in question . . . the belief that one is above that deeply contradictory situation is a fantasy.[172]

In *The Country and the City*, as well in a series of rural novels, William provided something more than clinical analysis. He offered a sense of the lived experience of place and community. His acid response to Eagleton shows an annoyance that this honesty had been turned into a political vulnerability, to be exploited by a less sentimental and less nostalgic critic.

Williams offers a distinction, familiar from Marx, between modern alienation and a lost human wholeness. The 'perception and affirmation of a world in which one is not necessarily a stranger and an agent, but can be a member, a discoverer, in a shared source of life', he argues, has been lost, for the 'process of human growth has in itself been deformed . . . in this kind of using, consuming, abstracting world'.[173] Yet, unlike Marx, Williams writes about this process in terms of direct personal involvement: of *his* memories; of *his* past; of *his* community. By doing so the nostalgia that is foundational but constantly scorned within Marx, creeps shyly towards centre-stage. Similarly, while Williams can often be seen considering memory as a political tool, his own memories cut across this reading. For Scanlan,

> Williams resists the urge, present in many Marxist critiques, to simply project his hopes and aspirations into the future . . . The conflict is left unresolved and in his theoretical work it becomes the tension between a 'militant particularism' devoted to the preservation of local identities and a socialist 'universalism' that has no place for the concern with historical and social singularity.[174]

Williams concludes that 'We must begin differently.'[175] But he does not offer us a single point from which to 'begin differently' but rather something broader; a place in which memory and modernity co-exist.

Perhaps, though, a project of acknowledging and recognizing nostalgia can do more than 'open up' the topic. It can actively challenge the neglect of nostalgia. It is a challenge taken up in one of the more provocative statements of radical thought of the past two decades, Trevor Blackwell and Jeremy Seabrook's *The Revolt against Change: Towards a Conserving Radicalism*.[176] Blackwell and Seabrook draw on their long experience of left activism to develop a manifesto for a different kind of relationship between radicalism and the past:

> [W]e were becoming uneasy about the recurring theme that 'people must change' . . . The experience of industrialisation had been of driven and relentless change, and continues to be so . . . So why should we expect exhortations to change will be welcomed by those who have known little else for at least two centuries? In this context, the desire to conserve, to protect, to safeguard, to rescue, to resist becomes the heart of a radical project.[177]

Blackwell and Seabrook's reclamation of the language of conserving and protecting for radicalism has to be understood in the context of the rise of environmentalism and increasing unease with the rapid refashioning of the urban landscape. The violence inflicted on memory and identity by the loss of place has been highlighted by many critics.[178] The constant upheaval and homogenization of townscapes has been described as a process that creates non-places, with multiple layers, of what Tamara Hareven and Randolph Langenbach, call 'social amnesia'.[179]

A new concern for the intimate spaces of locality and home also finds echoes in recent feminist reassessments of nostalgia. This connection may seem surprising. Feminists have rarely harboured illusions about a lost time of gender equality. For this reason it has sometimes been argued that the only truly forward-looking radical movement is feminism. Feminism, declares Michael Fischer has 'no tendency towards nostalgia, no illusion of a golden age of the past'.[180] However, this judgement has come to seem decidedly shaky in an era often declared to be post-feminist. The crisis of contemporary feminism appears to be linked to the revaluation of the topic. Since nostalgia is a condition that indicates a desire for home, it certainly appears ripe for a feminist counter-reading. Alexander Martin offers a psychological portrait of the masculinism of anti-nostalgia. Thus he finds in anti-nostalgia, compulsive reactions against the home and authority, against the past and tradition, against the emotional and the earthy non-intellectual, all being glorified as independence and expressions of healthy growth.[181]

Alison Blunt's examination of the search for community among Anglo-Indians makes the case that hostility to nostalgia draws on a gendered tendency to dismiss the importance of home. Thus for Blunt 'an antipathy towards nostalgia reflects a more pervasive and long-established "suppression of home"'.[182] Emphasizing the materiality of affective politics, Blunt also identifies the Anglo-Indian desire for 'home' as 'productive nostalgia': a term she uses 'to represent a longing for home that was embodied and enacted in practice rather than solely in narrative or imagination'.[183] This emphasis is taken up in other recent reassessments of nostalgia, which assert its corporeal and lived qualities and, hence, take issue with the claim, identified by Stephen Legg, that nostalgia 'is only "behind and before experience", not taking part in "lived experience"'.[184]

An interest in pre-discursive affective realms in recent cultural theory (sometimes termed the 'non-representational' turn) may be helping to create the intellectual space to challenge instrumental approaches to nostalgia. As Karen Till observes,

> [T]he affective materialities of a place or even an object – a unique quality resulting from particular social histories, interconnections to other places, and lasting human imprints – may surpass instrumental efforts to make selective pasts speak through them.[185]

The desire to locate and, in some way, affirm a realm beyond or outside of rational symbolic representation also offers less rational pleasures, of escape from authority into what the non-representational theorist, Nigel Thrift, calls 'wild new imaginaries', and regress into the 'purposefully immature'.[186] In as much as these hopes echo traditional romantic aspirations, these new critical trajectories are recognizable as not merely opening up discussion of nostalgia but as shaped by nostalgia. It seems that, as we begin to acknowledge nostalgia we may also begin to find it in some surprising places, including within the theories that reveal it to us.

The new currents identified in this section all offer the possibility of engaging nostalgia in more complex ways. They have all informed the arguments developed in this book. Yet their most profound influence lies in their power to dislodge some of the common-sense assumptions that still surround the topic. Along with historical reassessments of the place of romanticism and progressivism on the left, they have helped create an enabling and open-ended scepticism towards some of the central myths of modern radicalism. It should also be clear that *Left in the Past* carries its own set of questions and obsessions. It is the ambivalent presence of nostalgia within radicalism, its awkwardness and its reappearances, that fascinates me, and represents my own attempt to 'begin differently'.

Conclusion

In the late twentieth century the figure of the radical became something of a joke. The negative stereotypes that had emerged around radicalism, of self-important rigidity or narcissism, were mined to offer a cast of absurd and dislikable comic creations.[187] One idea that unites these humorous representations is that radicals are pompous, more specifically they make pompous claims on the future. In his wide-ranging and important challenge to the left's fetishization of the idea of progress, *The True and Only Heaven: Progress and Its Critics*, Christopher Lasch identified the psychological cost of maintaining a revulsion towards attachments to the past for those whose continued existence is cast by much of the wider world as an anachronism. It is the 'belief in progress', Lasch tells us, that explains 'the left's curious mixture of complacency and paranoia':

> Their confidence in being on the winning side of history made progressive people unbearably smug and superior, but they felt isolated and beleaguered in their own country, since it was so much less progressive than they were.[188]

The 'pretence of standing out against the prevailing intellectual fashion of sentimental regret' is, for Lasch, a left 'trademark', marked by a 'tone of bluff and jocular dismissal'.[189]

Lasch's ascerbic views of contemporary radicalism are testament to its declining power to speak convincingly about the future. They may also be indicative of the fact that hostility to nostalgia has also become less persuasive. There is a dated and curmudgeonly quality to what Raphael Samuel calls the 'heritage baiters'.[190] David Lowenthal's intervention in the 'Nostalgia strand' of the 'History Workshop' conference in 1985, may be taken as an early bell-weather of the changing mood. In his provocative chapter in *The Imagined Past*, the edited volume which emerged out of these sessions,[191] Lowenthal begins by describing the dominant theme:

> Diatribe upon diatribe denounced [nostalgia] as reactionary, regressive, ridiculous. The 'workshop' that yielded this very book deplored Britain's retreat into a cosy, pub-and-chocolate-box past, while our convenor termed nostalgia 'perhaps the most dangerous . . . of all ways of using history'.[192]

However, Lowenthal cheekily turns the tables on these assumptions. He points out that the idea of a 'History Workshop' is itself laden with nostalgia: an attempt at 'validating our endeavour by linking it with olden horney-handed toil'.[193] For Lowenthal there is something remarkable, deeply ironic and faintly ridiculous about a room full of nostalgic radicals berating nostalgia.

Today the identification of nostalgia with political conservatism invites scepticism. In a world where so many countries were once socialist but are no longer, it is this tradition, not capitalism, that evokes remembrance, fond and otherwise. A melancholic disposition within the left is not new. Indeed it chimes with a desire to withdraw from a hostile world that one can find throughout the history of radicalism. This is a desire that can be found even at times of political ascent. Writing in 1964, Ralph Miliband observed a prevalent mood 'of socialist decline, of the past as militant and committed, and the present as unregenerate'.[194] In his reminiscences about 'the immediate postwar years' (in the late 1940s) Raymond Williams recalls,

> feeling that except for certain simple kinds of idealising retrospect there was no main current of thought in the world which had not been incorporated within the fundamental forms of the capitalist and imperialist system . . . extreme subjectivism and fatalism . . . dominated our thought.[195]

The escalator of socialist decline and crisis can be followed much further. High expectations of popular uprising and social rebirth are easily brought low and turned into disappointment. The fact that defeat is familiar may explain why so many on the left seem inured to the collapse of the socialist tradition and, indeed, still seem to see their project as akin to a rocket blasting into the future. Yet, as we enter the second decade of the twenty-first century, the durability of this dramatic vision appears not only remarkable but myopic. The early optimism among radicals in the West that the collapse of communism, from 1989, would rescue the already faltering ambitions of social democracy (in part, by scotching the suggestion that social democracy was merely a less militant version of communism) was misplaced. The collapse of socialism was not simply of state socialism but of socialism as an ideology. Perry Anderson was, perhaps, exaggerating when in 2004 he spoke of 'three decades of nearly unbroken political defeats for every force that once fought against the established order'.[196] But his conclusion can hardly be disputed: by the 1990s, he argued, 'it was no longer even necessary to proclaim that capitalism was superior to socialism, as if there could be choice between them.'[197] With few exceptions, across the world, democratic workers and labour parties have moved away from state ownership and towards an economic outlook that a generation before would have been understood as centrist or right wing. The global financial meltdown of 2008–2009, which saw the banking and wider financial system, the central institutions of capitalism, humiliated and vulnerable, was also notable for the absence, in any major Western nation, of significant left mobilization. It seems that, for the time being at least, the term 'mainstream left' has become an oxymoron. Socialism as an idea – indeed *the* boldest and most influential political ideology of the twentieth century – has lost its role in modern politics. It is a thing of the past. And with that realization comes another: that the anti-nostalgic assumptions that have been sustained so easily and so uncritically for so many decades, need to be re-examined.

Notes

1. Dipankar Gupta, *Learning to Forget: The Anti-Memoirs of Modernity*, (New Delhi: Oxford University Press, 2005), 15.
2. Herbert Marcuse, *Eros and Civilization*, (London: Sphere, 1971), 163.
3. Williams, *The Country and the City*, 35.
4. Mario Jacoby, *The Longing for Paradise*, (Boston: Sigo Press, 1985), 12; Elihu Howland, 'Nostalgia', *Journal of Existential Psychiatry*, 3, (1962), 198.
5. Anthony D. Smith, *The Ethnic Origins of Nations*, (Oxford: Blackwell, 1986), 175.
6. Ibid.
7. Williams, *The Country and the City*, 12.
8. Cited by Williams (ibid., 14).
9. Smith, *The Ethnic Origins of Nations*, 176.
10. Ibid., 176–7.
11. Peter Fritzsche, *Stranded in the Present: Modern Time and the Melancholy of History*, (Cambridge: Harvard University Press, 2004), 30.
12. Cited by Richard Terdiman, 'Deconstructing memory: on representing the past and theorizing culture in France since the Revolution', *Diacritics*, 15, 4, (1985), 15.
13. Mill, 'The spirit of the age'.
14. Ibid.
15. Richard Horne (Ed.), *A New Spirit of the Age*, (London: Smith, Elder and Company, 1844); Thomas Carlyle, 'Signs of the Times', *Edinburgh Review*, 49, (June, 1829). See also Paul Schlicke, 'Hazlitt, Horne, and the Spirit of the Age', *Studies in English Literature*, 45, 4 (2005).

16. Carlyle, 'Signs of the Times', 58–9.
17. From 1901, the words *And After* were added to the title.
18. G. Lukács, *The Historical Novel*, (Lincoln: University of Nebraska Press, 1983), 23.
19. M. Weber, *From Max Weber: Essays in Sociology*, (New York: Oxford University Press, 1946), 155; F. Tönnies, *Community and Association*, (London: Routledge, 1955).
20. Weber cited by Arthur Mitzman, *The Iron Cage: An Historical Interpretation of Max Weber*, (New York: Knopf, 1970), 177–8.
21. G. Stauth and B. Turner, 'Nostalgia, postmodernism and the critique of mass culture', *Theory, Culture and Society*, 5, (1988), 517, 525.
22. Shaw and Chase, 'The dimensions of nostalgia', 8. It appears that Shaw and Chase have transposed the terms *Gemeinschaft* and *Gesellschaft*.
23. Ibid.
24. Marshall Berman cited by Chase and Shaw (ibid). The final words of the book, by Berman, that Chase and Shaw cite return to the same metaphor: 'I believe that we and those who come after us will go on fighting to make ourselves at home in this world, even as the homes we have made, the modern street, the modern spirit, go on melting into air.' M. Berman, *All That is Solid Melts into Air: The Experience of Modernity*, (London: Verso, 1983), 348.
25. Karl Marx, 'Letters from the Deutsch-Französische Jahrbücher', *Collected Works of Karl Marx and Friedrich Engels, Volume 3, Works of Karl Marx, March 1843–August 1844*, (New York: International Publishers, 1975), 142.
26. Karl Marx, 'The Eighteenth Brumaire of Louis Bonaparte', in *Karl Marx: Surveys from Exile: Political Writings: Volume 2*, (Harmondsworth: Penguin, 1992), 149.
27. It is one of the oddest and seemingly brutal of Christian teachings and is found twice in the Bible. Luke (9.59–60) '"Lord, suffer me first to go and bury my father". Jesus said unto him, "Let the dead bury their dead"'; Matthew (8. 22) 'Follow me; and let the dead bury their dead.'
28. Mikhail Bakunin, 'The reaction in Germany: from the notebooks of a Frenchman', http://www.marxists.org/reference/archive/bakunin/works/1842/reaction-germany. htm, accessed 09.09.2009.
29. Ibid.
30. Karl Marx, 'Montesquieu LVI', from *Collected Works of Karl Marx and Friedrich Engels, Volume 8, Articles from the Neue Rheinische Zeitung November 8, 1848–March 5, 1849*, (New York: International Publishers, 1975), 266.
31. Marx, 'The Eighteenth Brumaire of Louis Bonaparte', 147. Marx's 'The Eighteenth Brumaire of Louis Bonaparte' is an attack on Louis Bonaparte's attempt to rekindle nationalist sentiment. The title suggests that Louis Bonaparte's coup of 1851 sought to claim for itself the mantle of Napoleon I's coup against the Directory, a coup that occurred, according to the revolutionary calendar, on 18 Brumaire, Year VIII (9 November 1799).
32. Ibid., 146–8.
33. Cited by William Inge, *Outspoken Essays: Second Series*, (London: Longmans, Green and Company, 1927), 163.
34. Benjamin Kidd, *Principles of Western Civilisation: Being the First Volume of a System of Evolutionary Philosophy*, (London: Macmillan, 1902), 8.
35. Ibid., 340.
36. V. Widal, 'Nostalgie', *Dictionnaire Encyclopédie des Sciences Médicales*, (Paris: G. Masson and P. Asselin, 1879).

Bien plus, la nostalgie est en raison inverse de la civilisation et en raison directe de l'âpreté du pays regretté. Les peuplades simples, primitives, sauvages même, sont les plus sujettes au mal du pays.

37. K. Marx, *Karl Marx: Surveys from Exile: Political Writings: Volume 2*, (Harmondsworth: Penguin, 1992), 320.
38. Ibid., 306.
39. Ibid., 307.
40. Cited by Andrzej Walicki, *Marxism and the Leap to the Kingdom of Freedom: The Rise and Fall of the Communist Utopia*, (Stanford, CA: Stanford University Press, 1997), 158.
41. Marx, *Karl Marx: Surveys from Exile*, 264.
42. V. Lenin, *Imperialism: The Highest Stage of Capitalism*, (Chippendale: Resistance Books, 1999), 100.
43. L. Trotsky, 'Family relations under the Soviets: Fourteen questions answered', *The Class Struggle*, (June–July, 1934), 11.
44. Cited by I. Halfin, *From Darkness to Light: Class, Consciousness, and Salvation in Revolutionary Russia*, (Pittsburgh: University of Pittsburgh Press, 2000), 78.
45. *Peking Review*, 'Red Guards destroy the old and establish the new', *Peking Review*, (2 September, 1966), 17.
46. Cited by Roderick MacFarquhar and Michael Schoenhals, *Mao's Last Revolution*, (Cambridge: Harvard University Press, 2006), 102.
47. Jung Chang and Jon Halliday, *Mao: The Unknown Story*, (London: Random House, 2006). E. Vogel, 'From friendship to comradeship', *The China Quarterly*, 21, (1965). See also Thomas Gold, 'After comradeship: personal relations in China since the Cultural Revolution', *The China Quarterly*, 104, (December, 1985).
48. Edward Hyams, *A Dictionary of Modern Revolution*, (London: Allan Lane, 1973), 172; Peter Marris, *Loss and Change*, (London: Routledge and Kegan Paul, 1974).
49. Ibid.
50. Ibid., 170.
51. Ibid., 167.
52. S. Yekelchyk, *Stalin's Empire of Memory: Russian-Ukrainian Relations in the Soviet Historical Imagination*, (Toronto, University of Toronto Press, 2004); A. Weiner, 'Nature, nurture, and memory in a socialist utopia: delineating the Soviet socio-ethnic body in the age of socialism, *The American Historical Review*, 104, (1999); R. Bevan, *The Destruction of Memory: Architecture at War*, (London: Reaktion Books, 2006).
53. Bevan, *The Destruction of Memory*.
54. Ibid., 127.
55. Quoted in Ben Kierman, *The Pol Pot Regime: Race, Power, and Genocide in Cambodia under the Khmer Rouge, 1975–79*, (New Haven: Yale University Press, 1996), 57.
56. Clive Christie, *Ideology and Revolution in Southeast Asia, 1900–1980: Political Ideas of the Anti-Colonial Era*, (London: Routledge, 2001), 204; Kierman, *The Pol Pot Regime*, 26.
57. Georg Hegel, *The Philosophy of History*, (New York: Cosimo, 2007), 54.
58. Bruno Latour, *We Have Never Been Modern*, (Cambridge: Harvard University Press, 1993), 76.
59. Peter Fritzsche, 'How nostalgia narrates modernity', in P. Fritzsche and A. Confino (Eds), *The Work of Memory: New Directions in the Study of German Society and Culture*, (Champaign, IL: University of Illinois Press, 2002), 62.

60. K. Marx, *Early Writings*, (Harmondsworth, Penguin, 1975), 347. Marx continues,

> *Communism* is the *positive* supersession of *private property* as *human self-estrangement*, and hence the true *appropriation* of the *human* essence through and for man; it is the complete restoration of man to himself as a *social*, i.e., human, being, a restoration which has become conscious and which takes place within the entire wealth of previous periods of development. (348)

Marx's formulation in the *Grundrisse* reinforces the social and historical conditions that make this process possible while pulling back from the image of a 'return' and emphasizing, instead, that communism is a moment of social creation:

> individuals cannot gain mastery over their own social interconnections before they have created them . . . Universally developed individuals, whose social relations, as their own communal [*gemeinschaftlich*] relations, are hence also subordinated to their own communal control, are no product of nature, but of history. The degree and the universality of the development of wealth where *this* individuality becomes possible supposes production on the basis of exchange values as a prior condition, whose universality produces not only the alienation of the individual from himself and from others, but also the universality and the comprehensiveness of his relations and capacities. In earlier stages of development the single individual seems to be developed more fully, because he has not yet worked out his relationships in their fullness, or erected them as independent social powers and relations opposite himself. It is as ridiculous to yearn for a return to that original fullness as it is to believe that with this complete emptiness history has come to a standstill. (K. Marx, *Grundrisse: Foundations Of The Critique Of Political Economy*, Harmondsworth: Penguin, 1993, 160–1)

61. K. Marx and F. Engels, *Collected Works Volume 42*, (New York: International Publishers, 1975), 577.
62. Cited by Löwy and Sayre, *Romanticism against the Tide of Modernity*, 173.
63. Ibid., 97.
64. Karl Marx, *Pre-Capitalist Economic Formations*, (New York: International Publishers, 1965), 86–7.
65. Bertell Ollman, *Alienation: Marx's Conception of Man in Capitalist Society*, (Cambridge: Cambridge University Press, 1971), 135–6.
66. Karl Löwith, *Max Weber and Karl Marx*, (London: Routledge, 1993).
67. Halfin, *From Darkness to Light*.
68. F. Marc, 'The "savages" of Germany', in C. Harrison and P. Wood (Eds), *Art in Theory 1900–1990: An Anthology of Changing Ideas*, (Oxford: Blackwell, 1992), 99.
69. Tristan Tzara, 'Tristan Tzara: Lecture on Dada', in Robert Motherwell (Ed.), *The Dada Painters and Poets: An Anthology*, (Cambridge: Harvard University Press, 1981), 247.
70. Tristan Tzara, *Seven Dada Manifestos and Lampisteries*, (London: Calder Press, 1992), 63.
71. Cited by George Ribemont-Dessaignes, 'History of Dada', in Robert Motherwell (Ed.), *The Dada Painters and Poets: An Anthology*, (Cambridge: Harvard University Press, 1981), 108.

72. Cited by F. Rosemont, 'Surrealists on whiteness from 1925 to the present', *Race Traitor*, 9, (1998), 7.
73. Susan Buck-Morss, *Dreamworld and Catastrophe: The Passing of Mass Utopia in East and West*, (Cambridge, MA: MIT Press, 2000), 49.
74. For example, B. Wallis (Ed.), *If You Lived Here: The City in Art, Theory and Social Activism*, (Seattle, WA: Bay Press, 1991); A. Monroe, *Interrogation Machine: Laibach and NSK*, (Cambridge, MA: MIT Press, 2005).
75. W. Benjamin, *One-Way Street and Other Writings* (London: New Left Books, 1979), 229, 236.
76. L. Lerner, *The Uses of Nostalgia: Studies in Pastoral Poetry*, (London: Chatto and Windus, 1972); T. Wagner, *Longing: Narratives of Nostalgia in the British Novel, 1740–1890*, (Lewsiburg: Bucknell University Press, 2004).
77. T. Adorno, *Aesthetic Theory*, (Minneapolis: University of Minnesota Press, 1998).
78. For discussion see Allan Antliff, *Anarchist Modernism: Art, Politics, and the First American Avant-Garde*, (Chicago: University of Chicago Press, 2001); Richard Sonn, *Anarchism and Cultural Politics in Fin-De-Siècle France*, (Lincoln: University of Nebraska Press, 1989).
79. P. J. Proudhon, *What is Property?*, (Whitefish: Kessinger Publishing, 2004).
80. Cf. Walter Benjamin, 'Left-wing melancholy', in A. Kaes, M. Jay and E. Dimendberg (Eds), *The Weimer Republic Sourcebook*, (Berkeley: University of California Press, 1994).
81. Cited by David Frisby, *Fragments of Modernity*, (Cambridge: Polity Press, 1985), 139; S. Kracauer, *Strassen in Berlin und anderswo*, (Frankfurt am Main: Suhrkamp, 1964).
82. Ibid.
83. Ibid., 142.
84. Theodor Adorno and Max Horkheimer, *The Dialectic of Enlightenment*, (London: Verso, 1979), 9.
85. Ibid., xv. For Adorno, 'every reification is a forgetting'. Adorno cited by Martin Jay, 'Anamnestic totalization: reflections on Marcuse's theory of remembrance', *Theory and Society*, 11, 1, (1982), 5.
86. Herbert Marcuse, *One-Dimensional Man*, (London: Abacus, 1972); Herbert Marcuse, *Eros and Civilization*, (London: Sphere, 1971).
87. Marcuse, *One-Dimensional Man*, 14.
88. Henri Lefebvre, *Position: contre les technocrates*, (Paris: Gonthier, 1967).
89. Cited by Löwy and Sayre, *Romanticism against the Tide of Modernity*, 225. Löwy and Sayre also comment that a 'characteristic example' of 'Romanticism in action but without theory in May 1968 is of course the burning of cars' (225).
90. The following are useful sources: J. Hougan, *Decadence: Radical Nostalgia, Narcissism, and Decline in the Seventies*, (New York: William Morrow and Company, 1975); M. Brocken, *The British Folk Revival 1944–2002*, (Aldershot: Ashgate, 2003).
91. K. Melville, *Communes in the Counter Culture: Origins, Theories, Styles of Life*, (New York: William Morrow and Company, 1972), 100.
92. Theodore Roszak, *The Making of a Counter Culture: Reflections on the Technocratic Society and Its Youthful Opposition*, (New York: Anchor Books, 1969), 252; Löwy, 'The revolutionary romanticism of May 1968'.
93. György Lukács, *The Theory of the Novel*, (London: Merlin Press, 1971), 22.

94. I. Kristol, 'Capitalism, Socialism, and Nihilism', in R. Kirk (Ed.), *The Portable Conservative Reader*, (Harmondsworth: Penguin, 1982), 633. In more quixtoic vein, Tom Wolfe offered an intriguingly sartorially specific class analysis of the New Left's nostalgia:

> The New Left had a strictly old-fashioned conception of life on the streets, a romantic and nostalgic one somehow derived from literary images of proletarian life before World War II or even World War I. A lot of those white college boys, for example, would go for these chequered lumberjack shirts that are so heavy and woolly that you can wear them like a jacket. It was as if all the little lord Byrons had a hopeless nostalgia for the proletarians of about 1910. (Cited in Davis, *Yearning for Yesterday*, 100)

95. William Lecky, *The Rise and Influence of Rationalism in Europe*, (London: Longmans, Green and Company, 1910).
96. Ibid., 375.
97. Cited by Lasch, *The True and Only Heaven*, 41.
98. Richard Hofstadter, *The American Political Tradition and the Men Who Made It*, (New York: Vintage Books, 1989), xxxiii.
99. For example, Hewison, *The Heritage Industry*; Patrick Wright, *On Living in an Old Country: The National Past in Contemporary Britain*, (London: Verso, 1985).
100. Raphael Samuel, 'Introduction: exciting to be English', in Raphael Samuel (Ed.), *Patriotism: The Making and Unmaking of British National Identity: Volume I: History and Politics*, (London: Routledge), lv.
101. Simone Weil, *The Need for Roots: Prelude to a Declaration of Duties towards Mankind*, (London: Routledge, 2002), 51–2.
102. Many of Weils' concerns echo Orwell's critique of socialism as a 'materialistic Utopia'; George Orwell, *The Road to Wigan Pier*, (London: London: Secker & Warburg, 1973), 212.
103. Rachel Carson, *Silent Spring*, (Harmondsworth: Penguin, 1965), 21.
104. Fritz Schumacher, 'The problem of production', in Andrew Dodson (Ed.), *The Green Reader*, (London: Andre Deutsch, 1991), 33.
105. Donella Meadows, Dennis Meadows, Jorgen Randers and William Behrens, *The Limits of Growth*, (London: Pan Books, 1983), 23.
106. Stéphane Coutois (Ed.), *The Black Book Of Communism: Crimes, Terror, Repression*, (Cambridge: Harvard University Press, 1999); http://www.hawaii.edu/powerkills/COM.ART.HTM, accessed 09.09.2009; http://www.digitalsurvivors.com/archives/communistbodycount.php, accessed 09.09.2009.
107. Jens Jørgen Thorsen, Jørgen Nash and Hardy Strid, *CO-RITUS Manifesto*, available at: http://www.infopool.org.uk/6105.html, accessed 12.09.2009.
108. Cited by Stephen Brockman, *Literature and German Reunification*, (Cambridge: Cambridge University Press, 1999), 124–5.
109. A. Huyssen, *Present Pasts: Urban Palimpsests and the Politics of Memory*, (Stanford, CA: Stanford University Press, 2003), 2. See also Kerwin Klein, 'On the emergence of memory in historical discourse', *Representations*, 69 (2000).
110. Huyssen, *Present Pasts*, 4.
111. Ibid., 1–2. Pierre Nora has provided a different interpretation of the resurgence of memory. For Nora the cause of this phenomenon lies in a fundamental change in the social

institutionalization of memory. The 'conquest and eradication of memory by history' resulted in the loss of memory as something organic, embodied. Hence, 'We speak so much of memory because there is so little of it left.' Pierre Nora, 'Between memory and history: *Les Lieux de Mémoire*', *Representations*, 26, (1989), 7, 8.

112. L. Hutcheon, 'Irony, nostalgia and the postmodern', http://library.utoronto.ca/utel/criticism/hutchinp.html, accessed 03.03.2005.

113. W. Wheeler, 'Nostalgia isn't nasty: the postmodernising of Parliamentary Democracy', in M. Perryman (Ed.), *Altered States: Postmodernism, Politics, Culture*, (London: Lawrence & Wishart, 1994), 94, 97.

114. Marilyn Ivy, *Discourses of the Vanishing: Modernity, Phantasm, Japan*, (Chicago: University of Chicago Press, 1995), 65.

115. See also Esra Özyürek's study of nostalgic modernists in Turkey. Esra Özyürek, *Nostalgia for the Modern: State Secularism and Everyday Politics in Turkey*, (Durham, NC: Duke University Press, 2006). Özyürek traces the way 'Nostalgic citizens used the new legitimacy of privatization as they established private foundations to propagate the "original" ideology of the Turkish Republic' (17).

116. Judith Helmer and Florian Malzacher (Eds), *Not Even a Game Anymore: The Theatre of Forced Entertainment*, (Berlin: Alexander Verlag, 2004).

117. Stauth and Turner, 'Nostalgia, postmodernism and the critique of mass culture', 509.

118. F. Jameson, *Postmodernism, or the Cultural Logic of Late Capitalism*, (Durham, NC: Duke University Press, 1991), xvii, 19.

119. Hutcheon, 'Irony, nostalgia and the postmodern'.

120. Milan Kundera, *The Book of Laughter and Forgetting*, (New York: Alfred A. Knopf, 1980), 3.

121. Marx, 'The Eighteenth Brumaire of Louis Bonaparte', 146. In the German original, 'Marx writes "lastet wie ein Alp", that is, weighs like one of those ghosts that give nightmares', Jacques Derrida, *Spectre of Marx: The State of the Debt, the Work of Mourning, and the New International*, (London: Routledge, 1994), 108.

122. Derrida, *Spectre of Marx*.

123. For discussion see V. Geoghegan, ' "Let the dead bury the dead": Marx, Derrida and Bloch', *Contemporary Political Theory*, 1, (2002).

124. Derrida, *Spectre of Marx*, 110.

125. Ibid., 106.

126. Sayre and Löwy, 'Figures of romantic anti-capitalism'.

127. Ibid., 90.

128. Ibid., 85.

129. E. Bloch, *The Spirit of Utopia*, (Stanford, CA: Stanford University Press, 2000).

130. E. Bloch, *The Principle of Hope: Volume One*, (Cambridge, MA: MIT Press, 1995).

131. Sayre and Löwy, 'Figures of romantic anti-capitalism', 90.

132. Cited by Natali, 'History and politics of nostalgia'.

133. Sayre and Löwy, 'Figures of romantic anti-capitalism', 90.

134. Ibid., 91.

135. Ibid.

136. R. Samuel, 'Faith hope and struggle: the lost world of British communism, part one', *New Left Review*, 154, (1985); R. Samuel, 'Staying power: the lost world of British communism, part two', *New Left Review*, 156, (1986); R. Samuel, 'Class politics: the lost world of British communism, part three', *New Left Review*, 165, (1987); L. Segal, 'Lost

worlds: political memoirs of the left in Britain', *Radical Philosophy*, 121, (2003); L. Segal, 'Lost worlds: political memoirs of the left (II)', *Radical Philosophy*, 123, (2004).

137. Segal, 'Lost worlds: political memoirs of the left in Britain', 6.

138. Helen Graham, 'The radical as the past in the present: how to write histories of the British Women's Liberation Movement', paper presented to Gender and Power in the New Europe: Fifth European Feminist Research Conference, Lund University, (20–24 August, 2003).

139. Scanlan, 'Introduction: nostalgia'.

140. Henri Bergson, *Henri Bergson: Key Writings*, (London: Continuum, 2002), 133.

141. Henry Hyndman, *The Historical Basis of Socialism in England*, (London: Kegan Paul and Trench, 1883), 4; Tony Benn, 'Foreword', in Fenner Brockway, *Britain's First Socialists: The Levellers, Agitators and Diggers of the English Revolution*, (London: Quartet Books, 1980), x. The Englishness of the socialist tradition in Britain is explored by James Young in 'A very English socialism and the Celtic fringe 1880–1991', *History Workshop Journal*, 35, (1993).

142. P. Ward, *Red Flag and Union Jack: Englishness, Patriotism and the British Left, 1881–1924*, (Woodbridge: Boydell Press, 1998), 36. Ward draws our attention to the connections of past and future in English socialism. However, his emphasis on England's nostalgic socialism might mislead if taken to suggest that England, or Britain, was unique in this respect. Indeed, Peter Mandler has argued that, compared to other European countries, themes of ruralism and nostalgia were relatively undeveloped in England and that, 'the English political elite . . . was, in fact, by European standards peculiarly uninterested in its own national past'. P. Mandler, 'Against "Englishness": English culture and the limits to rural nostalgia, 1859–1940', *Transactions of the Royal Historical Society*, 6th series, 7, (1997), 157–8.

143. E. P. Thompson, *The Making of the English Working Class*, (London: Harmondsworth: Penguin, 1968), 13.

144. Jackson Lears, 'Looking backward: in defense of nostalgia', *Lingua Franca*, (December 1997/January 1998), 60, 60–1.

145. Tim Strangleman, 'The nostalgia of organisations and the organisation of nostalgia: past and present in the contemporary railway industry', *Sociology*, 33, 4, (1999), 743.

146. Ibid.

147. Glazer, *Radical Nostalgia*, 7.

148. Hayden White, *The Content of the Form: Narrative Discourse and Historical Representation*, (Baltimore: Johns Hopkins University Press, 1987), 149.

149. Marx, 'The Eighteenth Brumaire of Louis Bonaparte', 149; J. Ladino, 'Rediscovering nostalgia: the significance of counter-nostalgia in American literature', paper presented to the Nostalgia and Cultural Memory English Graduate Conference, University of Victoria, (4–5 March, 2005); J. Ladino, 'Longing for wonderland: nostalgia for nature in post-frontier America', *Iowa Journal of Cultural Studies*, 5, (2005).

150. Ladino, 'Rediscovering nostalgia'.

151. M. Foucault, *Language, Counter-Memory, Practice*, (Ithaca: Cornell University Press, 1977). The idea of counter-memory is drawn on in some of the essays collected in Katherine Hodkin and Susannah Radstone (Eds), *Contested Pasts: The Politics of Memory*, (London: Routledge, 2003) and Susannah Radstone and Katherine Hodkin (Eds), *Regimes of Memory*, (London: Routledge, 2003); S. Legg, 'Sites of counter-memory: the refusal to forget and the nationalist struggle in colonial Delhi', *Historical Geography*, 33,

(2005); T. Steiner, 'Strategic nostalgia, Islam and cultural translation in Leila Aboulela's *The Translator* and *Coloured Lights*', *Current Writing*, 20, 2, (2008), available at: http://currentwriting.ukzn.ac.za/index.php/archive/10-volume-20-number-2/78-strategic-nostalgia-islam-and-cultural-translation-in-leila-aboulelas-the-translator-and-coloured-lights.html, accessed 30.09.2009; L. Tabar, 'Memory, agency, counter-narrative: testimonies from Jenin refugee camp', *Critical Arts*, 21, 1, (2007).

152. Glazer, *Radical Nostalgia*, 9.
153. Davis, *Yearning for Yesterday*.
154. Boym, *The Future of Nostalgia*, 50.
155. S. Legg, 'Memory and nostalgia', *Cultural Geographies*, 11, (2004), 100.
156. Hutcheon, 'Irony, nostalgia and the postmodern'.
157. Andrew Hewitt, *Fascist Modernism: Aesthetics, Politics, and the Avant-Garde*, (Stanford, CA: Stanford University Press, 1996), 75.
158. Ernst Bloch, *Heritage of Our Times*, (Oxford: Polity Press, 1991), 67.
159. Hutcheon, 'Irony, nostalgia and the postmodern'.
160. Salman Rushdie, *The Ground Beneath Her Feet*, (London: Jonathan Cape, 1999), 55.
161. Lasch, *The True and Only Heaven*, 83.
162. Gayle Greene, 'Feminist fiction and the uses of memory', *Signs: Journal of Women in Culture and Society*, 16, (1991), 298.
163. This point is made by David Lowenthal, in 'Nostalgia tells it like it wasn't'.
164. Fritzsche, 'How nostalgia narrates modernity', 62.
165. Glazer, *Radical Nostalgia*, 9.
166. For case-studies of this process see K. Iwabuchi, 'Nostalgia for a (different) Asian modernity: media consumption of "Asia" in Japan', *Positions: East Asia Cultures Critique*, 10, 3, (2002). A. Bonnett, *White Identities: Historical and International Perspectives*, (Harlow: Prentice Hall, 2000).
167. Williams, *The Country and the City*, 37.
168. See http://www.svetlanaboym.com/main.htm, accessed 09.09.2009.
169. Williams, *The Country and the City*.
170. Cited by John Higgens, *Raymond Williams: Literature, Marxism and Cultural Materialism*, (London: Routledge, 1999), 4. The literary critics F. R. Leavis and Q. R. Leavis developed a form of critique centred on looking at art and writing as part of (and potentially reintegrating the alienated masses back into) a 'whole way of life'. The phrase 'left-Leavisite' denotes a lack of class analysis as well as an aspirational and somewhat judgemental perspective on the need to lift up and reintegrate the culture of 'the people'.
171. Ibid.
172. Ibid., 4–5.
173. Williams, *The Country and the City*, 298.
174. Scanlan, 'Introduction: nostalgia'.
175. Williams, *The Country and the City*, 37. Raymond Williams also exhibited more orthodox tendencies. *The Country and the City* ends in a Maoist flourish, with a polemical call to rescue the countryside as both a site of class struggle and a socialist resource. The to'ing and fro'ing between socialist progressivism and something less sure, less instrumental, that can be found in the book may be represented as a kind of 'opening up' of the issue of nostalgia. But it might also be portrayed as incoherence or hesitancy.
176. T. Blackwell and J. Seabrook, *The Revolt against Change: Towards a Conserving Radicalism*, (London: Vintage, 1993).

177. Ibid., 3–4.
178. Marc Auge, *Non-Places: Introduction to an Anthropology of Supermodernity*, (London: Verso, 1995); James Kunstler, *The Geography of Nowhere*, (New York: Simon and Schuster, 1993).
179. Tamara Hareven and Randolph Langenbach, ' Living places, work places and historical identity', in D. Lowenthal and M. Binney (Eds), *Our Past before Us: Why Do We Save It?*, (London: Temple, 1981), 114. In *How Modernity Forgets*, Paul Connerton uses the term 'cultural amnesia' to depict 'topographies of forgetting' (Cambridge: Cambridge University Press, 2009, 99).
180. Cited by Hutcheon, 'Irony, nostalgia and the postmodern'. See also Janice Doane and Devon Hodges, *Nostalgia and Sexual Difference: The Resistance to Contemporary Feminism*, (New York: Methuen, 1987).
181. Alexander R. Martin, 'Nostalgia', *American Journal of Psychoanalysis*, 14, (1954), 101. See also Meaghan Morris, 'At Henry Parkes Motel', *Cultural Studies*, 2, (1988); Craig Thompson and Siok Tambyah, 'Trying to be cosmopolitan', *Journal of Consumer Research*, 26, (1999).
182. A. Blunt, 'Collective memory and productive nostalgia: Anglo-Indian homemaking at McCluskieganj', *Environment and Planning D: Society and Space*, 21, (2003), 721. See also R. Rubenstein, *Home Matters: Longing and Belonging, Nostalgia and Mourning in Women's Fiction*, (London: Palgrave, 2001).
183. Ibid., 722.
184. Cited by S. Legg, 'Contesting and surviving memory: space, nation and nostalgia in *Les Lieux de Mémoire*', *Environment and Planning D: Society and Space*, 23, (2005), 486.
185. K. Till, 'Memory studies', *History Workshop Journal*, 62, (2006), 330.
186. N. Thrift, 'Performance and . . . ', *Environment and Planning A*, 35, (2003), 2019; N. Thrift, 'Summoning life', in Paul Cloke, Philip Crang and Mike Goodwin (Eds), *Envisioning Human Geography* , (London: Arnold, 2004), 84.
187. Examples include the portrayal of the Peoples' Front of Judea in the 1979 film, 'Life of Brian', the portrayal of liberal celebrities in the 2004 film 'Team America' and the character of Eddy in the BBC comedy 'Absolutely Fabulous'.
188. Lasch, *The True and Only Heaven*, 36.
189. Ibid., 57.
190. R. Samuel, *Theatres of Memory*, (London: Verso, 1994).
191. Christopher Shaw and Malcolm Chase (Eds), *The Imagined Past: History and Nostalgia*, (Manchester: Manchester University Press, 1989).
192. Lowenthal, 'Nostalgia tells it like it wasn't', 20.
193. Ibid., 28.
194. R. Miliband, 'Socialism and the myth of the golden past', *The Socialist Register*, (1964), 92.
195. Williams, *The Country and the City*, 305.
196. P. Anderson, 'The river of time', *New Left Review*, 26, (2004), 71.
197. Ibid.

CHAPTER TWO

Nostalgia in and against English Socialism, 1775–1894

Introduction

In this chapter I explore a rupture in the politics of the past. Drawing on three English examples, I argue that, in the late nineteenth century, the relationship of the left to the past began to change. The past was increasingly filtered through an anti-nostalgic world-view. Thus nostalgia became a site of anxiety and transgression. This argument is developed around portraits of three of the foundational figures in English socialism, Thomas Spence (1750–1814), William Morris (1834–1896) and Robert Blatchford (1851–1943).

The first of the two dates that bookend this chapter refers to the publication of *Property in Land Every One's Right*, by one of English history's authentic examples of 'radicalism from below', Thomas Spence.[1] I discuss Spence's politics in terms he would recognize: not in the anachronistic language of socialism or class struggle but in terms of the natural and historical right of the people to the common ownership of the land. I also intend to emphasize the unselfconscious role of continuity, memory and tradition in Spence's radicalism. When we turn to the *rediscovery* of Spence, from the early 1880s to the present day, we see these themes being put aside. They were neglected in favour of a vision of Spence as a proletarian, an embryonic class warrior. Thus, in tracing the socialist invention of Spence, I chart a developing anti-nostalgic political orthodoxy. It is an orthodoxy that demanded that the early heroes of a maturing movement be duly celebrated but also that the backward-looking components of their contribution be either ignored or identified as residual.

As this implies, I offer the difference between the politics of the past found in Spence, and the politics of the past found among his later admirers, as evidence of a schism between the populist radicalism of the former and the progressive world of the latter. The argument that the late nineteenth century witnessed the emergence of a culture of suspicion towards nostalgia is explored further in my other two case-studies. In each I focus upon the difficulty of sustaining nostalgia in an increasingly anti-nostalgic political milieu. Thus I show that William Morris was involved in an uneasy negotiation with, through and against nostalgia. His *self-consciously* romantic yearnings reflected a *defensive* attachment to the past. The defensive nature of this attachment can be witnessed in Morris's compartmentalization of his nostalgic interests. By offering his nostalgic vision as an aesthetic and cultural sensibility, Morris found a way to express loss within and against an increasingly dominant modernist culture of the left.

The second of the dates in my title refers to the publication of Robert Blatchford's *Merrie England* (1894, although the book had been published in parts the previous year in *The Clarion*).[2] *Merrie England* remains by far the most popular introduction to socialism written by an Englishman. Over two million copies were sold over the decade following its publication, many at public meetings and football matches. Blatchford's book, subtitled *A Series of Letters to John Smith, of Oldham – a Practical Working Man*, combines an anti-industrial spirit with a demand for modern state socialism. The book was the centrepiece of Blatchford's celebrity. 'No honest man will deny', wrote Albert Lyons in his enthusiastic biography, 'that Blatchford's pen alone has produced – has invented if you like – "the rank and file" of Socialism'.[3] The *Manchester Guardian* pointed out that 'For every convert made by *Das Kapital*, there were a hundred made by *Merrie England*.'[4] These claims are interesting, in part, because Blatchford's Clarion movement appears so strikingly unusual and unorthodox when set beside the dominant forms of modern socialism. With Blatchford we again encounter the defensive dilemma of expressing nostalgia in an anti-nostalgic political milieu. However, Blatchford's populism offers a different context for the negotiation of this paradox. I will explore what appears as the oddity of the Clarion movement – its emphasis on personal fulfilment and its idealization of a jovial clubbiness – as a way of bringing together revolutionary modernity and revolutionary nostalgia. More specifically, it is suggested that the rendering of political transformation into convivial 'fellowship' and individual 'salvation' allowed the 'Clarionettes' to assert a radical message while laying claim to a British tradition of bonhomie and pride in place and nation.

The Politics of Loss in English Socialist History

The history of nostalgia might allow us to look back at modern history not solely searching for newness and technological progress but for unrealized potentialities, unpredictable turns and crossroads.

Svetlana Boym[5]

Boym's aspiration offers a familiar message. In Britain the search for 'unrealized potentialities' grew to prominence with the rediscovery of the diverse political heritage of the working class, associated with E. P. Thompson and kindred historians. 'In some of the lost causes of the people of the Industrial Revolution', Thompson explained, 'we may discover insights into social evils which we have yet to cure.'[6] However, to evoke Thompson's exploration of the birth of class consciousness, in the late eighteenth century and the first three decades of the nineteenth century, is also to invite further refinement of my argument that a rupture in the politics of the past can be identified later in the nineteenth century. In celebrating early English radicals, Thompson offers them as attractive, yet primal, figures at the beginning of a story which concludes with the accomplishment of a recognizably modern socialist identity. Nostalgia, if admitted at all – for even Cobbett is said by Thompson to be only 'seemingly "nostalgic"' – becomes a strategic device; the weapon of memory against capitalism.[7]

The progressivism found (but also sometimes questioned) in Thompson has much bolder expression in Hobsbawm, for whom 'primitive rebels' are

> *pre-political* people who have not yet found, or are have only begun to find a specific language to which to express their aspirations about the world. Though their movements are thus in many respects blind and groping, by the standards of modern ones, they are neither unimportant nor marginal.[8]

The attempt to locate *transitions* towards class identity, or of periods which offer us a *turning point* towards the political organization of class struggle, is characteristic of socialist history.[9] This task has been complemented by the expectation that capitalist processes of social disembedding and dispossession have been followed by political processes of segregation and affiliation around antagonistic class identities. Although often connected with Marx, one can find intimations of this chain of association throughout nineteenth-century radical thought. In the 1850s, the Chartist leader, Ernest Jones, repeatedly wrote about the emergence of class conflict in the context of the fact that the 'intervening classes are melting away'.[10] Although Jones's repetition of the point suggests he believed it to be a novel one, it had in fact been observed decades earlier. Indeed, Thompson finds comparable ideas being voiced from the last decades of the eighteenth century, as connections were forged between 'the clamour of the mill' and a new population among whom 'levelling systems are the discourse; and rebellion may be near at hand'.[11]

By 1869, when John Stuart Mill started planning his major study of socialism, the term had been in circulation for over four decades.[12] It was clear to Mill that, 'the fundamental doctrines which were assumed as incontestable by former generations, are now put again on their trial.'[13] Moreover, he believed that a new dispossessed and alienated class had emerged that was the agent of a new 'standpoint':

> [C]lasses who have next to no property of their own . . . will not allow anything to be taken for granted – certainly not the principle of private property, the legitimacy and utility of which are denied by many of the reasoners who look out from the standpoint of the working classes.[14]

Mill's analysis suggests that feelings of loss and attachment can best be described as residual. In placing nostalgia as a dying form, his narrative both problematizes and marginalizes it within the bigger story of a maturing class movement. Thus the persistent desire voiced by the radical poor, especially in the turbulent decades at the start of the nineteenth century (but echoed many times in later years), to see a transition, in the words of the *Poor Man's Guardian* (of November, 1831), back 'from a state worse than slavery to the old system of old England',[15] is rendered anachronistic.

A key figure in the expression of such supposedly anachronistic attitudes is the journalist and farmer William Cobbett (1763–1835). In the 1810s and 1820s, Cobbett was the most widely read and influential radical in English politics. His *Political Register* campaigned against the immiseration of the labouring population as well as the corrupt nature of the new commercial society Cobbett saw growing around him. Cobbett also made it crystal clear that,

> [W]e want *nothing new*. We have great constitutional laws and principles, to which we are immovably attached. We want *great alteration*, but we want nothing new . . . the great principles ought to be, and must be the same, or else confusion will follow.[16]

It was on this basis that Cobbett denounced the new 'race of merchants and manufacturers, and bankers and loan-jobbers and contractors' which he saw as destroying the well-being and fine traditions of rural life.[17] 'Unnatural changes' are Cobbett's target throughout his *Rural Rides*. He foresees with horror 'the long oak-table' of village life disposed of at the 'bottom of a bridge that some stock-jobber will stick up over an artificial river in his cockney garden'.

'Nowadays the limits of Cobbett's outlook are obvious', John Derry confidently informed us in 1967: 'he idealised the England of his youth'.[18] This verdict accords with the widespread late modern assumption that Cobbett is part of an inherently conservative tradition of rural and national mythology. The fact that 'Cobbett most always had in mind the village labourer or small farmer', explains Richard Johnson, means that 'his prescriptions have an old-fashioned or "Tory" ring'.[19] More boldly, Linda Colley finds in Cobbett's nostalgic evocations of popular solidarity a precursor of fascism: he was, she suggests, a 'forerunner . . . ultimately of the National Front'.[20]

Ian Dyck has effectively challenged many of these associations by making the case that, by 1805, Cobbett was 'an unqualified Radical'.[21] Dyck links the modern difficulty in accepting this political identity to the fact that 'folk tradition and cottage politics . . . have become increasingly estranged from the theory and practice of left-wing radicalism'.[22] Dyck opens out Cobbett's nostalgia to show that, idealized as it undoubtedly was, it nevertheless referred to concrete experiences and specific memories. 'It was not country workers but middle-class rural writers', Dyck argues,

> who lapsed into vague and romantic effusions about the past. Cobbett and the labourers were not vague: their sense of the eighteenth-century past was grounded in experience and oral traditions rather than in a chronic and wistful impulse to recover the past for the past's sake.[23]

Surveying the evidence for generational differences in living standards between 1790–1840 E. P. Thompson found that 'there was a slight improvement in average material standards.'[24] However, looking beyond the statistics of income and prices, he comes down on the same side as Dyck.

> Over the same period there was intensified exploitation, greater insecurity, and increasing human misery. By 1840 most people were 'better off' than their forerunners had been fifty years before, but they had suffered and continued to suffer this slight improvement as a catastrophic experience.[25]

Dyck's argument also finds support in the portrait of Thomas Spence I offer later in this chapter. He too had 'grounded' experience to draw on when he criticized the changes he saw around him. However, in turning to Spence we can also make a broader attempt to challenge the identification of early nostalgic radicalism with the right. For unlike Cobbett, whose thumping rhetoric and ruddy farmer's demeanour allow him to be easily rendered as 'really a Tory', Spence is the poorest and most determined militant in English history; an unassailable icon of revolutionary integrity.

To identify and understand the role of nostalgia in Spence's politics might seem, then, a disquieting prospect. However, as Dyck's intervention suggests, over recent years the history of socialism in Britain has become far more receptive to the complexity of radical identity. One of the most influential interdisciplinary contributions to this new mood was Craig Calhoun's *The Question of Class Struggle*. Calhoun unpicks the fabric of Marxist analysis by arguing that it was not the factory worker but the artisan, deeply embedded in locality and tradition and rebelling against the destruction of his whole way of life, that provided the most active revolutionary agent.[26] The 'reactionary radicalism' of such workers, best exemplified for Calhoun by the Luddite movement of the 1810–1820 period, was a fight for survival: 'what they sought could not be granted except by fundamentally altering the structure of power and rewards in English society.'[27] Hence such 'workers were not fighting for control of the industrial revolution as much as against that revolution itself.'[28] Contrary to Mill and Marx's idea that radicalism emerged from deracination (when people have 'nothing but their chains' to loose), Calhoun suggests that 'revolutionary and other radical mobilisations take place when people do have something to defend'.[29]

Turning one of the assumptions of class history on its head, Calhoun goes on to conclude that 'reformism is the characteristic stance of the working class': for the 'new working class could gain an indefinite range of ameliorative reforms without fundamentally altering its collective existence.[30] Although Calhoun's assessment of defensive radicalism is compelling his notion that the proletariat are essentially reformist is less convincing. While the former argument captures the specific social experience of artisan radicals in the early nineteenth century, the latter is sweeping. Moreover, it makes it difficult to understand why the proletariat in Britain were later to play a central role in non-reformist radicalism. Nevertheless, Calhoun's wider thesis opens up the question of whether later working-class radicalism emerged in spite of, or because of, the diminution of cultural ties and traditional attachments. *The Question of Class Struggle* unsettles and convincingly challenges the *expectation* that authentic radicalism is tied to the loss of cultural embeddedness.

Perhaps the most comprehensive and influential recent revision of English popular history has been offered by Patrick Joyce. In *Visions of the People* Joyce questions the existing 'emphasis on the onward march of class, or class as the only or the main outcome of historical change'.[31] Indeed, for Joyce, the idea of 'class consciousness' has 'an antiquated ring to it' and may be placed alongside 'hopelessly idealised categories such as "revolutionary" or "labour consciousness" '.[32] Joyce's version of English radical history from 1848 up to 1914 emphasizes the continuity of populism. Thus he is interested in the mobilizing power of discourses about 'the people' and popular autonomy, as well as the interconnections between liberal, radical and socialist perspectives. Joyce's pluralistic approach has helped open the door for more sympathetic and nuanced approaches to radical nostalgia. This is evident from his appraisal – which focuses upon but is not restricted to the Independent Labour Party (ILP) – of the way the 'romantic, moral and aesthetic critique of "industrialism" was taken over intact by socialists'.

> The pantheon of Liberalism and radicalism was the pantheon of socialism – Dickens, Bunyan, Carlyle, Ruskin, and, later, Emerson, Thoreau and Tolstoy. Marx and Morris were not much bothered with. Strands of socialist thinking influential beyond as well as within the ILP preached a similar message: MacDonald's anti-urbanism was as evident as Blatchford's evocation of a 'merrie England' in which 'pre-industrial values' were exalted. Edward Carpenter attacked 'modern civilisation' rather than capitalism as a system.[33]

However, although Joyce's shared 'pantheon' usefully highlights continuities, it smoothes over the rupture in the radical attitude to nostalgia that occurred in the late nineteenth century. For one of the things that is striking about the politics of nostalgia found in Blatchford and Morris is its self-conscious and defensive nature. By the end of the nineteenth century, the common-sense, practical turn to the past found in earlier periods was no longer possible. In its place a kind of injured yearning came occasionally to the fore and, more commonly, into an awkward, broken, dialogue with anti-nostalgic and modernist aspirations.

Over recent years, the names of E. P. Thompson and Patrick Joyce have often been used to mark out opposing poles in the debate on the evolution of radical politics. The difference between them has been framed as an argument between materialist and postmaterialist/post-modern approaches to the nature and production of social meaning.[34] However, our interest in the dilemma of radical nostalgia points to political connections rather than theoretical distinctions. The dispute over the nature of social meaning between materialists and postma-terialists should not blind us to the fact that Thompson and Joyce (and Calhoun) all seek to rescue forms of popular resistance from the 'condescension of prosperity'. Indeed, while Joyce and Calhoun have subverted the fetishization of developmental narratives, it is Thompson who comes closest to, not simply recording, but offering a politics of nostalgia. Thompson's history has a vulnerable quality that finds space and accords value to sentiments of loss and yearning. 'I like these Muggletonians', he writes in his book about William Blake, *Witness against the Beast*, 'but it is clear that they were not among history's winners. Nor did they wish to be.'[35] The following wistful passage at the end of *The Making of the English Working Class* suggests a powerful sense of nostalgia for missed pathways within English political culture:

> both the Romantic and the Radical craftsmen opposed the annunciation of Acquisitive Man. In the failure of the two traditions to come to a point of junction, something was lost. How much we cannot be sure, for we are among the losers.[36]

From Poorman's Advocate to Proletarian: Thomas Spence and Radical Tradition

Spence was born in 1750 on the Quayside in Newcastle-upon-Tyne. He was one of 19 children. His mother sold stockings, his father made fishing nets. Spence received no formal education. At the age of 10 he joined his father's trade. When Spence was thrown out of the Newcastle Philosophical Society for hawking his pamphlet – *Property in Land Every One's Right* – on the streets of the city it was the start of a long and impoverished life on the margins of British politics. One of his biographers, Francis Place, observed that Spence was 'a typical specimen of those political poor preachers' and that he was 'as poor as any man could well be. And with some trifling fluctuation in his affairs he continued in this state to the day of his death.'[37]

Spence's politics centred on his 'Plan', which he set out in his pamphlet and stuck to throughout his life. Spence's Plan was a scheme to take the ownership of land away from individuals and place it under local (parish) ownership as common property. The model of self-government Spence foresaw was, as Mary Ashraf notes, based on the 'well-tested experi-ence of the common people in organizing their numerous benefit clubs and societies'.[38] For Spence, who saw himself as 'the poorman's advocate', autonomy was part of the political heritage of ordinary people.[39] Spence's implacability on the capacity of ordinary people to control their own affairs earned him a reputation as an extremist and an eccentric. Indeed, he worried that only the Government took him seriously. Imprisoned for a year for seditious libel in 1801, he complained,

> The people without treat me with the contempt due to a Lunatic . . . it is only the Government that wishes to make me appear of consequence, and the people within [the prison] treat me as bad or worse than the most notorious Felons among them.[40]

However, Spence's disappointment with his countrymen must be judged in the context of his ambition. In fact, he had many followers. The term 'Spencean' was, in the first two decades of the nineteenth century, synonymous with ultra-radical opinion. Such was the Government's fear of the spread of his doctrines that three years after his death, an Act of Parliament was passed prohibiting 'all Societies or Clubs calling themselves *Spenceans* or *Spencean Philanthropists*'.[41] In the same year, 1817, Thomas Malthus observed that,

> [I]t is generally known that an idea has lately prevailed among some of the lower classes of society, that the land is the people's farm, the rent of which ought to be divided equally among them; and that they have been deprived of the benefits which belong to them, from this their natural inheritance, by the injustice and oppression of their stewards, the landlords.[42]

Spence's intransigent hostility to aristocrats and landlords was based on two historical claims. First, that they had stolen the land from the people and second, that the power of this 'band of robbers' was a transgression of the people's 'native state' of natural, God-given, freedom.[43] The former argument was based on Spence's personal experience, the latter on a sweeping sense of rights being established and defended 'from the beginning'.[44]

Spence's active interest in politics appears to have begun in 1771, when the Corporation of Newcastle attempted to enclose the city's common, the Town Moor. Lessee's fences were knocked down by irate town folk while the city's Freemen challenged the legality of the Corporation's actions. The defeat of enclosure took two years to achieve. When it came it was celebrated as a victory of common ownership over private interests. Signet rings issued to mark the occasion were inscribed *vox populi vox dei*. Though not a Freeman, the fight for the Town Moor had a tremendous impact on Spence. His life-long conviction that the common ownership of land is possible was based on his experience of the way common ownership had been defended in his native city. In later life he recalled that he 'took a lesson' from the Town Moor affair 'which I shall never forget'.[45]

For Spence, the enclosure of common land represented an attack on the traditional rights of the people. Today, he explained in his lecture of 1775, 'men may not live in any part of this world, nor even where they are born, but as strangers'.[46] Under his Plan this situation would be reversed, for 'All would be little farmers and little Mastermen.'[47] Despite being a city dweller himself, Spence's model for the future was almost entirely agrarian. As H. T. Dickinson notes, 'Mines, factories and cotton mills had no place in Spence's vision of Britain's green and pleasant land.'[48] Spence's idealized images of egalitarian and autonomous village communities, in which land was held in common, emerged from, and appealed to, a predominantly rural society in which attachments to the land remained strong. In his 1775 lecture he looks forward to a time when there is 'perfect freedom from every imposition'; a time when,

> there no more nor other lands in the whole country than the parishes; and each of them is sovereign lord of its own territories.[49]

It is important to note, in the light of later interpretations of his work, that Spence explicitly ruled out land nationalization. His experience of political struggle and belief in popular democracy expressed itself as a distrust of national government,

> [A] Government that draws great Riches from sources which do not immediately affect the people, as from Loans, Mines, Foreign Tribute or Subsidies is sure to creep by Degrees

into absolute power and overturn everything. It is for this reason I would not have the Land national, nor provincial, but parochial property.[50]

When Spence looked forward to the implementation of his Plan he was applying and developing his direct knowledge of co-operation and common ownership. This aspect of his nostalgia, like Cobbett's, offered a critique of the present that was based upon knowledge of the recent past. However, there is another, broader, aspect to Spence's nostalgia, an aspect which arose from the idea that there once existed a Golden Age of freedom and that the people had been brought low from this state by being deprived of their natural and God-given rights. Tracing the developing of the myths of the Norman Yoke and Golden Age in radical thought, Christopher Hill writes that,

> One of the great revolutions of radical thought, secularising Winstanley's demand for heaven on earth, was Thomas Spence's claim in 1783 that 'The Golden Age, so fam'd by Men of Yore/Shall soon be counted fabulous no more.'[51]

However, although Spence's religious convictions may not have been as dominant as those found among earlier radicals, it is misleading to ignore them entirely. Spence was brought up in an egalitarian dissident sect called the Glassites and often referred to the biblical teaching that 'God hath given the earth to the children of men, given it to mankind in common.'[52] Seeking to explain Spence's frequent biblical references T. M. Parssinen suggests that 'The cry of revolution entailed a new rhetoric' and that Spence 'found in his fundamentalist religious background a ready source of language to suit his purpose'.[53] However, in his detailed study of Spenceanism, Malcolm Chase corrects the suggestion that Spence was merely deploying Christian language for political ends. Spence's 'religious terminology', he notes 'meant more than a cynical means of self-promotion',

> A tendency to see Spence within the context of the development of socialist theory, as a far-sighted 'pioneer' and 'forerunner', has encouraged in historians an anachronistic disbelief that he actually *meant* what he wrote.[54]

When we do listen to Spence we hear an unselfconscious, 'common-sense' assertion of the people's political heritage.

> [T]he country of the people, in a native state, is properly their common, in which each of them has an equal property, with free liberty to sustain himself and family with the animals, fruits and other products thereof.[55]

Spence identified his Plan with 'Nature's plan'.[56] One notices again and again in his work a sense of nature that goes beyond biblical teaching or political imperative and suggests a specific identification with animals as a repository of incorruptible freedom and defiance against novelty. The title of Spence's journal *Pigs Meat*, was a response to Burke's dismissal of the revolutionary masses as the 'swinish multitude'. But Spence's frequent use of the image of an angry hog, stamping upon the symbols of authority (a motif also found on many of the hundreds of political tokens he minted and distributed) and the abundance and diversity of references to other animals throughout his work, suggests that he found within the animal kingdom the kind of unchanging, primordial integrity that he wished to find in people.

When Spence – who liked to describe himself as 'free as a cat' – writes about dispossession it is towards a comparison with other creatures that he turns:

> A worm pays no rent: the Earth while he lives is his portion, and he riots in untaxed Luxuries. And, if perchance, a Crow, or other creature, should pick him up, why that is only Death, which may come in some shape or other to us all as well as he. But in this respect he had the advantage of us that while he lived he paid no Rent! And herein are all the Creatures to be envied.[57]

Spence took the idea of natural rights further in *The Rights of Infants* (1796). Like many of Spence's tracts this pamphlet portrays a dialogue, on this occasion between a contemptuous Aristocrat and a Spencean woman.

> '*AND pray what are the Rights of Infants?*' cry the haughty Aristocracy, sneering and tossing up their noses.

> Woman: Ask the she-bears, and every she-monster, and they will tell you what the rights of every species of young are. – They will tell you, in resolute language and actions too, that their rights extend to a full participation of the fruits of the earth.[58]

Spence goes on to claim that women were the natural defenders 'from the beginning' not only of the rights of children but rights in general.

> *Aristocracy (sneering): And is your sex also set up for pleaders of rights?*

> Woman. Yes, Molochs! Our sex were defenders of rights from the beginning. And though men, like other he-brutes, sink calmly into apathy . . . You shall find that we not only know our rights, but have spirit to assert them, to the downfall of you and all tyrants.[59]

Spence's precise impact on later radicals is difficult to gauge. In *The People's Farm* Chase argues that Spence's agrarian radicalism, including elements of his Plan, fed into Chartism. Spence's fundamental conviction – that the land should be returned to the people as common property – retained a place in English socialism into the last century.[60] However, by the late nineteenth century, this idea had been largely absorbed by campaigns for the nationalization of land. Moreover, the interpretation of Spence was increasingly shaped by socialist progressivism and socialist modernity. These interpretations suggested that Spence was, at best, an embryonic figure in a maturing class movement. Spence's nostalgic concern with the popular experience of co-operation and with reviving a Golden Age of natural rights were filtered out. What remained was an early working-class militant, fumbling towards the future. This image was open to both negative or positive representations. Spence was rendered by some critics into a simple-minded misfit. Thus in *The Socialist Tradition* Alexander Gray writes that Spence was 'in himself a poor creature of little capacity and less gifts'. Gray adds that 'oddly, he became a symbol and played a certain part in history'.[61] The idea that Spence was an oddity is repeated by E. P. Thompson and G. D. H. Cole. Thompson says that '[i]t is easy to see Spence . . . as little more than a crank',[62] while for Cole he had 'little practical bearing on the contemporary development of British radical or working-class thought'.[63] A final stinging blow comes from Knox, who argues, on the basis of Spence's localism, that he was 'less a harbinger of modern revolutionism than a mutation of the past'.[64]

However, more positive interpretations could call on the authority of Marx. In *The German Ideology*, Marx included Spence in his short roll call of early English communists. In *Theories of Surplus Value* he speaks warmly of him as the author of a tract called *Private Property in Land* and as a 'deadly enemy' of this form of property.[65] The emergence of land nationalization campaigns in the 1880s also provided fertile soil for Spence's rehabilitation.[66] The English Marxist Henry Mayers Hyndman came across Spence's work in the early 1880s and immediately identified it as an important indigenous statement of socialism. Hyndman's discovery of Spence shaped his interpretation for the next one hundred years. Hyndman issued a work, in 1882, called *The Nationalisation of the Land in 1775 and 1882*, which reprinted Spence's 1775 lecture.[67] Spence was to become a key figure in Hyndman's argument that 'In England . . . there was perhaps more practical Socialism than in any other nation.'[68]

From generation to generation the idea of nationalising the land has been kept alive among the people. A hundred years ago, Thomas Spence of Newcastle formulated a complete scheme to bring about this result through the action of parishes and municipalities. The time was not ripe.[69]

Frederick Engels enthused to Hyndman (in a letter of 13 March 1882) that he was 'very glad that glorious old Tom Spence has been brought out again'.[70] But what had happened to Tom Spence? He had developed what the Marxist historian Max Beer eulogized as a 'thoroughly honest, proletarian and consistent character'.[71] He was being turned into an authentic working-class revolutionary.

To understand the growth of interest in Spence it is also useful to be reminded that Hyndman's main concern was to translate Marx into the common language of ordinary people. His worry was that Marxism was too theoretical to be readily comprehended. Indeed, in his *The Historical Basis of Socialism in England*, Hyndman notes that even the *Communist Manifesto* 'is by no means written in a popular form'.[72] With his non-nonsense rhetoric and irascible style Spence had the kind of common touch Hyndman considered to be absent from Marx. Hence, within an increasingly intellectual and abstract radical discourse, his plain-speaking populism took on a class value. Yet it is a value that reinforces the argument that Spence was being cast in the role of rudimentary forerunner; a primitive prototype that confirmed the more educated and advanced status of later radical thinkers.

The most diligent attempt to pull Spence into a Marxist lineage was to come in the 1960s, with the research of Mary Ashraf, an English communist historian based in the German Democratic Republic.[73] A number of Marxist historians in the Soviet Union were already familiar with Spence. He was a reference point in an existing debate on the origins of revolutionary communist consciousness. Ashraf was attempting to challenge the view, associated with V. P. Volgin, that Spence was an egalitarian but not a socialist, because he did not reject private property in anything other than land.[74] Ashraf's attempt to turn Spence into a modern socialist demanded that she counter this view and insert into his work her own conjecture:

It seems clear that Spence intended large-scale industry to be public property or if not managed by the Parish as a whole, to be run by 'corporations' of workers collectively. From land confiscation which included these larger industries intimately associated with land tenure but already long established on capitalist lines, there is not a great step to the concept of the workers' ownership of the means of production.[75]

However, Spence will always disappoint this kind of appropriation. Indeed, there is an undertow of frustration in Ashraf's attempts to corral him. Spence's backward-looking evocations of better times and natural rights, along with his determined parochialism, make him an unconvincing proto-Marxist. He is, says a suddenly unenthused Ashraf, ultimately part of an 'inchoate tendency' of 'working class eccentrics' whose 'passionate denunciations . . . made no distinction between one method of accumulation and another'.[76]

The rupture between the street-level organic politics of Spence and the socialist modernity offered by his later critics and admirers, renders him incomplete and incoherent. It is only with the disintegration of Marxism's certainties, over the past few decades, that Spence's voice has re-emerged and been allowed to speak in terms which he might have recognized. The new attention he is receiving today is notable for its openness to the localist and anti-authoritarian aspects of his political message.[77] The commemorative Blue Plaque put up at the Quayside in Newcastle in 2010 to celebrate his birth symbolizes a new interest in this once forgotten 'poorman's advocate'. It may also mark a new willingness to listen to Spence and his deeply rooted plans for the future.

William Morris: Revolutionary Nostalgia in an Age of Progress

Morris is the best known example of a nostalgic radical. He concluded his socialist ode *The Pilgrims of Hope* in characteristic style with the lines,

> I cling to the love of the past and the love of the day to be,
>
> And the present, it is but the building of the man to be strong in me.[78]

And yet, as Mark Bevir notes, 'Morris is an icon of the left. Everyone wants to have him on their side.'[79] Morris's unembarrassed love of beauty, craftsmanship and nature makes him an intriguing hero for modern politics. It is, perhaps, precisely because we find such themes so difficult to voice that he has become so necessary.

Morris's broadly Marxist understanding of the division of labour, art and life emerged, in the early 1880s, directly from having 'studied socialism from the scientific point of view'.[80] However, his consistent eulogies for medieval society and repugnance at the ugliness of industrial existence were problematic and paradoxical within a movement and wider society that had come to identify nostalgia with conservatism. For Engels he was 'good for nothing but sentiment'.[81] Slightly more sympathetically, Raymond Williams said of Morris that he suffered from a 'fragmentary consciousness'. The 'larger part of his literary work', he continued, 'bears witness only to the disorder which he felt so acutely'.[82] Another approach to Morris has been to trace his evolution, as the subtitle of E. P. Thompson's book on Morris has it, from *Romantic to Revolutionary*.[83] Nevertheless, the unorthodox nature of Morris's socialism has enthralled generations of commentators. Indeed, in more recent years his 'disorder' has been construed positively. Fiona MacCarthy hopes that 'in the light of our own mellow postmodern eclecticism we can accept Morris more easily as the conservative radical he really was.'[84] It is a transition in which the nostalgic part of Morris is cast as playing both an early and limiting role. By contrast, Ruth Kinna offers an integrative perspective on Morris's 'art of socialism'.[85] Kinna argues that Morris's romanticism was integral to his socialism, leading him to a cultural and creative critique of the experience of alienation in industrialized capitalist society.

These different interpretations of Morris reflect the fact that radical nostalgia has been established as a site of anxiety but also of fascination. From the late nineteenth century onwards, the figure of the romantic revolutionary took on an anachronistic charm. Questions and worries about being backward-looking that never troubled Thomas Spence swarm around Morris, attracting our attention but also making him appear remote from the mainstream of twentieth-century socialism. I am going to look at how Morris responded to some of these concerns. More specifically, I will suggest a number of ways that Morris managed his revolutionary nostalgia in the context of an increasingly anti-nostalgic movement. As this implies, it is the self-conscious and defensive quality of Morris's socialism that interests me. I identify two ways Morris brought nostalgia and socialism together: first, by identifying socialism as an overcoming of modernity (a point explored in the company of Morris' utopian novel *News from Nowhere*); second, by concentrating his nostalgic concerns into particular periods of his life (e.g. in the 1890s) and spheres of activity (notably, the aesthetic and cultural). These distinctions are, of course, a descriptive and analytical device and not at all in keeping with Morris's own holistic ambitions and sensibility.

Morris's most celebrated depiction of a utopian future, *News from Nowhere; or, an Epoch of Rest* (published in 1890) is also a bold escape from modernity.[86] It was written in response to Edward Bellamy's *Looking Backward*, a state socialist, industrial utopia set in the year 2000, published in 1888.[87] Morris's vulnerable sense of being overtaken by modernity, leaps off the page of the biting criticisms of this new 'Socialist bible' he contributed to *The Commonweal* in 1889 and 1890.[88] Although 'attracting general attention', and although its 'temperament is that of many thousands of people', Morris despises the book and is clearly upset that its technocratic solutions are in the ascendant.[89]

The success of Mr. Bellamy's utopian book, deadly dull as it is, is a straw to show which way the wind blows. The general attention paid to our clever friends, the Fabian lecturers and pamphleteers, is not altogether due to their literary ability; people have really got their heads turned more of less in their direction.[90]

Bellamy's 'temperament', Morris explains,

may be called the unmixed modern one, unhistoric and unartistic; it makes its owner (if a Socialist) perfectly satisfied with modern civilisation, if only the injustice, misery, and waste of the class society could be got rid of; which half-change seems possible to him . . . it is necessary to point out that there are some socialists who do not think that the problem of the organisation of life and necessary labour can be dealt with by a huge national centralisation.[91]

News from Nowhere offers a bold, alternative, vision. Morris wishes to make the case that radicalism and a dissatisfaction with 'modern civilization' are mutually sustaining. It may be argued that he was, thereby, elaborating Marx's vision of class revolution as returning society to a time beyond time and beyond alienation. Yet *News from Nowhere* is no formal or orthodox exercise in Marxism. It draws out the nostalgic content within Marxism to the point where it transgresses and subverts Marx's modern spirit.

In the ideal society presented in *News from Nowhere*, modern techniques are acknowledged and selectively employed, but only so as to allow the integration of art and life and the disappearance of industrialization. Although Morris conceded elsewhere that 'machinery . . . has been, and for some time yet will be, indispensable', the pastoral utopia depicted in *News from*

Nowhere is a place where the sight and smell of factories is just a bad memory.[92] Looking back on the 'labour-saving machines' of the capitalist era, one elder recalls that they,

> were meant to 'save labour' (or, to speak more plainly, the lives of men) on one piece of work in order that it might be expended – I will say wasted – on another, probably useless, piece of work. Friend, all their devices for cheapening labour simply resulted in increasing the burden of labour.[93]

The new world Morris envisages is one in which the division between intellectual and non-intellectual labour has also ended. Asking a weaver about his craft, the novel's narrator-protagonist, William Guest, hears that he has, for the time being, 'taken to mathematics'.[94] Morris's distaste for intellectuals as a distinct social caste and for a library bound life of books and criticism, also finds full expression in the remembrance of how, in capitalist society,

> [T]he prevailing feeling amongst intellectual persons was a kind of sour distaste for the changing drama of the year, for the life of earth and its dealings with men. Indeed, in those days it was thought poetic and imaginative to look upon life as a thing to be borne, rather than enjoyed.[95]

Morris's utopia is a changeless *Epoch of Rest* in which social and natural harmony have been achieved. Revolutions and turmoil are at an end and a state of 'bliss' commenced that has no need for eras or ages, other than a vague foundational comparison between the present and the pseudo-civilization of the capitalist past. Thus the overcoming of modernity is also an overcoming of time: 'You see, guest, this is not an age of inventions.'[96] An 'old man' muses that he does not think his

> [T]ales of the past interest [the young] much. The last harvest, the last baby, the last knot of carving in the market-place is history enough for them. It was different, I think, when I was a lad, when we were not so assured of peace and continuous plenty as we are now.[97]

As I have already noted, Morris's communist utopia can be portrayed as developing themes found in Marx. However, one of the reasons that Morris has excited so much debate over the years is that his imaginative journey both touches and challenges many different political traditions. Arguments that suggest Morris is really a Marxist, or really a conservative, or really an anarchist or green libertarian, have all been put forward, pulling us towards particular ways of approaching his work. By contrast, an emphasis on the way that nostalgia had become a site of counter-orthodoxy, while not necessarily assisting any one of these claims, may help explain why the political image of Morris appears so mutable and alluring. Morris's revolutionary nostalgia offers, not a resolution, but a kind of negotiation with and through an awkward terrain. In more concrete terms, we find that Morris concentrated his nostalgia into particular areas, notably into his artistic and creative output but also into the less political years that preceded and followed his burst of socialist activism between 1883–1890. Indeed, it is pertinent to note the dramatic shifts in focus that characterized his life course. His life-long friend Edward Burne-Jones observed,

> When I first knew Morris nothing would content him but being a monk . . . and then wanted to smash everything up and begin the world anew, and now it is printing he cares for, and to make wonderful rich-looking books.[98]

In the 1880s Morris was dismissive of the arts and crafts movement that he had inspired: 'the general public don't care a damn about arts and crafts.'[99] However, from 1890, his withdrawal from active involvement in socialism was, as Burne-Jones's depiction suggests, matched by a re-engagement with the revivalist craft movement and with romantic literature. This is not to suggest that, for Morris, old-age and nostalgia were connected. However, it is to find significance in the fact that Morris gave over certain years to the pursuit of revolution and others to the pursuit of lost arts and high romance.

Another way Morris's nostalgic yearnings were compartmentalized was by assigning them to the realm of the aesthetic and the cultural (as distinct from the political and economic). Carole Silver has argued that in the fantasy lands of Morris's late romances, such as *The Wood beyond the World* (1894), *The Well at the World's End* (1896) and *The Water of the Wondrous Isles* (1897), we find an 'internalisation' of his socialism.[100] *News from Nowhere* (written when Morris was still actively involved in the socialist movement) looks forward to his withdrawal from politics. Although it charts the dream of a member of the Socialist League (founded by Morris in 1885), it is also a journey towards a purely creative and organic form of community. William Guest enters his dream after an unsatisfactory and irritating meeting with members of the League:

> [T]here were six persons present, and consequently six sections of the party were represented, four of which had strong but divergent Anarchist opinions.[101]

Guest's dream takes him away from the tedium and backbiting of politics and towards a restful realm where useful and fully human lives are being enjoyed. We do not have to accept Philip Henderson's claim that, in *News from Nowhere*, Morris is 'abolishing everything he disliked in the nineteenth century and replacing it by everything he nostalgically longed for', in order to appreciate that the book functioned not just as an outlet for politics but against politics.[102] In *News from Nowhere* Morris takes us to an intimate and imaginative realm, waving goodbye to scientific socialism and political struggle in the knowledge that we must return to them once the dream is over.[103]

Morris did not heal the rupture between progress and nostalgia but, given his popularity with so many sections of the British left, he may be said to have successfully negotiated it. The urge to forgive Morris's supposed quirkiness tells its own story. Indeed, many critics offer a tone of indulgence towards Morris. They like him not *despite* but *because* of his non-conformity. Morris himself seems to have played up to the role of maverick. 'Does Comrade Morris accept Marx's theory of value?' he was asked at one public lecture in Glasgow in 1884:

> I am asked if I believe in Marx's theory of value. To speak quite frankly, I do not know what Marx's theory of value is, and I'm damned if I want to know . . . political economy is not my line, and much of it appears to be dreary rubbish.[104]

Morris's irreverence has tended to elicit more tolerant smiles than tuts of disapproval. Morris has been claimed by so many different political traditions because he lends them humanity. In an era when politics appears ideological and bureaucratic this is a valuable asset. The image of Morris as the grand old man of English socialism, as the Labour Party's father-figure, is rooted not just in his ability to synthesize Marxism with cultural creativity but with the desire to identify with someone who is so clearly both in and against the modern age.

Speaking in 1895, the year before he died, to one of the architects of democratic state socialism, Sidney Webb, Morris grumbled 'the world is going your way, Webb, but it is not the right way in the end'.[105] My argument suggests that in Morris we see resistance to, and a negotiation of, the emergence of socialist modernity. His self-conscious, romantic yearnings reflect a new, defensive and self-marginalizing politics of the past. It was a political form that deployed the creative and the aesthetic (and, hence, the anti-political) as a way of allowing loss to be expressed within and against the forward-looking culture of the left. And yet it also disturbs and excites that culture, leaving a sense of discomfort and longing.

Robert Blatchford: The New Life and Old Traditions of Socialist Fellowship

With Robert Blatchford we meet another radical nostalgic. And we again encounter the negotiation of the dilemma of expressing a sense of loss in an increasingly anti-nostalgic political milieu. Blatchford saw himself as a follower of Morris. When Morris died Blatchford wrote in the paper that he edited: 'I cannot help thinking that it does not matter what goes into *The Clarion* this week, because William Morris is dead . . . he was our best man.'[106]

The Morrisian themes that thread their way through the Clarion movement, that Blatchford presided over, include anti-parliamentarianism, anti-reformism, a focus on 'making socialists' rather than participation in party politics and a semi-spiritual sense of solidarity. *The Clarion* used Morris's slogan for its banners: 'Fellowship is Life: Lack of Fellowship is Death.' Morris's assertion of socialism as a politics of beauty was also important to Blatchford. In *Merrie England* he demands a country where all can enjoy 'beautiful fields, woods and gardens':

> And let me ask you is any carpet so beautiful or so pleasant as a carpet of grass and daisies? Is the fifth-rate music you play upon your cheap pianos as sweet as the songs of the gushing streams and joyous birds? And does a week at a spoiled and vulgar watering-place repay you for fifty-one weeks' toil and smother in a hideous and dirty town?[107]

The querulous tone Blatchford adopts in this passage is found throughout much of his work. This defensive stance also suggests that, like *News from Nowhere*, *Merrie England* is self-consciously situated against the spectre of more technocratic forms of socialist reasoning. The 'ugly, disagreeable, and mechanical' factory system is a target throughout Blatchford's novels and journalism.[108] However, Blatchford was not anti-modern. Indeed, he looked forward to the total resources of the country being run efficiently and effectively by a central socialist state. In-between railing against the factory system Blatchford sets out a model of a bright, clean new society, in which national ownership and public control will sweep away the past and ensure decent housing and living conditions for the working class.

Moreover, unlike Morris, Blatchford was a populist. The dilemmas of radical nostalgia that he negotiated were approached within the context of a unique mass movement that he inspired and helped lead. The 'Clarion movement' remains the largest extra-parliamentary socialist movement in British history (the movement may be dated from the first issue of the magazine around which it centred, *The Clarion* in 1891). Joyce suggests that the Clarion movement was 'perhaps the single greatest source of mass inspiration in early socialism'.[109] For Preben Kaarsholm,

> The movement surrounding the socialist weekly *Clarion* was probably the most peculiar and original left-wing organisational milieu of the period. It was also without doubt the most influential socialist movement; whereas the significance of the ILP and the SDF was surely restricted to their approximate 7,000 and 3,000 members respectively. *Clarion* with its sale of about 40,000 a week and wide-range of cultural activities was in contact with a much wider range of working-class and 'plebeian' opinion.[110]

It is intriguing therefore, that the Clarion movement is little more than a footnote in many histories of the early years of British socialism. The movement's 'Bible', *Merrie England*, appears indigestible to later critics. Following a well-trodden tradition of casual dismissal of the book, Roger Ebbatson refers to it as 'socialist-inclined' and is clearly bemused by its 'paradoxical popularity'.[111] Once claimed as 'the most widely read man in the world', by the late 1910s, Blatchford had lost much of his former appeal.[112] There may be good reasons for this. Blatchford's favoured rhetorical mode is bluff banter; a barrack-room form that alternates between the whimsical and the hearty and is both too arcane and self-consciously ingratiating for twentieth-century tastes. Moreover, he combined this backslapping mode of address with a deep sense of patriotism. As the title of *Merrie England*, as well as its follow up volume, *Britain for the British*, attest, Blatchford offered an insular vision of a self-supporting country. This sentiment also found expression in the familiar radical *cri de coeur*: 'the land of England should be restored to the English people from whom it was stolen.'[113] Laurence Thompson's biography *Robert Blatchford: Portrait of an Englishman* pinpoints Blatchford allegiance: 'It was this loved England, then that was to be merry, Great Britain possibly as an afterthought, but not the British Empire, and certainly not the united workers of the world.'[114]

There is a defensive and peevish quality to Blatchford's patriotic attachments. His nationalism was stubborn and often belligerently resistant to the internationalism that he considered was coming to typify the mainstream and radical left. Offering himself as 'an ancient and quiet watchman' in the mid-1920s, he complained,

> In these days of the cosmopolitan cult it is bad form to think nationally, but I am an old dog and cannot easily learn new tricks.[115]

Somewhat confirming his suspicions, Blatchford's patriotism has meant that, despite his ultra-left utopianism, his trenchant hostility to eugenics (as seen in *Not Guilty: A Defence of the Bottom Dog*, 1906)[116] and prominence as a campaigning atheist (*God and My Neighbour*, 1903),[117] he has long been treated as a compromised and conservative figure.[118] The idea that Blatchford was right wing may be supported by reference to the fact that even his friends regarded him a patrician moralist (he was, said Lyons 'spiritually – a Tory').[119] Moreover, his controversial pro-British position in both the Boer War and First World War, and his movement to the right in later life (Blatchford voted Conservative in 1924), also lend credence to the label. Indeed, his journey to the right might be seen to put him in the company of socialist conservatives, such as Penty and Chesterton.[120]

However, both the urge to locate Blatchford as really a Tory or, indeed, really a revolutionary, miss what is interesting about him as a political figure, for Blatchford cannot be understood in isolation. The Clarion movement surrounded and sustained him and it is through an understanding of this movement that he must be approached. What appeared to later eyes as the oddity of the movement – notably its idealization of a jovial 'clubbiness' – provides us with an example of a popular form of nostalgic radicalism.

The Clarion movement was an attempt to *create a sense of community around political ideals and social bonds*. In sociological terms it appears as a response to *Gesellschaft* and a recreation of *Gemeinschaft*. This portrait also implies that the informality of the Clarion movement, its lack of official structures, membership or leadership, should not be understood as a failure of organization but a conscious attempt to enable an organic and spontaneous social form. Another aspect of Clarion politics was the movement's *emphasis on the political transformation of the clubbable individual*. This emphasis allowed Blatchford and the wider Clarion movement to both assert a revolutionary message while laying claim to a national tradition of popular conviviality. Within the Clarion movement the agent of revolution, the point of change, was the individual who, coming together with like-minded people in bonds of friendship and loyalty, entered into a 'new life' of 'socialist fellowship'. The Clarion Fellowship, formed by Blatchford in 1900, centred on active identification with other readers of *The Clarion*. The Clarion Fellowship offered the socialism of friendship to Clarionettes. However, unlike the Australian model of socialist 'mateship', the Fellowship was not entirely dominated by models of masculine comradeship. Indeed, it attracted a significant following among socialist women. From 1896 a number of Clarion Women's Vans toured the country promoting socialism. They were one part of an elaborate network of largely autonomous Clarion social organizations. The Handicraft Guilds, Field Clubs, Rambling Clubs, Camping Clubs and Camera Clubs of the Clarion movement are a reminder just how social socialism once was.[121] The movement also incorporated Clarion Glee Clubs and the philanthropic activities of Cinderella Clubs (the latter provided food and entertainment for poor children and pre-dated *The Clarion*, being started by Blatchford in 1890). However, the most popular Clarion clubs were the Clarion Choirs and Clarion Cycling Clubs. There were 32 Clarion Cycling Clubs in 1895 and 70 by 1897. Cycling was a natural form of affiliation, in part, because it was the favoured means of travel for the propaganda and fly-posting activities of the Clarion Scouts (formed in 1894; by 1895 there were 38 Scouting 'Corps').

Keir Hardie, who disliked Blatchford, surely had the Clarion movement in mind when he noted, in 1903, that 'For a time in England, the fibre of the Socialist movement was almost destroyed by a spirit of irresponsible levity.'[122] For his part Blatchford argued that he regarded Hardie and his followers at the *Labour Leader*, as 'Puritans; narrow, bigoted, puffed up with sour cant'. He contrasted *Labour Leader* with *The Clarion* which 'loved the humour and colour of the old English tradition'.[123] 'There never was a paper like it' agreed Margaret Cole,

[I]t was not in the least the preconceived idea of a socialist journal. It was not solemn; it was not highbrow . . . It was full of stories, jokes and verses – sometimes pretty bad verses and pretty bad jokes – as well as articles.[124]

Bernard Shaw described *The Clarion* as 'a very good family joke' and the circle which surrounded Blatchford appear to have approached it in similar vein.[125] A list of the pen names used on *The Clarion* – Nunquam (Blatchford), The Bounder (Edward Fay), Dangle (A. M. Thompson), Mont Blong (Montague Blatchford) and Whiffly Puncto (William

Palmer) – indicates much about the tone of the paper. The Clarion movement was understood by Blatchford to sustain the 'old English tradition' against the alienating forces that beset the nation. Humour was central to this endeavour precisely because it was irrational, non-instrumental and created bonds among strangers. The Clarion movement offered political education and transformation within a spirit of friendship. Blatchford's hazy summation of the Fellowship explained that,

[T]he Clarion fellowship [should] be an association for social intercourse, and for the realisation of *Clarion* ideals. It is necessary that we should not be tied up in cast-iron rules, and this resolution is both clear and vague. The *Clarion* ideals belong to *Clarion* readers, and as ideals change it is thought best not to define what they are. . . . the Fellowship exists to promote social intercourse, and to work for whatever is thought desirable at the time.[126]

In 1910, Albert Lyons offered a portrait of the Fellowship that fleshes out Blatchford vision, while maintaining his contrarian manner.

The Clarion Fellowship is absurd and inexplicable, and – wholly charming. It is Socialism – real Socialism – this bond of genuine sympathy and kindness which exists between the readers of the paper which Mr. Blatchford edits. A stranger entering almost any town in England has but to proclaim himself a *Clarion* reader ('Clarionette' is a popular phrase) to be assured of welcome and hospitality in the houses of friends whom he has never seen before. This is not practical; but it *is* Socialism.[127]

The Fellowship was understood to create socialists and make socialism, to bring it into being in microcosm. It offered and enabled a new community based not simply on political activism but also on traditional bonds of intimacy and pleasure. Thus the challenges of modernity – of deracination and revolution – could be both accommodated and refused. The transformation that needed to happen could be imagined to be created and managed within and through the enthusiasm of individuals acting together.

John Trevor, describing the 'Clarionettes', explained that,

[I]t has not been to a new economic theory, merely, that these converts have been introduced. It has been to a new life. Their eyes shine with the gladness of a new birth.[128]

In a section of *The Clarion*, from February 1896, titled 'How I Became a Socialist', readers wrote in with their personal narratives of how, as one put it, they had 'found salvation'.[129] As another reader writes, 'I found our chief's articles, read them, took the *Clarion* (good old *Clarion*) from the first number, and finally found salvation.'[130] In many ways the Clarion movement is an excellent example of the kind of 'religion of socialism' Stephen Yeo has charted in the last two decades of the nineteenth century.[131] However, Yeo's suggestion that, from the mid-1890s, the Clarion movement 'gradually became what is now remembered as – a recreational society' is doubly misleading.[132] For not only do the reminiscences of those who knew the movement show that it was recalled as both a social and political phenomenon, but the splitting of the two forms was what the Clarion movement brought into question.[133] The offer of a 'new life' within the Clarion Fellowship cannot be properly understood without a political appreciation of the convivial pleasures it also offered.

Conclusion

I have been encountering the paradox that many of the people whom 'reality' has proved to be wrong, still seem to me to have been better people than those who were, with a facile and conformist realism, right.

E. P. Thompson[134]

Towards the end of the nineteenth century, those forms of radicalism that claimed to be rooted in the history and the natural rights of the people were being displaced by modernist radicalisms that viewed nostalgia with intense suspicion. It was awkward moment. But the power of the modernist imagination was, if not overwhelming, the stronger force. Before long the radical nostalgia of William Morris would be treated as a charming contradiction in terms and the convivial socialism of the Clarion movement a whimsical footnote in the story of mainstream socialism.

This chapter has offered portraits of three English radicals. Two of the three (Morris and Blatchford) are commonly portrayed as nostalgic radicals. Yet it is precisely the emergence of self-consciousness around a sense of loss and attachment to the past that has provided the focus of this chapter. Spence escaped being labelled as a nostalgic only by being translated into the progressive language and ambitions of state socialists with whom he had little in common. In this way Spence's parochialism and traditionalism were stripped away and an image of a honest proletarian, a forward-looking if embryonic communist, offered in their place.

Since this book has claimed to be reading nostalgia against the grain of socialist history my decision to explore the work of Morris and Blatchford may be judged an evasion of duty. However, my reading of both men has been designed to emphasize the difficulty of articulating nostalgic radicalism in an age of progress. It has not been my intention to offer Morris or Blatchford simply as nostalgics, even less as politically confused or 'mixed-up'. Rather, what is revealed in their work is the management or negotiation of nostalgia and modernity. In both men we find a relatively self-conscious defence of tradition within and against a socialist movement that appeared to them to be turning away from such themes. With Morris I highlighted how he offered a distinct, aesthetic and cultural, radical sphere for the development of increasingly suspect nostalgic themes. In the previous chapter I identified the transgressive nature of the avant-garde's use of nostalgia. The portrait of Morris offered in this chapter suggests that he could be claimed as an early incarnation of this counter-cultural tradition. This interpretation would also accord with the extensive deployment of Morris's ideas within the environmentalist and anti-authoritarian movements of the last century.

After his death, in 1943, Robert Blatchford suffered no radical reincarnations. This is, in part, a reflection of the fact that it is easier to appropriate and reinvent the vision and spirit of intellectuals, such as Morris, than of historically specific and tub-thumbing populists, such as Blatchford. However, if we broaden our view of Blatchford to place him within the Clarion movement we find one of the more intriguing moments in British socialist history. Deeply conservative in many ways, the Clarionettes also spoke in the language of transformation, revolution and salvation. By making the self – not the isolated self but the social, clubbable self – the axis of change, the Clarion movement combined nostalgia and anti-nostalgia, modernity and anti-modernity. It appears, with hindsight, a strange combination. It was also the last major effusion of radical nostalgia within British socialism. For the rest of the century, the most significant forms of radical nostalgia were to be found well beyond the shores of 'merrie England'.

Notes

1. *Property in Land Every One's Right, Proved in a Lecture Read at the Philosophical Society in Newcastle, on the 8th of Nov. 1775.* In later editions Spence's first work was titled 'The Rights of Man' or 'The Real Rights of Man'. It can be found in T. Spence, *Pigs' Meat: Selected Writings of Thomas Spence*, (Nottingham: Spokesman, 1982). The original pamphlet had been presumed lost for many decades but was rediscovered in 2005. For a report of the discovery see Alastair Bonnett, 'Thomas Spence, *Property in Land Every One's Right* (1775)', *Labour History Review*, 74, 1, (2009).
2. R. Blatchford, *Merrie England*, (London: Clarion Press, 1908).
3. A. Lyons, *Robert Blatchford: The Sketch of a Personality: An Estimate of Some Achievements*, (London: Clarion Press, 1910), 5.
4. Cited by A. Thompson, 'Preface', R. Blatchford, *My Eighty Years*, (London: Cassell and Company, 1931), xiii.
5. Boym, *The Future of Nostalgia*, xvi.
6. Thompson, *The Making of the English Working Class*, 13.
7. Ibid., 836.
8   E. Hobsbawm, *Primitive Rebels*, (Manchester: Manchester University Press, 1959), 2.
9   Dated by Hobsbawm to 1880–1900. Hobsbawm, *Labour's Turning Point*.
10. E. Jones, *Notes to the People: Volume I*, (London: J. Pavey, 1851), 245.
11. 'An aristocrat traveller who visited the Yorkshire Dales in 1792', cited by Thompson, *The Making of the English Working Class*, 207. Thompson asserts that 'the outstanding fact of the period between 1790 and 1830 is the formation of "the working class"' (212).
12. Max Beer identifies its first use with Robert Owen: the word 'socialism', he notes, 'is found for the first time in *The Co-Operative Magazine* of November, 1827'. M. Beer, *A History of British Socialism*, (New York: Ayer Publishing, 1979), 187.
13. J. Mill, *Socialism*, (New York: John B. Alden, 1886), 260.
14. Ibid.
15. *Poor Man's Guardian*, (19 November, 1831), 174.
16. W. Cobbett, 'To the Blanketteers', *Cobbett's Weekly Political Register*, (27 March, 1819), 830–1.
17. W. Cobbett, *Rural Rides*, Volume 1, (London: J. M. Dent, 1917), 6.
18. J. Derry, *The Radical Tradition: Tom Paine to Lloyd George*, (London: Macmillan, 1967), 46.
19. R. Johnson, '"Really useful knowledge": radical education and working-class culture', in J. Clarke, C. Critcher and R. Johnson (Eds), *Working-Class Culture: Studies in History and Theory*, (London: Hutchinson, 1979), 89.
20. L. Colley, 'I am the watchman', *London Review of Books*, (20 November, 2003), 17.
21. Dyck, *William Cobbett*, 214.
22. Ibid.
23. Ibid., 147.
24. Thompson, *The Making of the English Working Class*, 231.
25. Ibid., 231.
26. C. Calhoun, *The Question of Class Struggle: Social Foundations of Popular Radicalism during the Industrial Revolution*, (Chicago: University of Chicago Press, 1982), 55.
27. Ibid., 60.
28. Ibid., 55.

29. C. Calhoun, 'The radicalism of tradition: community strength or venerable disguise and borrowed language?', *American Journal of Sociology*, 88, 5, (1983), 911.
30. Calhoun, *The Question of Class Struggle*, 140.
31. P. Joyce, *Visions of the People: Industrial England and the Question of Class, 1848–1914*, (Cambridge: Cambridge University Press, 1991), 8.
32. Ibid., 9.
33. Ibid., 77.
34. See, for example, Marc Steinberg, 'Culturally speaking: finding a commons between post-structuralism and the Thompsonian perspective', *Social History*, 21, 2, (1996), 193–214. Neville Kirk, 'History, language, ideas and post-modernism: a materialist view', *Social History*, 19, 2, (1994), 221–40.
35. E. P. Thompson, *Witness against the Beast: William Blake and the Moral Law*, (Cambridge: Cambridge University Press, 1993), 90. The Muggletonians were a millenarian free-thinking non-scriptural English sect of Dissenters. Thompson argues they were influenced by Blake.
36. Thompson, *The Making of the English Working Class*, 915.
37. Cited by P. M. Ashraf's *The Life and Times of Thomas Spence*, (Newcastle: Frank Graham, 1983), 287.
38. Ibid., 128.
39. The full title of Spence's journal was *Pigs' Meat; or, Lessons for the Swinish Multitude: Collected by the Poor Man's Advocate (an Old Veteran in the Cause of Freedom) in the Course of His Reading for More than Twenty Years.*
40. Cited by Ashraf, *The Life and Times of Thomas Spence*, 81.
41. House of Commons, *An Act for the More Effectually Preventing Seditious Meetings and Assemblies*, 17 March, 1817. The *Act* further explains that,

    certain Societies or Clubs calling themselves *Spenceans* or *Spencean Philanthropists*, hold and profess for their Object the Confiscation and Division of the Land, and the Extinction of the Funded Property of the Kingdom . . . it is expedient and necessary that all such Societies or Clubs as foresaid should be utterly suppressed and prohibited.

42. T. Malthus, *Additions to the Fourth and Former Editions of an Essay on the Principle of Population*, (London: John Murray, 1817), 40.
43. T. Spence, 'The rights of infants written in the latter end of the year 1796', in T. Spence, *Pigs' Meat: Selected Writings of Thomas Spence*, (Nottingham: Spokesman, 1982), 116.
44. Ibid., 115.
45. T. Spence, 'The restorer of society to its natural state (1803)', in T. Spence, *Pigs' Meat: Selected Writings of Thomas Spence*, (Nottingham: Spokesman, 1982), 163.
46. T. Spence, 'The rights of man', 61–2.
47. Cited by G. I. Gallop, 'Introductory essay: Thomas Spence and the real rights of man', in T. Spence, *Pigs' Meat: Selected Writings of Thomas Spence*, (Nottingham: Spokesman, 1982), 33.
48. H. T. Dickinson, *Liberty and Property: Political Ideology in Eighteenth-Century Britain*, (London: Weidenfeld and Nicolson, 1977), 268.
49. T. Spence, 'The rights of man', 63.
50. T. Spence, 'The restorer of society to its natural state', 146.

51. C. Hill, *Puritanism and Revolution: Studies in Interpretation of the English Revolution of the 17th Century*, (London: Pimilco, 2001), 49. The lines are from T. Spence, 'The rights of infants', 120.
52. T. Spence, 'The rights of infants', 111.
53. T. M. Parssinen, 'Thomas Spence and the origins of English land nationalisation', *Journal of the History of Ideas*, 34, (1973), 139, 135–41.
54. M. Chase, *The People's Farm: English Radical Agrarianism 1775–1840*, (Oxford: Clarendon Press, 1988), 51.
55. T. Spence, 'The rights of man', 59.
56. T. Spence, 'The rights of infants', 121.
57. T. Spence, 'The restorer of society to its natural state', 144.
58. T. Spence, 'The rights of infants', 114.
59. Ibid., 115.
60. Chase, *The People's Farm*.
61. A. Gray, *The Socialist Tradition: Moses to Lenin*, (London: Longmans, 1963), 257.
62. Thompson, *The Making of the English Working Class*, 177.
63. G. D. H. Cole, *Socialist Thought: The Forerunners 1789–1850*, (London: Macmillan, 1959), 25.
64. T. Knox, 'Thomas Spence: the trumpet of jubilee', *Past and Present*, 76, (1977), 98.
65. K. Marx, *Theories Of Surplus Value*, Volume 1, (London: Lawrence & Wishart, 1969), 382.
66. The idea of land nationalization was popular in the 1880s, influenced by the work of, among other, Alfred Russel Wallace, Henry George, The Land Nationalisation Society and the English Land Restoration League. However, it is also pertinent to be reminded that the association, so important to Spence, between freedom, independence and land ownership also remained in the mind of some labour leaders. For Keir Hardie speaking in 1909,

> the peasant who has even three acres of land, a well filled pig sty, a cows grass on the common and a cottage which is his to use and hold so long as he pays the rent, is to all intents and purposes a free man. He cannot be starved into submission nor be coerced by eviction. It is an ideal worth fighting for. (Cited by Michael Tichelar, 'Socialists, Labour and the land: the response of the Labour Party to the Land Campaign of Lloyd George before the First World War', *Twentieth Century British History*, 8, 2, 1997, 127)

67. H. Hyndman, *The Nationalization of the Land in 1775 and 1882: Being a Lecture Delivered at Newcastle-upon-Tyne by Thomas Spence, 1775* (London: E. W. Allen, 1882). Hyndman later noted the pamphlet 'has sold to the number of many thousands'. (Hyndman, *The Historical Basis of Socialism in England*, 448)
68. Hyndman, *The Historical Basis of Socialism in England*, 409.
69. Ibid., 448.
70. The letter is reproduced in Ashraf, *Thomas Spence*, plate XIX.
71. Beer continues, 'and to the end of his days took part in all revolutionary Labour movements at the cost of heavy sacrifices and sufferings'. M. Beer, *Social Struggles and Thought (1750–1860)*, (London: Leonard Parsons, 1925), 27.
72. Hyndman, *The Historical Basis of Socialism in England*, 409.
73. Ashraf was a researcher at the Institute for Marxism-Leninism in Moscow, where she undertook a study on the history of black radicals in Britain. She then moved to a university post in the GDR.

74. See Ashraf, *Thomas Spence*, 141, note 2 (1), 143, note 18.

75. Ashraf, *Thomas Spence*, 121.

76. Ibid., 139–40.

77. See, for example, Brian Morris, 'The agarian socialism of Thomas Spence', in Brian Morris, *Ecology and Anarchism* (London: Images Publishing, 1996); see also the website which I run http://thomas-spence-society.co.uk

78. W. Morris, *The Pilgrims of Hope and Chants for Socialists*, (London: Longmans, Green and Company, 1915), 57.

79. M. Bevir, 'William Morris: the modern self, art, and politics', http://repositories.cdlib.org/postprints/1097/, accessed 09.09.2009.

80. Cited by Fiona MacCarthy, *William Morris*, (London: Faber and Faber, 1994), 476.

81. Ruth Kinna, *William Morris: The Art of Socialism*, (Cardiff: University of Wales Press, 2000), 124.

82. R. Williams, *Culture and Society, 1790–1950*, (Harmondsworth: Penguin, 1971), 159–60.

83. E. P. Thompson, *William Morris, Romantic to Revolutionary*, (New York: Pantheon Books, 1976).

84. MacCarthy, *William Morris*, 605.

85. Kinna, *William Morris*.

86. W. Morris, *News from Nowhere; or, an Epoch of Rest* News from Nowhere, (London: Routledge, 1972).

87. E. Bellamy, *Looking Backward 2000–1887* (Oxford: Oxford University Press, 2009).

88. W. Morris, *Political Writings: Contributions to 'Justice' and 'Commonweal' 1883–1890*, (Bristol: Thoemmes Press, 1994), 425.

89. Ibid., 419, 420.

90. Ibid., 493.

91. Ibid., 420–4.

92. Cited by Kinna, *William Morris*, 150.

93. Morris, *News from Nowhere*, 80.

94. Ibid., 16.

95. Ibid., 179.

96. Ibid., 146.

97. Ibid., 45. The dream land described in *News from Nowhere* is not entirely without the possibility of change, although the prospect is an ominous one:

    people are too careless of the history of the past – too apt to leave it in the hands of old learned men . . . Who knows? happy as we are, times may alter; we may be bitten with some impulse towards change, and many things may seem too wonderful for us to resist, too exciting not to catch at, if we do not know that they are but phases of what has been before; and withal ruinous, deceitful, and sordid. (167–8)

98. Cited by MacCarthy, *William Morris*, 598.

99. Cited by MacCarthy, *William Morris*, 595.

100. W. Morris, *The Wood beyond the World*, (London: Kelmscott Press, 1894); W. Morris, *The Well at the World's End*, (London: Kelmscott Press, 1896); W. Morris, *The Water of the Wondrous Isles*, (London: Kelmscott Press, 1897); C. Silver, 'Socialism, internalised: the last romances of William Morris', in F. Boos and C. Silver (Eds), *Socialism and the Literary Artistry of William Morris*, (Columbia: University of Missouri Press,

1990). See also Christine Bolus-Reichert, 'Aestheticism in the late romances of William Morris', *English Literature in Transition, 1880–1920*, 50, 1, (2007), 73–95.

101. Morris, *News from Nowhere*, 1.

102. P. Henderson, *William Morris: His Life, Work and Friends*, (Harmondsworth: Penguin, 1973), 387.

103. Another outlet was Morris shop. Shaw called it 'a highly select shop in Oxford Street where he sold furniture of a rum aesthetic sort and decorated houses with extraordinary wallpapers' (cited by MacCarthy, *William Morris*, 471).

104. Cited by John Glasier, *William Morris and the Early Days of the Socialist Movement*, (London: Longmans, Green and Company, 1921), 32.

105. Cited by MacCarthy, *William Morris*, 644.

106. Cited by MacCarthy, *William Morris*, 672.

107. Blatchford, *Merrie England*, 27.

108. Ibid., 25.

109. Joyce, *Visions of the People*, 83.

110. P. Kaarsholm, 'Pro-Boers', in Raphael Samuel (Ed.), *Patriotism: The Making and Unmaking of British National Identity: Volume I: History and Politics*, (London: Routledge, 1989), 116. In the 1908 edited version of *Merrie England* a circulation of over 80,000 was being claimed for *The Clarion* (back inside cover).

111. R. Ebbatson, *An Imaginary England: Nation, Landscape and Literature, 1840–1920*, (Aldershot: Ashgate, 2005), 10.

112. L. Thompson, *Robert Blatchford: Portrait of an Englishman*, (London: Victor Gollancz, 1951), 224.

113. Blatchford, *Merrie England*, 68–9. Despite the rupture within the politics of the past, the natural and historical right of the people to the common ownership of the land was still considered important within the more class conscious popular radical/socialist constituency of the decades spanning the turn of the nineteenth century. *The Clarion Song Book* offers the typical refrain, 'The People to Their Land', by Edward Carpenter, with its chorus of 'A robber band has seize'd the land, and we are exiles here'. The song contains a set of images that could have been chosen by Spence:

> The cattle in the sun may lie
>
> The fox by night may roam
>
> The lark may sing all day on high
>
> Between its heaven and home;
>
> But we have no place here, to die
>
> Is the one right we need not buy:
>
> Then high heaven our vows be given,
>
> We'll have our land or die.

(*The Clarion Song Book*, London: Clarion Press, undated, 19).

114. Thompson, *Robert Blatchford*, 111.

115. R. Blatchford, *As I Lay A-Thinking: Some Memories and Reflections of an Ancient and Quiet Watchman*, (London: Hodder and Stoughton, 1926), 114.

116. R. Blatchford, *Not Guilty: A Defence of the Bottom Dog*, (London: Clarion Press, 1906).

117. R. Blatchford, *God and my Neighbour,* (London: Clarion Press, 1903).
118. For example, see H. Cunningham, 'The language of patriotism', in Raphael Samuel (Ed.), *Patriotism: The Making and Unmaking of British National Identity: Volume I: History and Politics,* (London: Routledge, 1989).
119. Lyons, *Robert Blatchford,* 186.
120. Arthur Penty, *Old Worlds for New: A Study of the Post-Industrial State,* (London: George Allen and Unwin, 1917). Penty and G. K. Chesterton's 'redistributionist' theories for a 'third way' between capitalism and socialism were disseminated in, among other places, Chesterton's journal, *G. K.'s Weekly.*
121. For further reading see David Prym, 'The Clarion Clubs, rambling and the Holiday Associations in Britain since the 1890s', *Journal of Contemporary History,* 11, 2/3, (1976). Denis Pye, *'Fellowship is Life': The National Clarion Cycling Club 1895–1995,* (Halliwell: Clarion Publishing, 1995).
122. Cited by Thompson, *Robert Blatchford,* 117.
123. Cited by Thompson, *Robert Blatchford,* 230.
124. Cited by Martin Wright, 'Robert Blatchford, the Clarion Movement and the crucial years of British socialism, 1891–1900', in Tony Brown (Ed.), *Edward Carpenter and Late Victorian Radicalism,* (London: Frank Cass, 1990), 75.
125. Cited by Thompson, *Robert Blatchford,* 166.
126. Cited by Thompson, *Robert Blatchford,* 159.
127. Lyons, *Robert Blatchford,* 112–3.
128. Cited by Thompson, *Robert Blatchford,* 101.
129. *The Clarion,* 'How I became a socialist', (February, 1896), available at: http://www.wcml.org.uk/group/scout.htm, accessed 07.09.2006.
130. Ibid.
131. S. Yeo, 'A new life: the religion of socialism in Britain, 1883–1896', *History Workshop Journal,* 4, 1, (1977), 5–56.
132. Yeo, 'A new life: the religion of socialism in Britain', 38.
133. For example, Thompson, *Robert Blatchford.* It is also pertinent to note that the *New Clarion,* published from 1931, was dominated by serious socialist commentary and activism while maintaining Clarion Fellowship ideals and social activities, notably the Cycling clubs and Choirs. Moreover, even in the early 1890s *The Clarion* combined its socialism with non-political and humorous work. See, for example, the collection offered by The Staff of the 'Clarion', *Contraptions,* (London: Walter Scott, circa 1895),
134. E. P. Thompson, *The Poverty of Theory and Other Essays,* (London: Merlin, 1978), 109.

PART TWO

CHAPTER THREE

Worlds We Have Lost: Nostalgia in Anti-colonialism and Post-colonialism

Introduction

This chapter explores two interconnected forms of radical nostalgia. First, the nostalgia of anti-colonialism and, second, the nostalgia of post-colonial critical scholarship. It is argued that anti-colonial nostalgia provided a transgression of, and a challenge to, monolithic visions of modernity (both Western and communist). As this implies, anti-colonial nostalgia is portrayed as marking a break with the repression of themes of loss and attachments to the past. The portrait of post-colonialism that I offer, by contrast, suggests that its characteristic hostility to 'essentialism' has created a new lexicon for suspicion of nostalgia. At the same time, post-colonialism displays powerful nostalgic commitments. Some of these echo anti-colonial claims for the value of indigenous knowledge. However, a more distinct and characteristic nostalgic theme may be identified in the post-colonial yearning for the political drama and moral clarity of the era of socialist revolutionary anti-colonial struggle.

Threading through these arguments is a claim about the nature of the impact of modernity upon colonized societies. We have seen how profound the impact was of capitalism in nineteenth-century England and how it provoked radical reaction. The temptation is to suggest that something similar happened in colonial contexts: that in the one we find an echo of the other. We might also be reminded of E. P. Thompson's hopeful prediction that 'Causes which were lost in England might, in Asia or Africa, yet be won.'[1] The comparison is not entirely without merit. However, the scale and intensity of the upheaval wrought by colonialism is on such a greater scale and reached so much more deeply through the entire fabric of colonized societies, that the suggestion that it offers merely a set of echoes of an older, European pattern, should be resisted. For, while the story of England remains one characterized by powerful continuities – in language, culture and institutional forms – the story of many of the new nations of Africa, America and Asia is very different. Entire pre-colonial histories were obliterated and novel entities, with new structures, new names and often new languages were set in motion. The resultant sense of loss is so far-reaching that it remains difficult to grasp. As Gérard Chaliand suggests,

[N]o historical phenomenon of modern times has been so traumatic and so destructive of the mental structures of entire societies. Everywhere, but most especially in nations whose own history dated back to antiquity – China, Egypt, Vietnam, Persia, the onslaught of European colonialism stunned, bewildered, and overwhelmed the traditional elites . . . answers were no longer adduced from traditional sources and, instead, began to be inspired by western models (and Marxism, despite its universality, is an integral part of the West).[2]

The profound nature of this trauma is indicated by the fact that, whereas for the radicals discussed in the previous chapter, modernity, however resented, was understood to have emerged from *within* existing society, in much of the colonial world (most notably that majority part which came to be called the Third World or developing world) modernity was understood as something entirely foreign. In the words of the Namibian scholar Tjama Tjivikua,

> For citizens of most occidental societies 'progress' is an immanent concept. Its symbols do not represent a threat. For cultures rooted in non-modern symbols, however, the situation is different.[3]

Tjivikua emphasizes the collapse of what came to be regarded as 'local languages'. The 'younger generations', he says, have come to disdain their own culture and 'speak foreign languages, and lose their culture as their native languages die out'.[4] Another critic of the cultural onslaught of Westernization, the Iranian writer Jalal Al-e Ahmad, explained that,

> [T]he onslaught of Colonialism is not merely to plunder the raw mineral material and human powers . . . from the colonies. It also devastates the language, the customs, the music, the ethics, and the religion of the colonized lands.[5]

Thus modernity is cast as overwhelming and alien, a tsunami arising from far away that has engulfed and destroyed the traditional and existential order of things. Stanley Diamond's 'conscripts of civilization' are also 'conscripts of modernity'.[6]

Ashis Nandy has spoken of the 'concept of modernity' as being 'sterile in the South because there is little understanding of the loss that is brought about by the victory of modernity itself'.[7] Yet, the power of modernity makes Nandy's depiction of it as 'sterile' unconvincing. It is precisely because it is so fertile, because it is so invasive, attractive, creative and adaptive that modernity is so powerful. This power also implies there are strong incentives for claiming modernity as inevitable and narrating the identity of one's own society through it. Once underway, this new narrative also opens up the possibility that modernity can be reidentified as something with indigenous roots, or at least connections. The idea that the tautology 'Western modernity' should be broken apart and that other forms of modernity brought into view is one that has, over recent years, generated a considerable body of literature on what are variously described as 'multiple modernities', 'alternative modernities' and 'co-evolving modernities'.[8] Moreover, we can identify it both in the kind of spiritual modernity offered by Tagore, as well as in attempts to claim an indigenous trajectory for socialism witnessed in Asia, Africa and Latin America. However, although these indigenizing and appropriative trends were significant to many intellectuals, their role in anti-colonialism should not be exaggerated. For much of the last century, the explicit and self-conscious rescription of modernity as local and diverse remained a marginal current. As with so many anti-colonial critics, what is more notable within Tagore is his profound sense of loss.

Anti-colonial Nostalgia: Roots against Empire

A minimal definition of colonialism is that it refers to the direct control of foreign territory. Colonialism encounters many social responses, including acceptance and adaptation.

But perhaps the most noticeable – either for its presence or absence – is resistance. The idea that freedom from colonialism is the same thing as, or contains, a desire for, a return to an older, pre-colonial era, can be found in most anti-colonial movements. The strength and abundance of this nostalgic current suggests that anti-colonialism provides the most vigorous example of radical nostalgia in the twentieth century. For against the tide of Western modernity and of anti-nostalgic orthodoxy, anti-colonial leaders often spoke explicitly about the value of organic traditions and the importance of cultural roots.

In turning to the nostalgic expression of anti-colonialism we encounter a landscape of humbling dimensions. It is important to recognize that the territories under colonial control included many parts of Europe and Central Asia, under the control of dominant nations in Europe or of the Soviet Union. All I can claim of the following account is that it identifies some key themes that are apparent across, if not all, then at least a significant proportion of the anti-colonial commentary of politicians and intellectuals from the last century. Three themes are identified: the use of images of a pre-colonial Golden Age; the identification of socialism as a indigenous tradition; and the need for anti-colonial intellectuals and political leaders to go 'back to the people'.

In 1892, the Irish nationalist and historian, George Sigerson, addressed the Irish National Literary Society:

Our deliverance from this thraldom of an enemy's judgement abides in the monuments of the ancient Irish past.[9]

Sigerson found the authentic voice of Ireland in its distant past. There is, he explained, 'a tone of sincerity in the ancient narratives which cannot exist in imported thought'.[10] The necessity of knowing one's 'own past' is seen to lie not only in its intrinsic worth but also in the relationship between such knowledge and a willingness to challenge colonial power. Thus cultural nationalism is translated into political militancy. The journey from the former to the latter is also seen in the Basque nationalist movement, which emerged in Bilbao in the 1890s. When the armed faction of this movement was formed, in 1959 (ETA: Euskadi Ta Askatsuna), it sought to combine cultural identification with a socialist and insurgent identity. In an ETA statement from 1960 it was explained that,

A people that do not know their different characteristics can hardly establish a nation because they are not aware of the benefit of forming one. Once this is accomplished, a collective appreciation of these values, of these differences and peculiarities must follow.[11]

Anthony Smith suggests that the different parts of nationalist historical ideology form a mutually sustaining 'triad': (a) a myth of the Golden Age; (b) a myth of decline; and (c) a myth of regeneration or salvation.[12] Diego Muro corroborates Smith's depiction with the following depiction of the mythology of Basque nationalism:

That in the remote past all Basques were equal and noble . . . That Basques had eternally been independent . . . That the Basque nation had been occupied by two different states, the Spanish and the French.[13]

The themes found in these European examples can be identified across numerous anti-colonial movements. They may also be found at a larger scale, as a foundation for the international ideology of Third Worldism. Mark Berger depicts the latter as a hybrid form which,

> emerged out of the activities and ideas of anti-colonial nationalists and their efforts to mesh often highly romanticized interpretations of pre-colonial traditions and cultures with the utopianism embodied by Marxism and socialism specifically, and 'Western' versions of modernisation and development more generally.[14]

However, the categorization of such forces as romantic and myth-based should not lead us to conclude that they lacked insight or precision. Indeed, discussion of a pre-industrial Golden Age often turned upon the particular. An example of this is the place of the machine in national life. When Gandhi argued, in 1909, that '[i]t is machinery that has impoverished India', he was not just offering a hazy gesture of defiance but also a focused assessment of the damage done by English manufacturing.[15] 'The workers in the mills of Bombay have become slaves', went on Gandhi, 'When there were no mills, these women were not starving. If the machinery craze grows in our country, it will become an unhappy land.'[16]

The similarity between the anti-industrial radicalism encountered in Chapter Two and Gandhi's vision of a pastoral Eden have suggested to some commentators 'the Anglo-Indian hybridity of the idea of postindustrialism'.[17] Both Gandhi and Coomaraswamy were influenced by William Morris and Ruskin while, in turn, the vision of a postindustrial future was taken up in Britain, in part, due to the influence of Gandhi and Coomaraswamy. The idea of tracing such patterns of cross-fertilization is an attractive one, in part because it presents us with the paradox of attachments to the local and the culturally specific being part of a global resistance movement. However, there is another geographical aspect of anti-colonial nostalgia to consider. The idea of a pastoral Golden Age is both historical and spatial. More specifically, it implies that nostalgia is being mapped onto a distinction between rural and urban life. The belief that within the countryside the soul of the people was preserved while within the cities it was polluted is found again and again in anti-colonial activism and literature. The 'seven hundred thousand villages' of India were, for Gandhi, not simply the bedrock of Indian civilization but daily proof of the possibility of a postindustrial future.[18] The Indian poet Rabindranath Tagore returned to this comparison on many occasions, arguing that,

> [U]nlike a living heart, these cities imprison and kill the blood and create poison centers filled with the accumulation of death . . . The reckless waste of humanity which ambition produces, is best seen in the villages, where the light of life is being dimmed, the joy of existence dulled, the natural threads of social communion snapped every day.[19]

Tagore's vision of authentic village life suggests a more communal and ethical mode of existence. However, the stark caste inequalities that mark rural India may help explain why that country offered difficult ground for the thesis that socialism was an *indigenous* tradition. Gandhi may have promised that India could 'evolve indigenous socialism of the purest type'. But it was a claim that laid more emphasis on the future than on the past.[20]

By contrast, in many other parts of the world, the idea that socialism is not a metropolitan invention but rooted in traditional, pre-colonial, society, had enormous appeal. Such claims were sometimes provocatively bold. The Peruvian journalist, José Carlos Mariátegui, claimed, in 1928, that 'Socialism is ultimately in the American tradition. Incan civilization was the most advanced primitive communist organization that history had known.'[21] In 1959, the year before he was elected as the first president of Senegal, Léopold Senghor, declared that 'we had already realized *socialism* before the coming of the European'.[22] Another first president, Julius Nyerere of Tanganyika (later Tanzania) made the same point in a speech delivered in 1962:

> We, in Africa, have no more need of being 'converted' to socialism than we have of being 'taught' democracy. Both are rooted in our own past – in the traditional society which produced us. Modern African Socialism can draw from its traditional heritage the recognition of 'society' as an extension of the basic family unit.[23]

'Traditional society', for Nyerere, as for nearly all anti-colonialists, meant rural society. To turn away from the West is also to turn away from an urban, industrial economy. There was 'too much emphasis on industries' argued Nyerere.[24] The socialist Africa he envisaged grew from the soil. The Kenyan trade unionist, Tom Mboya, also spoke of African socialism as an 'organic tradition' arising from Africa's 'sons of the soil'. He found its moral philosophy in what he called,

> proved codes of conduct in the African societies which have, over the ages, conferred dignity on our people and afforded them security regardless of their station in life. I refer to universal charity which characterized our societies and I refer to the African's thought processes and cosmological ideas which regard man, not as a social means but as an end and entity in the society.[25]

Nyerere framed the anti-colonial struggle as an attempt to 'regain our former attitude of mind – our traditional African socialism'.[26] Yet this restoration was not merely a matter of psychological recovery. For Nyerere, to 'reactivate the philosophy of co-operation' meant public ownership, notably a return to the communal ownership of land.[27] With the coming of independence in Tanganyika, freehold possession of land had been abolished. 'All land now belongs to the nation', declared Nyerere, adding: 'But this was not an affront to our people; communal ownership of land is traditional in our country.'[28]

Occasionally the resilience and success of socialist anti-colonial warfare also strengthened the notion that left-wing ideologies had deep and indigenous roots. This can be seen in the case of communist insurgency in Vietnam. In *Tradition and Revolution in Vietnam*, Nguyen Khac Vien, a leading intellectual of the Vietnamese Communist Party, sought to explain the success of the war against the United States. He argued that there existed a 'fairly smooth transition from Confucianism to Marxism'.

> Confucianism having for centuries accustomed minds not to speculate on the great beyond, Marxism had less trouble being accepted than in Islamic or Christian countries.[29]

Perhaps the most influential American analysis of the unexpected tenacity of the Vietnamese communists, Frances Fitzgerald's *Fire in the Lake*, also found part of the explanation in the militant synthesis of Confucianism and Marxism.[30] Another Western commentator, Gérard Chaliand, emphasized the country's 'village commune traditions', such as the militarily valuable 'ability to keep secrets'. This tradition, he wrote,

> stems from the fact that a person who betrayed the authority recognized by the village would find himself excluded from the community, which is the worst thing that could happen to a Vietnamese peasant.[31]

Chaliand also repeats as, at least, 'partly accurate', the connection often made during the Vietnam war between success in anti-colonial operations and the low-tech, 'primitive', nature of Vietnamese society. The revolutionary forces, he explains, were 'able to hold out because the country had not yet been industrialized and had few needs, in terms of both its infrastructure and its population'.[32]

The third and last of the themes within anti-colonial nostalgia to be considered here is the call for a 'return to the people'. The characteristic unit of political appeal and insurrection within anti-colonial movements is 'the people'. One of the anti-colonial intellectuals who explored the problem of the deracinated elite most doggedly was the Iranian leftist Jalal Al-e Ahmed. For Al-e Ahmed, writing in the early 1960s, a 'west-stricken man' is,

> like a dust particle flowing in space, or a straw floating on water. He has severed his ties with the essence of society, culture, and custom. He is not a bond between antiquity and modernity. He is not a dividing line between the old and the new. He is something unrelated to the past and someone with no understanding of the future.[33]

Al-e Ahmed contrasts such lonely, misinformed creatures with the 'ordinary man': 'his voice is not heard, his record is clean.'[34] As part of his attempt to reconnect with his own culture, to stop being a 'straw floating on water', Al-e Ahmed broke with the secular left in Iran. He attacked industrial modernity as cursed by 'machinitis' and began to take an interest in Islam. His 1964 pilgrimage to Mecca was a moment of exploration but also of personal reconnection, not simply to Islam, but to the traditions of 'the people' who, Al-e Ahmed felt, socialist modernizers did not understand or respect.[35]

The urge to 'go to the people' has a revolutionary as well as a cultural impetus. Mao instructed communists to '[t]rust the masses, rely on them and respect their initiative'.[36] Frantz Fanon's anguished pleas to the 'native intellectual' to plunge into 'his own people' suggested that the alternative was a life of damaging and ineffectual alienation:

> If it is not accomplished there will be serious psycho-affective injuries and the result will be individuals without an anchor, without a horizon, colourless, stateless, rootless – a race of angles . . . Going back to your own people means to become a dirty wog, to go native as much as you can, to become unrecognizable, and to cut off those wings that before you had allowed to grow.[37]

For Fanon to 'cut off those wings' means that one

> accepts everything, decides to take all for granted and confirms everything, even though he may lose body and soul . . . He not only turns himself into the defender of the people's past; he is willing to be counted as one of them.[38]

In part, the determination to 'go to the people' reflects the fact that socialism and Marxism, although presented as liberating 'the people', were foreign ideologies developed by, and associated with, a Westernized elite. In Chaliand terms: 'to the ideology of revolution – nationalist, by definition – falls the therapeutic task of cleansing . . . shame, providing a new identity, a new face, of restoring dignity.'[39] Thus the desire to emerse oneself in the people salves the sharpest edges of a radical paradox. Fanon was particularly acute in his observation of the power of alienation to stimulate a passion for connection. The 'passionate search for a national culture which existed before the colonial era', he explained,

> finds its legitimate reason in the anxiety shared by the native intellectuals to shrink away from that Western culture in which they all risk being swamped. Because they realize they are in danger of losing their lives and thus becoming lost to their people, these men, hot-headed and with anger in their hearts, relentlessly determine to renew contact once more with the oldest and most pre-colonial springs of life of their people.[40]

Fanon is not only describing but also affirming, willing the act of connection to the 'pre-colonial springs of life'.

Yet anti-colonial nostalgia was no sooner articulated than it became a site of concern and nervousness. Radical nostalgia in an anti-nostalgic age is always a vulnerable form, self-conscious and defensive. The inevitable criticisms, both from within and from outside the anti-colonial project, could be dismissive. Many simply claimed that all forms of nostalgic attachment were irrelevant and conservative. However, critiques also often took the form of instrumental analyses of nostalgia as representing a strategically useful *early stage* of resistance: something that could and should be quickly overcome. In this way, the longing for a pre-colonial past could be both acknowledged and denied. For Chaliand,

> [The] first response to the shock of colonialism, in all societies with a traditional state organization, was to take refuge in tradition as an ideology of resistance, to exalt the past and teach patience while awaiting better times . . . Following defeat or occupation, this rigid clinging to old values became the basis of a kind of ideology of resistance.[41]

Chaliand's identification of nostalgia as a 'refuge' and his image of a 'rigid clinging' to the past, are designed to remind us that a *modern* response to colonialism is supposed to transcend such attachments. Fanon can also be heard voicing the same argument. He often expressed a desire to surpass local attachments, or to treat them instrumentally, as a therapeutically and politically necessary but initial stage in a bigger project of total liberation. It is a mistake he advises 'to skip the national period'.[42] Thus the past becomes a resource to be employed and deployed: 'The colonized man who writes for his people ought to use the past with the intention of opening the future, as an initiation to action and a basis for hope.'[43] This kind of strategic deployment of ethnicity and nationalism echoed a dominant perspective within European Marxist circles, a perspective that dryly accorded the search for roots a temporary and instrumental function. Summarizing the debate, Igor Kopytoff noted that, although there was little evidence for pre-colonial 'African socialism',

> [T]he low predicative value of the concept of traditional African socialism in dealing with specific problems has nothing to do with its role as an instrument of policy at the ideological level. The myth of traditional socialism . . . will shape the readiness of the population at large to accept socialist forms when new institutions, serving new functions, are created or when old institutions are made to serve new functions.[44]

But Fanon invests too much in cutting away his Western, intellectual, 'wings', for the dilemma of nostalgia to be smoothed away this easily. When he read Satre's opinion that 'negritude appears as the minor term of a dialectical progression' he was appalled: 'I had been robbed of my last chance . . . black consciousness is immanent in its own eyes'.[45] Fanon can be read as a clear, bold voice of revolutionary action. However, when we approach him from the perspective of the transgressive narrative of radical nostalgia, his voice appears vulnerable and uncertain. In the light of this anxiety, the redemptive revolutionary message offered by Fanon in *Wretched of the Earth* takes on a particular poignancy. Fanon finds a new Third World context for Marx's vision of the 'return of man'. After Europe's 'negations of man', he argues, '[d]ecolonisation is the veritable creation of new men': 'It is a question of the Third World starting a new history of Man' against and after '[Europe's] pathological tearing apart of his functions and crumbling away of his unity'.[46] The nostalgia of 'reintroducing mankind into this world' is premised on the fact of alienation, on a world of 'individuals without an anchor'.[47] Yet this argument connects awkwardly with Fanon's nostalgia for 'the people'. Can a 'new history of Man' be achieved by 'defender[s] of the peoples' past'? Perhaps so. But the question also suggests that Fanon's anti-colonialism is a site of multiple narratives of loss.

Nationalist Nostalgia and Communist Colonialism

Fanon presented himself as engaged in a struggle of small nations and oppressed peoples for socialism and against colonial power. His contemporary popularity in post-colonial studies recycles this image. However, in so doing it continues to dodge an uncomfortable question: 'Why does Fanon not write about existing socialism?'. Part of the answer lies in the fact that Fanon was a spokesperson for the Algerian National Liberation Front (FLN), an organization which was supported by the Soviet Union, as part of its geopolitical ambitions to secure influence in Africa. Although Fanon's communism has an ultra-left dimension out of keeping with Soviet orthodoxy, it remains the case that his analysis of colonialism could not be seen to offend one of the FLN's principle backers.[48]

To contemporary eyes, colonial power is inherently illegitimate. Hence, its identification is a political act.[49] In 'Communist parlance', Kulski noted, 'Anti-colonialism means anti-Westernism'.[50] This identification was fostered by the Soviet Union and other communist states in order to subvert Western power. However, if colonialism is understood as the control and subjugation of foreign territory, then the Soviet Union was a colonial entity, containing numerous subject nations. The 'Soviet bloc' contained another set of states subject to colonial control. The Soviet Union supported *anti-Western* anti-colonialism around the world in order to extend and defend this bloc.

Although Marxism was presented as an anti-colonial force by Lenin, for the Bolsheviks the right of self-determination was always subsidiary to the larger, historical, issue of progress towards communism. 'The aim of Socialism', Lenin noted in 1916,

> is not only to abolish the present division of mankind into small states, and all-national isolation, not only to bring the nations closer to each other, but also to merge them.[51]

However, the differences between communist and Western colonialism do not only turn on issues of political ideology. Indeed, it is worth remembering that Western empires also made extensive use of discourses of emancipation and global unity. If we restrict our view to the twentieth century, it would appear that the main difference between Western and communist colonialism is that the latter was more complete and authoritarian. What Kārlis Račevskis calls 'totalitarian colonialism' was invasive, draconian and unyielding.[52] By comparison, by the mid-twentieth century, pluralism and open criticism of the colonial authorities were, if not well developed, clear and important features of political life in many British and French colonies. The fact that the British and French empires fell apart in the two decades following the end of the Second World War, while the Soviet colonial system survived until 1989–1991, is another testament to the severity Soviet power.

Once we admit the fact of communist colonialism, a new landscape of left resistance and nostalgic radicalism comes into view. As one might expect, this history turns on the national-ist ambitions of socialists working in and against colonial power. My examples turn on the anti-colonial ambitions of socialist nationalists in Ukraine, Poland and Hungary.

Over the past two decades anti-colonialism has been reclaimed in Ukraine as part of a heritage of nationalist revolt. However, the most active period of *left* anti-colonialism took place during the period in which the old Russian empire was disintegrating and the new Soviet Bolshevik state had not yet secured domination. An independent Ukrainian council or soviet, the Tsentralna Rada, came into existence in 1917 and lasted into the next year. The Rada was led by a Ukrainian socialist patriot, Mykhailo Hrushevsky. Hrushevsky was a historian whose epic, multivolume, history of Ukraine weaves socialism and nationalism together into a radical story of national heroes and popular uprisings.[53] Under Hrushevsky's leadership the Rada initially sided with the Russian Bolsheviks. However, the Bolsheviks in Ukraine were a minority force and Bolshevism began to be suspected of having colonialist tendencies (identified by the Ukrainian communists Serhii Mazlakh and Vasyl' Shakhrai in their 1918 book, *On the Current Situation in the Ukraine*).[54] The Ukrainian Bolsheviks sort to seize power in December 1917, announcing the formation of All-Ukrainian Council of Soviets and inviting the Red Army into the country. In reaction, on 22 January 1918, the Tsentralna Rada declared independence. Although Ukrainian independence was recognized by Lenin, the country was already partly occupied by Red Army troops. Ukraine had entered into a long period of Soviet colonial domination. The agitation for national independence that characterized the early years of this era, and persisted beyond the formal federation of Russia and Ukraine in 1920, may be characterized as both socialist and nationalist. As expressed by Hrushevsky it also contained a commitment to a form of international plu-ralism that opposed Bolshevik centralism. In 1921 Hrushevsky wrote of the prevalence of 'sectarian exclusiveness and intolerance of non-communist parties' under the new regime.[55] He continued to argue for a form of international soviet federation in which Ukraine's rela-tionship with Russia would be no closer than with any other soviet state. However, like other left nationalists, Hrushevsky soon found himself effectively banned from political office. He died in mysterious circumstances in 1934.

For much of the twentieth century, anti-colonialism in Ukraine can hardly be called a movement. In part this is because the smallest signs of any such tendency were thor-oughly suppressed. The association of authentic Ukrainian socialism as a popular, nation-alist, underground phenomenon which must battle against overwhelming force, is rooted in this experience. This melancholic history suggests a form of nostalgic anti-colonialism that, while looking back and gaining strength from images of a continuous struggle for a free, independent country, is shot through with a profound sense of betrayal and humili-ation. Compared to the open declarations of defiance issued from many Western colonies, Ukrainians had to content themselves with ambivalent memories and compromised ges-tures. The seemingly undramatic nature of such gestures may be another explanation of why these forms of anti-colonialism have failed to capture the attention of Western scholars. Yet in the context of 'totalitarian colonialism', symbolic acts of resistance should be understood as often having considerable significance. When, in October 1956, as part of an attempted 'thaw' in hard-line communism, Polish communist leaders removed a Soviet Marshall from the Polish government and Defence Ministry, it was interpreted by Moscow as a hostile act. Soviet troops were put in alert for a possible invasion. For a while the Polish communists enjoyed considerable domestic popular praise and support for their stand against the Soviet Union. The Soviet authorities understood that the Polish leaders had attempted, as Kulski notes, to '[regain] emotional links with their nation'.[56] In *The Rise and Fall of the Soviet Empire*, Raymond Pearson suggests that the October events signalled Poland's shift from colonial to dominion status.[57] However, given the pervasive and institutionalized nature of Soviet influence in the country, this distinction seems like a point of detail. Indeed, the anti-colonial revolt of rebellious communists in Hungary, in the same year, clearly demonstrated the limits of Soviet toleration. Although ending in open revolt, the brief Hungarian uprising also illustrates the complexity of socialists' struggles over the past. The pro-Soviet regime in Hungary was fond of employing Hungary's 1848–1849 war of independence as a symbol of the people's sympathy with its political project. The 1956 uprising took this symbol and appropriated it, turning the 1848–1849 struggle for independence into a sign of anti-Soviet and anti-colonial intent:

[T]he memory of the 1848 Revolution was the yeast in the 1956 ferment. The 1956 Revolution did not begin at the radio building where the first shots were fired, but at a demonstration of solidarity with Poland around the statue of Joseph Bern, a Polish general who commanded one of the rebel Hungarian armies in 1848–49. The next stop was at the statue of Petöfi, where the poet's 108-year-old – but again apropos – poem was recited, and proclamations were read recalling the Manifesto of 15 March 1848.[58]

Anti-colonial struggle yearns for a return to the pre-colonial. The moment of colonial power is a moment of rupture that can only be healed by deploying symbols that evoke a return to, and continuation from, an image of a better, independent past. In many parts of the world, the story of anti-colonialism is also the story of the left: they are two sides of the same nationalist coin. Within the communist colonies the situation is more complicated. But the nation remained the central site of left-wing anti-colonial activism. It was in the name of the nation that the hope of freedom was maintained over decades of extreme repression. And the name of the nation was also the name of the past. Across the large swath of the globe once subject to 'actually existing socialism', nostalgia often remained the only possible form of resistance.

Post-colonial Nostalgias: Yearning for Resistance

In a post-socialist era, what can the left believe in? The obvious answer is the past. In this section I consider post-colonial critical scholarship as a form of nostalgic politics. Before encountering post-colonialism we need to address its origins. In part these become immediately clear when we compare what kind of material we have been looking at to understand anti-colonialism and what kind of material we must address to explore post-colonialism. The former was, in large part, composed of the speeches of politicians, the analyses of activists or reportage of ongoing conflict. By contrast, the evidence of post-colonialism that I survey consists of academic commentary. In shifting from anti-colonialism to post-colonialism we are shifting from primary to secondary data and between two different sites of intellectual production. We are also shifting in time. 'Post-colonial studies' (a term which is widely understood to be synonymous with post-colonia*lism*) is an academic trend that appeared from the late 1980s onwards.

David Chioni Moore offers a broad, institutional designation of post-colonialism as 'the principal designator for a range of activities formally known as the study of the Third World, non-Western world, emergent, or minority literatures'.[59] Although this definition does not shed any light on the theoretical content of post-colonialism, it does help us get a sense of its politics of dislocation; of post-colonialism as offering an alternative geography within the Western academy. What I shall term 'left post-colonialism' complements this alternative perspective with an insurgent and broadly anti-capitalist sensibility. The prominence of this radical perspective in the 1990s and 2000s is intriguing, for socialist movements in the 'majority world' were, by this time, few and far between. In Africa, Europe and across Asia, anti-capitalist anti-colonialism had been largely supplanted by neo-liberal, state capitalist and/or liberal democratic agendas. Moreover, socialism had become widely associated with a range of problems, including corruption, totalitarianism and economic stagnation. Berger notes that, 'by the late 1970s successful capitalist development in East Asia had displaced the socialist agenda contained in the idea of the Third World and Third Worldism.'[60] As this implies, when the Prime Minister of Singapore, Lee Kuan Yew, wrote *From Third World to First: The Singapore Story, 1965–2000*, he was expressing a wider mood which eschewed the revolutionary ideologies of the 1960s and took the increased living standards obtained in East Asia as testament to the success of state led capitalism.[61] Arif Dirlik represents the resultant problem for the anti-colonial left in the following terms:

> To recall the Third [World] is to recover memories of those utopian projects that are essential to imagining radical alternatives to the present. On the other hand, it is necessarily also to disassociate those radical alternatives from the Third World which, in its present reconfiguration, may have become an obstacle to the imagination, let alone the realization, of any such radical alternatives.[62]

It is striking, then, that at the very moment that the wider constituency for Third Worldist insurgency disappeared, that so many academics seem to have discovered the anti-colonial struggle. Chandra and Larsen argue that,

> It seems almost as if postcolonial theory was fated to discover Third Worldist . . . national liberation doctrine just when its last flickerings of political and social viability were about to be extinguished, just when the real historical contours of Third Worldist *ideology* were coming into plain view.[63]

Chanda and Larsen go on to offer a comparison between post-colonial appropriations of anti-colonialism with Marx's depiction of Louis Bonaparte's attempt to evoke the spirit of the French Revolution. Thus they suggest that post-colonialism, 'arriving long after' the moment of insurgent anti-colonialism, 'seeks à la *The Eighteenth Brumaire*, to "make its ghost walk about again"'.[64] David Scott has developed this critique in a number of important interventions which seeks to identify 'the nostalgia and clinging resentment that attaches to the fading narrative of anticolonial Romance'.[65]

Hélène Gill argues that post-colonialism 'defines itself as a strand of oppositional, radical thought'. She adds that,

> [I]t is tempted to adopt strongly contrasted binary positions. By the same token, it tends to be uncomfortable with in-between situations: unclear ethical dilemmas, ambivalent political attitudes, divided loyalties.[66]

It seems that the same discourse, that many consider the home of hybridity and anti-essentialism, is imagined by Gill to be so wedded to one particular set of political loyalties, that it is 'uncomfortable' with split allegiances. Gill's provocative depiction is a response, in part, to post-colonial theorist's attraction to fiery radical rhetoric. One example of this tendency can be found in post-colonialists' fascination with Fanon and his troubled affirmations of the cathartic power of revolutionary violence. Fanon's idealization of violence has been sympathetically read by a number of post-colonial Fanonists. For example, Lewis Gordon argues that '*any* response that portends real change will take the form of violence . . . Nonviolent transformation of power boils down to no transformation of power.'[67] However, the disjuncture between the context of Fanon's work, in the midst of a revolutionary war, and the quiet campuses from which post-colonial studies has emerged is, perhaps, too stark to allow this kind of appropriation not to be dogged by doubts about its audience and authenticity. For David Scott, it is 'a romance, the self-indulgent nostalgia of late modernity, to read Fanon as though we were about to join him in the trenches of the anti-colonial national liberation struggles'.[68]

In fact, if one's only source of information was the major texts of academic post-colonialism, one would probably conclude that the only form of colonialism the world has ever known emanated from a few, uniquely culpable, Western nations.[69] Račevskis claims that the relationship between the Western left and communist colonialism is one of denial and complicity. He argues that 'leftist critical theory is implicated in a long history of misperception or miscomprehension of the Soviet system'.[70] The chief source of this complicity, says Račevskis, is the fact that,

> [A]ccording to the Western critical canon, it is not possible to be both a victim of Marxism *and* colonialism, since Marxism has always belonged to the tradition of anti-colonial discourse.[71]

The recent turn towards a critical encounter with 'actually existing socialism', is not merely a scholarly supplement. It contains a clear accusation that Western intellectuals have ignored communist colonialism because they have found it politically convenient to do so. David Chioni Moore develops this theme by way of an analysis of the geography of colonialism found in post-colonial theory. Finding that communist regimes occupy a blank space on the post-colonial map, he searches for answers in the rare and marginal remarks that do address the topic. Thus, for example, he finds Edward Said, in *Culture and Imperialism*, explaining why the book's 'focus' on 'the projection of far-flung interests', dictates an exclusive interest in British and French imperialism. Said argues that,

> Russia . . . acquired its imperial territories almost exclusively by adjacence. Unlike Britain or France, which jumped thousand of miles beyond their own borders to other continents, Russia moved to swallow whatever land or peoples stood next to its border, which in the process kept moving further east and south.[72]

As Moore suggests, Said seems here to be giving an 'odd primacy to water'. It is, after all, an 'infinitely rougher path from Moscow to Tashkent' than between Europe and Africa.[73] It should be noted, in defence of Said, that he is explicit that it is only Western imperialism that 'is the subject of this book'.[74] Yet Moore's criticisms arise from the fact that this focus and this kind of omission have been routinized and, hence, become a form of avoidance. Indeed, we may add to Moore's reading, by pointing out that Said's mention of the way *Russia* first acquired its territories, is itself indicative of a politically myopic representation of colonialism. For while it acknowledges that pre-communist Russia was an imperial state, it draws a veil over the possibility that the Soviet Union might also have been a colonial regime. Indeed, the only substantive mention that the Soviet Union gets in *Culture and Imperialism* refers to its *anti-colonial* agitation.[75]

Another example from Moore's critique is, perhaps, even more telling. He cites Ella Shohat from her 1992 paper 'Notes on the "Post-Colonial"', responding to the disintegration of the Soviet Union,

The collapse of Second World socialism, it should be pointed out, has not altered neo-colonial policies, and on some levels, has generated increased anxiety among such Third World communities as the Palestinians and South African Blacks concerning their struggle for independence without a Second World counter-balance.[76]

In response to this passage Moore writes,

What is remarkable or, rather remarkably ordinary here is the way in which a scholar enormously concerned with the fate of colonized and recently decolonized peoples across the planet should treat events that were widely perceived, at least in the twenty-seven nations from Lithuania to Uzbekistan, as a *decolonization*, instead as a distant . . . *non*colonial event, and as a loss, since it has increased the anxieties of, for example Palestinians and Black South Africans.[77]

However, Moore, like other critics of post-colonialism's communist blind spot makes little attempt – beyond references to post-colonial orthodoxy – to explain why there should have arisen in the West, at almost the precise moment when communism was collapsing as a political alternative, a new literature that erased the experience of communism and resurrected the political dramas of a previous generation. It is towards the idea of nostalgia that I believe we can usefully look to find some of the answers.

Orianna Baddeley identifies a certain healing balm in post-colonial militancy: for 'the right and wrongs of colonial history are still reducible to moral certainties at a time when certainty of any sort is in short supply'.[78] Perhaps so. Yet the nostalgia for these particular 'moral certainties' is not a general phenomenon but something much more socially specific. The disciplinary emergence of post-colonialism in the humanities, more especially within literary studies, has sometimes been evoked to explain its focus and rhetorical style. This focus might also help explain why post-colonialism has such a wide-eyed, celebratory approach to the heroes and fighters of anti-colonialism. For within Western literary studies, these figures were, until recently, relatively unknown. Thus a tradition of indifference to colonialism could be offered as an explanation of the revelation of its discovery.

However, this disciplinary explanation is too narrow. Post-colonialism has been taken up across the humanities and many of the social sciences. A more plausible explanation suggests that the impact of majority world diasporas upon Western societies and, more specifically the entry of diasporic intellectuals into the Western academy, has been a deciding factor. Robert Young argues that post-colonialism is 'a diasporic production'.[79] Yet this explanation is also not sufficient. For although this migratory flow may help to explain why issues concerning the global south have gained new prominence, it does not take us very far in understanding the nostalgic radicalism of post-colonialism. The idea that it is the nostalgia of diasporic intellectuals that is at the root of the matter is an obvious resolution of this problem. However, it appears to be doubly unwarranted: for not only is the notion that post-colonialism is led or dominated by diasporic intellectuals a gross overgeneralization but the kind of nostalgia found within post-colonialism does not suggest a nostalgia for the global south but, rather, a nostalgia for a politics of another time.

Some further answers may be found in the social consequences of recent political history. More specifically, in the dislocation of the political experience of the left-leaning class faction that provides the social base for the production of post-colonial studies. There are a number of stages to this argument. First, it is useful to acknowledge that the politics of public professionals are relatively left-leaning. The causes of this disposition have been the subject of much sociological debate.[80] However, although the causes are disputed, there remains consistent evidence, not only that this disposition exists, but also that it was sustained through the Reagan and Thatcher years and beyond. Thus in noting that post-colonial studies has arisen within the academy we are also noting that it has arisen from within a social group with a particular political disposition. At this point the question posed at the start of this section – 'In a post-socialist era, what can the left believe in? – comes into view. For it is relatively clear that while leftism is being reproduced in the academy, the wider constituency for such views – hence the links between this faction and rest of the world – have diminished. The result is a recipe for political isolation and bewilderment. Although there are many pathways through this paradoxical landscape – and many different institutional forms and pressures – the combination of forces it contains suggests the likelihood of a strengthening of less militant and more reformist perspectives. However, it also suggests another possibility: that leftism may undergo a crisis of attachment but not necessarily of political conviction. Both these outcomes can be found in post-colonialism. Indeed, its liberal 'identity politics' are favourite target of Marxist criticism while its displays of revolutionary fervour have been portrayed as anachronistic by some non-Marxist critics. Thus, for example, in *Beyond Postcolonial Theory*, Epifanio San Juan attacked post-colonialism as a form of identity politics that subverted international socialism and liberation struggles.[81] By contrast, in *Refashioning Futures: Criticism after Postcoloniality* David Scott rejects post-colonialism's adherence to the outmoded discourses of liberation that San Juan accuses it of abandoning.[82] The uncertain and fragile nature of post-colonial politics is captured in a comparison of these two different challenges.

An interplay of anxiety and conviction can also be seen in the post-colonial interpretation of anti-colonialism. For many post-colonialists, the anti-colonial struggles of previous decades have a talismanic status. At the same time, post-colonialism is characterized by hostility to essentialism. It is suspicious of attempts to 'construct' or 'invent' identities as fixed or rooted. Indeed, it may be said to represent a culmination of the anti-nostalgic imagination. For while Marx looked upon deracination as positive only because it would lead to a final healing and reintegration of life, many post-colonialists tend to subscribe to a post-modern ethic that offers fragmentedness and uprootedness as political destinations. It will be recalled that Fanon had doubts about the prospect of such a new 'race of angles'. Reading against the grain, we can find similar doubts among post-colonial theorists. The post-colonial political vision is replete with signs of tension and uncertainty, of cool loyalties, vernacular cosmopolitanisms and detached attachments.[83] These ambivalent terms suggest that post-colonialism may also be seen as a site of crisis within the anti-nostalgic tradition. This is, perhaps, most starkly evident from the fact that post-colonialism contains within it a series of attempts to continue the essentialist claims on indigenous knowledge found in anti-colonialism. Although such claims are translated into a new rhetoric of cultural incommensurability, and spliced with anti-essentialist evocations of hybridity, they evoke and make use of the symbolic power of roots. The other main trajectory within post-colonial studies is far more progressivist and has produced a contemporary rebirth, or at least a rearticulation, of Marxist revolutionary anti-colonialism. However, both these tendencies combine avowals of militancy with a deep, yet unacknowledged, sense of loss.

Post-colonial Nostalgias I: The Return to Indigenism

Meera Nanda has argued that,

> [W]hat distinguishes a specifically *post-colonial* critique of (neo)-colonialism and Third World modernization from all previous critiques is that it posits an irreconcilable and 'incommensurable' . . . difference in rationalities between modern 'Western' science on the one hand and on the other, the rationalities of 'other' groups occupying different cultural spaces or different class/caste/gender positions in the same culture.[84]

A good example of this kind of post-colonial project is Walter Mignolo's *Local Histories/ Global Designs*. Mignolo's post-colonial project has a clear restitutionist agenda. Thus post-colonialism becomes a project of rediscovering tradition and asserting non-Western cultures as providing distinct cultural paradigms. '[D]iversity as a universal project', he argues, 'allows us to imagine alternatives to universalism', or what he calls elsewhere, 'a new medievalism, a pluricentric world built on the ruins of ancient, non-Western cultures and civilizations with the debris of Western civilization'.[85] In more specific terms, Mignolo calls for the 'restitution of Amerindian philosophy of life and conceptualization of society'; a 'symbolic restitution of the past in view of a better future'.[86] He suggests that,

> [T]he organic intellectuals of the Amerindian social movements (as well as Latino, Afro-American, and women) are precisely the primary agents of the movement in which 'barbarism' appropriates the theoretical practices and elaborated projects, engulfing and superseding the discourse of the civilizing mission and its theoretical foundations.[87]

Boaventura de Sousa Santos has pursued a similar argument, categorizing 'modern knowledge and modern law' as irredeemably oppressive and pitting them against 'popular, lay, plebeian, peasant or indigenous knowledges'.[88]

Perhaps the first thing that strikes us about these ideas is their similarity to anti-colonial reclamations of tradition. Indeed, the chain of resemblance may be extended further, for the kind of radical populism found in early English socialism and again in anti-colonialism resurfaces in post-colonialism as a politics of 'the people'. Thus Nanda can write that,

> The 'people' have acquired an unprecedented centrality in contemporary social theory. Their 'emancipation' from the West as well as all institutions of modern nation-states,

even democratically elected, developmentalist states, has become the cherished end of every post-colonial social project.[89]

However, whereas most anti-colonialists had no trouble in straightforwardly celebrating the organic social roots and identities of the past, post-colonial theorists are more or less wedded to a political suspicion of essentialism. Authenticity is represented as a 'cult' or a 'myth' by post-colonialists. Appiah notes that 'its *post* like post-modernism's, is also a post that challenges earlier legitimizing narratives'.[90] Indeed, David Scott rather acidly remarks that 'Postcolonial theorists have made a considerable name for themselves by criticizing their predecessors, the anti-colonial nationalists, for their essentialism'.[91]

Post-colonialism, we may conclude, contains an uneasy combination of forces. The resultant mixture appears to be populist yet omnivorously critical, traditionalist yet imaginatively and continuously insurgent. A fine example is Akhil Gupta's account of the hybrid modern-traditionalists of the Indian peasantry. The conception of post-colonial development Gupta identifies is one of,

> multivalent genealogies of modernity, at the limits of 'The West', where incommensurable conceptions and ways of life implode into one another, scattering, rather than fusing, into strangely contradictory yet eminently 'sensible' hybridities.[92]

Gupta's swirling prose reminds us that the intended readership for post-colonial studies is highly restricted. Whereas anti-colonialism sought to speak to 'the people', post-colonialists evoke 'the people' but speak to the academy. Yet the romantic, post-modern, spectacle of implosions and scatterings presented by Gupta is, perhaps, just too baroque for those academic readers impatient for some sign that post-colonialism is a worthy heir to the anti-colonial tradition. In an exasperated review of Gupta's book, Meera Nanda parodies its political claims: 'We are hybrids, and we are dangerous! Just by being our hybrid selves, we are threatening to bring down Western civilization!'[93]

However, it is indicative of how dominant the suspicion of nostalgia continues to be among intellectuals on the left, that critics of post-colonialism have tended to identify its Achilles heel, not in its failure to acknowledge its own nostalgia, but in its inability to completely pull itself out of the mire of the past. Thus, for example, Hélène Gill's critique of post-colonial images of Algeria, turns on the fact that they have an 'uncanny resemblance to the positive types lovingly put on canvas by socially conservatives or reactionary Orientalists during the colonial era'.[94] Nanda also suggests that,

> Postmodern/postcolonial theory's animus against the Enlightenment values, and its indulgence towards contradictions make it eminently compatible with a typically right-wing resolution of the asynchronicity (or time-lag) between advanced technology and backward social context.[95]

Nanda and Gill's criticisms imply that post-colonialism is nostalgic and, therefore, to be deplored. By contrast, I would suggest that it is precisely because post-colonialism has not taken the nostalgia of anti-colonialism seriously, because it tries to continually pull back from it to avoid contamination with essentialism, that makes its indigenist trajectory appear implausible. The post in post-colonialism does not neutralize the nostalgia of anti-colonialism. The tension between its hostility to, and deployment of, such yearnings is too open, too ragged, to allow any such sense of resolution. We are left with a sense of uncertainty, of post-colonialism being troubled by the memory of anti-colonialism. However, post-colonial longings come in a variety of forms. Indigenism is one. Another is anti-imperialist communism.

Post-colonial Nostalgia II: Communism and the 'Great Tricontinental'

The resurrection of socialism within post-colonial studies provides one of the more interesting expressions of nostalgia in contemporary radical theory. The example I shall explore in some detail is a book by one of the best known British post-colonial theorists, Robert Young's *Postcolonialism: An Historical Introduction* (published in 2001).[96] It must first be admitted that this work is unusual in that it brings out explicitly the idea that post-colonialism is a continuation of revolutionary politics. Its politics are clear in a genre often marked by the absence of clarity. However, I take this distinctive quality, not as an indication of uniqueness, but rather as a methodological opportunity. For the kind of political premises that are to the fore in *Postcolonialism* can be found at work in many post-colonial texts as a set of assumptions. One reflection of this fact is that Young's book has been greeted as a major and mainstream statement of post-colonial thought. It is, noted Peter Morey and James Procter in 2003, 'the most substantial, scholarly contribution to colonial and postcolonial theory this year'.[97]

Unlike most examples of post-colonial study, *Postcolonialism: An Historical Introduction*, pays a great deal of attention to the Soviet Union. Moreover, Robert Young acknowledges that, 'With regard to the old Russian Empire . . . the Soviet government was at once anti-colonist and colonist.'[98] However, this admission is not developed. Indeed, if we ignore, for the moment, the final two chapters on post-structuralism, Young's history is unswervingly Leninist. The bulk of the book charts the upward path from the First to the Third Internationals and the 'transculturation' of this tradition around the world. Bolshevism is presented as offering the authentic path towards liberation. The difficulty of communist colonialism is overcome by Young by sticking closely to the conventional Leninist view (a) that the Soviet Union offered independence to the old Russian Empire's colonial possessions and (b) that their retention within the Soviet Union reflected the need to marry political expediency with a desire to meet the wishes of the communist workers of these nations. 'The federal structure, which then remained until the dissolution of the Soviet Union', Young tells us, 'was made up of a federation which the individual nations had freely joined at the request of their parties'.[99] As this portrait implies, the issue of communist colonialism is raised by Young only to be pushed aside. Indeed, it is only encountered over a few pages, under the rubric of Lenin's handling of the 'national question', within a chapter that unfolds a narrative on the Bolshevik revolution as the founding moment of international anti-colonialism.

> It was largely Lenin himself who changed the situation . . . in which in 1914, few colonised countries could realistically seek complete independence.[100]

In the context of post-colonial discourse, with its emphasis on transgression and hybridity, the orthodoxy of Young's Leninism is interesting. The light of Bolshevism shines from the pages of *Postcolonialism: An Historical Introduction* like a distant and very brilliant star: pure and powerful. It is as if Marxist-Leninism were being retold as a beautiful legend. This is, though, a rather stern tale. When turning to the many acts of revolutionary violence required to sustain Bolshevism, Young's orthodoxy can make for uncomfortable reading.

Indeed, he repeats the official line that the punishment and invasion meted out to periph-eral nations was a consequence of their reactionary allegiance to counter-revolutionary forces.

Although Bolshevik interventions against national governments (for example in the Ukraine and the Central Asian republics) have been seen as a betrayal of the original principle of national self-determination, such actions also need to be seen in the context of the civil war in which several such governments had sided with the counter-revo-lutionary White Russians and Entente powers in an effort to overthrow the Bolshevik regime.[101]

Despite his hard-line on the consequences of counter-revolutionary activity, Young's commitment and loyalty to the cause has an infectious quality. His book is alive with enthusi-asms. Young is particularly excited about 'the great Havana Tricontinental' of 1966.[102] Indeed, he suggests that,

[P]ostcolonialism might well be better named 'tricontinentalism', a term which exactly cap-tures its internationalist political identifications, as well as the source of its epistemologies.[103]

'Tricontinental Marxism', Young tells us, provides 'the foundation for postcolonial theory'.[104]

Today, tricontinental or 'postcolonial', theory and its political practices seek to build on that rich inheritance, the radical legacy of its political determination, its refusal to accept the status quo, its transformation of epistemologies, its establishment of new forms of discursive and political power.[105]

For Young the 'identification of exploited nations as proletarian people' is 'the central thesis of tricontinental Marxism, most forcibly embodied in Mao's and Guevara's global campaign against imperialism'.[106] Hence, post-colonialism becomes a straightforward con-tinuation of anti-colonialism. Indeed, Young goes to considerable lengths to identify the two. Thus, for example, he claims that anti-colonialism was, like post-colonialism, created in the capitals of the West: that it was 'thoroughly metropolitan', and that 'like postcolonialism, tricontinental anti-colonialism has always been a diasporic production'.[107] In this way anti-colonialism ceases to exist as a set of national struggles, or as a form of popular or mass politics, and comes to resemble post-colonialism, the creation of metropolitan intellectuals. The same argument also means that post-colonialism ceases to exist merely as a form of criti-cal scholarship and becomes the voice of the oppressed. The identification of the two forms encourages Young to continually meld and run them together.

'We, the dispossessed' . . . We, postcolonial subjects. With Guevara's Message to the Tricontinental, the epistemology of the postcolonial subject had been born.[108]

Indeed, the logical conclusion of Young's chain of association is that post-colonialism is, or should be, a form of armed insurgency. The contrast with the academic context in which post-colonialism has been articulated and developed is striking. Indeed, it speaks of a power-ful attraction to the more muscular political identities of yesteryear. A number of Young's chapters conclude with ringing revolutionary declarations from Ho Chi Minh and Castro that speak of struggle and sacrifice. Unframed by analysis they are offered as sage mediations and moments of inspiration. Indeed, Young's favoured appellation for the revolutionary moments of the past – 'great' ('the great Havana Tricontinental'; the 'great Indian Marxist M. N. Roy'; the 'great Kenyan novelist Ngugi wa Thiong'o') – might be found patronizing but for the romantic reverence with which he approaches the revolutionary past.[109]

Young interprets the indigenist and pastoral currents within anti-colonialism as dialectical moments to be overcome and suppressed. He turns nostalgic anti-colonialism into a nursery incantation, a moment of immaturity:

> [T]he return-to-the-authentic-tradition-untrammelled-by-the west variety that responds to the present by seeking to deny the past while invoking the European Romantic trope of a return to a true, authentic, indigenous culture.[110]

The pure past Young is attracted to is one in which 'great' revolutionary figures always saw through appeals to primitivism and nationalism. '[N]ationalism was a subsidiary in a more politically and theoretically innovative practice'.[111] Thus authentic African socialism is presented as a continuation of the Leninist tradition. Given the extraordinary depth and range of the nostalgic themes within anti-colonialism, Young's attempt to despatch it to the margins of history requires a certain dexterity. One of the devices he employs is to pile the nostalgic sins of anti-colonialism onto the shoulders of one man – Gandhi – and treat him as 'the most extraordinary phenomenon of a unique history'.[112] Gandhi's 'anomalous position' is central to the plausibility of Young's account.[113] Yet, given the weight of evidence that suggests how important the themes Gandhi raised were to anti-colonial movements in many parts of the world, it is also a point of vulnerability.

However, perhaps the most intriguing point of vulnerability found within *Postcolonialism* centres on the relationship between tricontinental Marxism and post-structuralism. Much of the book offers a conventional Third World Leninist perspective. Yet this journey culminates in post-structuralism. Thus the final chapters are titled 'Foucault in Tunisia' and 'Derrida in Algeria'. Having rolled together post-colonialism and anti-colonialism in earlier chapters Young now absorbs both into post-structuralism. Thus we are told that, 'Structuralism came from the east, poststructuralism from the south'.[114] To verify this statement Young notes that Foucault wrote the *Archeology of Knowledge* in Tunisia, while Derrida was born in Algeria. Indeed, 'Fanon, Memmi, Bourdieu, Althusser, Lyotard, Derrida, Cixous – they were all in or from Algeria'.[115] Addressing Derrida in the first person he draws his book to a close with the claim that,

> [Y]ours were the ideas that, against all apparent odds, against all patronising assumptions that only the simplest language and ideas could ever inspire people to self-assertion and struggle towards social and political transformation, were taken up by many refugees and minorities, migrant and immigrant groups.[116]

Post-structuralism is even represented by Young as a kind of continuation of the armed struggle by other means: for,

> [It] represented one echo of the violence of Algeria playing itself out in an insurrection against the calm philosophical and political certainties of the metropolis.[117]

What are we to make of these claims? At one level they seem like examples of wishful thinking. Certainly for Chandra and Larsen this is the most baffling part of Young's book. 'We are seriously asked to believe that the late patriarch of deconstruction', they write, 'is in fact the post-colonial Other like no other'.[118] They add that,

> [I]t is as if, for Young, tricontinetalism's now blatantly obvious ideological aspect could be effectively cancelled out by its cultural and intellectual redemption in the form of a Foucauldian 'counter-knowledge' dubbed 'postcolonial theory'.[119]

What Chandra and Larsen find troubling is that Young concludes his book in such a way as to make the entire history of anti-colonialism appear as a kind of clumsy empirical prologue for one particular episode of Western social theory (the aggravation being made worse by the insultingly gestural nature of his attempts to show that post-structuralism is 'from the south').

Yet the spectacle of Leninist post-structuralism that Young provides us with does not set out to mock but revere. It exhibits the trauma of its time. Caught between anti-essentialism and profound currents of loss and yearning, it has produced an unlikely set of images: of the glorious march of Bolshevism freeing the world and of the post-colonial scholars continuing the fight. In one fleeting passage, Young points to the contemporary context that has shaped his endeavours.

> From capitalism's point of view, the postsocialist era involves the adoption and then the subsequent renunciation of the anti-colonial, anti-capitalist ideology of Marxism by many newly independent states.[120]

Young's explanation is a curious one. After all, if the collapse of Marxism has only occurred from 'capitalism's point of view', then why are Young's examples of socialist liberation all from so long ago? Young's statement is an act of political self-insulation; a cutting off and away, a refusal of the present. Yet it is precisely because loss and yearning are not admitted to – banished into an anomaly in the history of anti-colonialism and deeply buried in the progressivist discourse of anti-capitalist revolution – that they come to reek such havoc. The insurgent voice that results is jarring and anachronistic; the political representation of post-colonialism convincing only as a form of longing.

Conclusion

This chapter has charted the journey of radical nostalgia from anti-colonialism to post-colonialism. It began with the struggle against colonialism. It is within such struggles that we find some of the clearest twentieth-century examples of the politics of radical nostalgia. While nostalgia had been marginalized in the Western socialist tradition, it obtained a far more vibrant and important role in many of the forms of activism that sought to reclaim political autonomy and cultural identity from the colonial powers.

This process of rediscovery contained many aspects that may be termed traditionalist and backward-looking. The diversity of these currents makes gestures of carte blanch approval or disapproval both ridiculous and presumptuous. To make the claim that the yearning and sense of loss of this period offered an important political reclamation of nostalgia is not to try and offer a post-facto gesture of endorsement. However, it is to argue that these nostalgic radicalisms need to be taken seriously, to be judged on their own terms and not dismissed as varieties of primitivism. The latter concept is to be objected to on a number of levels, not least because it is fundamentally misleading. To conflate, for example, Gandhi or Tagore's concern with the maintenance of roots and organic community with primitivism is to indulge in precisely the kind of Eurocentrism that they sought to challenge. The need to think about such anti-colonial traditionalists, not simply as reacting against modernity, but as charting a path through it, has been emphasized by Ashis Nandy.

> Some Western thinkers, artists and writers have located the idea of loss in a revitalised concept of primitivism. Thus, the pastoral becomes an infantile, pre-rational utopia. The South has no obligation to accept the current global hierarchy of scholars and their work; it can reassess Western thought. The South may decide that the so-called Romantic is a valid stratagem to counter the social evolutionary presumptions of urban-industrial society. In this case, the pastoral becomes the starting point for a vision of post-industrial life. Secondly, Romanticism suggests the possibility of subverting the linear concept of time. In so doing, a future becomes possible that is not an edited version of contemporary Europe and North America. It was probably for these reasons that the idea of the pastoral was picked up by a number of non-Western scholars. Rabindranath Tagore and Gandhi being two of India's most prominent examples. What looks like a lament for the past in Gandhi and Tagore can be read as an attempt to conceptualise the future of Southern societies outside the steel frame of history as it was forged in nineteenth-century Europe.[121]

Unlike post-colonial indigenists Nandy does not try and duck the issue of loss with talk of hybridity and anti-essentialism. Indeed, in depicting his agenda as 'critical traditionalism' he places himself in an anti-colonial lineage that postcolonialism often appears embarrassed by.

> My intention is to reinstate the dignity and intellectual relevance of the everyday lives of people and communities who live with and in traditions, reinvented or otherwise. In order to comprehend the sense of loss that accompanies modernity, we need something that, whilst not entirely beyond the intellect, is closer to intuition. An understanding of loss will serve as a corrective to the easy optimism of the currently dominant theories of progress.[122]

However, despite the reclamation of the topic that has occurred over recent years, Nandy's ability to speak about loss remains unusual. Post-colonial theorists appear ill-equipped to broach themes of longing and nostalgia. Indeed, post-colonialism may be seen to traduce anti-colonialism by completing the modernist project of hostility to nostalgia and affirmation of alienation. And yet, as we have seen, a sense of loss permeates the post-colonial canon. Indeed, the flow of nostalgias at work within it can have a heady quality. In Robert Young's introduction to the topic, for example, we are confronted with a form of anti-nostalgic nostalgic radicalism that feels simultaneously contemporary and out of kilter with its age.

Homi Bhabha once advised post-colonialists that they 'must get beyond the rhetoric of continuance and inheritance', and embrace a less linear of struggle.[123] Yet it seems that 'continuance and inheritance' is the site of post-colonialism's most ardent desires. Its burden of loss is both awkward and heavy. Recently, I came across a second-hand book titled *Africa: Problems in the Transition to Socialism*. It was not old, being an academic collection published in 1986. Yet what drew me to it – what gave it its aura of fascination – was its historical remoteness. The title, full of a predictive certainty (given more emphasis by the admission of mere 'problems'), seems to come from a very different and inaccessible age. It tells us how clear the upward path once seemed but also, perhaps, how ill-prepared the left was for the political realities of the twenty-first century. Post-colonialism is a response to these new political realities yet also a reflection of the left's inability with dealing with them.

Post-colonial theorists have sometimes sought to make a virtue of the incoherence of its disparate elements, by resorting to the notion that discordancy is a positive outcome. Young argues that the 'most challenging post-colonial theory' offers,

[A]n unresolved tension between colonialism as an institutional performative discourse of power-knowledge and colonialism understood according to the dialectical formations elaborated in tricontinental Marxism. Indeed . . . such a disjunctive articulation could be said to operate as the theoretical kernel of postcolonial theory itself.[124]

Yet the odd metaphor of a 'kernel' being 'unresolved' and 'disjunctive' does little to make Young's post-structural Leninism politically or theoretically any clearer. Indeed, after many pages of tricontinental instruction, it is a little disappointing to hear that the academy is safe from revolution. Perhaps, though, we can describe the 'unresolved tension' of post-colonialism in rather different and more critical terms. Instead of acknowledging loss post-colonialism refuses and stereotypes it. Post-colonial studies provides a clear example that, despite its revaluation in some quarters, nostalgia still remains a site of transgression and discomfort. In the next chapter we explore this dilemma further in the company of Paul Gilroy's attempt to pit cosmopolitan conviviality against imperial melancholia.

Notes

1. Thompson, *The Making of the English Working Class*, 13.
2. G. Chaliand, *Revolution in the Third World: Myths and Prospects*, (Hassocks: Harvester Press, 1977), 7–8.
3. Tjama Tjivikua, 'Fighting on', *Zeitschrift für Kulturaustausch*, 1, (2005), 23.
4. Ibid.
5. Cited by H. Dabashi, *The Theology of Discontent: The Ideological Foundations of the Islamic Revolution in Iran*, (New York: New York University Press, 1993), 93.
6. S. Scott, *In Search of the Primitive: A Critique of Civilization*, (New Brunswick: Transaction Books, 1974, 2004), 204. Cited in David Scott, *Conscripts of Modernity: The Tragedy of Colonial Enlightenment*, (Durham, NC: Duke University Press, 2004), 8.
7. A. Nandy, 'Modernity and the sense of loss', *Zeitschrift für Kulturaustausch*, 1, (2005), 41.
8. S. Eisenstadt, 'Multiple modernities', *Daedalus*, 129, 1, (2000); D. Gaonkar, 'On alternative modernities', *Public Culture*, 11, 1, (1999); H. Harootunian, *Overcome by Modernity: History, Culture and Community in Interwar Japan*, (Princeton: Princeton University Press, 2000).
9. Cited by Shaun Richards, 'Polemics on the Irish past: the "return to the source" in Irish literary revivals', *History Workshop Journal*, 31, 1, (1991), 120.
10. Cited by Richards, 'Polemics on the Irish past', 123. The identification of the *authentic* part of the people is a common anti-colonial problematic. The dilemma is exacerbated

by the fact that anti-colonial myths of a Golden Age create cultural reference points that appear arcane and superior when compared to the existing culture of the mass of the people. In his essay 'The necessity of de-anglicizing Ireland', the future president of an independent Ireland, Douglas Hyde, warned in stern tones that 'We must set our face sternly against penny dreadfuls, shilling shockers, and still more, the garbage of vulgar English weeklies.' Yet the most renowned Irish literary nationalist, W. B. Yeats, argued that it is 'from the beliefs and emotions of the common people' that the Irish could rediscover 'the habit of mind that created the religion of the muses'. But who are the 'common people'? Neither Yeats nor Hyde seem to have imagined that the 'religion of the muses' could be found among the urban working class. The thoroughness of colonization finds its reflection in the scarcity and remoteness of those who have been least touched by foreign culture. (Hyde and Yeats citations from Richards, 'Polemics on the Irish past', 123, 124.)

11. Cited by D. Muro, 'Nationalism and nostalgia: the case of radical Basque nationalism', *Nations and Nationalism*, 11, 4, (2005), 579.
12. A. Smith, *Myths and Memories of the Nation*, (Oxford: Oxford University Press, 1999).
13. Muro, 'Nationalism and nostalgia', 580.
14. M. Berger, 'After the Third World? History, destiny and the fate of Third Worldism', *Third World Quarterly*, 25, 1, (2004), 11.
15. Gandhi, *Gandhi's Experiments With Truth: Essential Writings by and about Mahatma Gandhi*, (Lanham: Lexington Books, 2006), 87.
16. Ibid.
17. Patrick Brantlinger, 'A postindustrial prelude to postcolonialism: John Ruskin, William Morris, and Gandhism', *Critical Inquiry*, 22, 3, (1996), 481.
18. Cited by Brantlinger, 'A postindustrial prelude to postcolonialism', 479.
19. Cited by S. Hay, *Asian Ideas of East and West: Tagore and his Critics in Japan, China, and India*, (Cambridge: Harvard University Press, 1970), 180.
20. Gandhi, *The Collected Works of Mahatma Gandhi: Volume 58*, (New Delhi: Ministry of Information and Broadcasting, 1984), 248.
21. J. Mariátegui, *The Heroic and Creative Meaning of Socialism*, (Atlantic Highlands: Humanities Press, 1996), 89.
22. Cited by Igor Kopytoff, 'Socialism and traditional African societies', in W. Frieland and C. Rosberg (Eds), *African Socialism*, (Stanford, CA: Stanford University Press, 1964), 53.
23. J. Nyerere, *Ujamaa: Essays on Socialism*, (Dar es Salaam: Oxford University Press, 1968, first published 1962), 12.
24. Ibid., 26.
25. T. Mboya, 'African socialism', in W. Frieland and C. Rosberg (Eds), *African Socialism*, (Stanford, CA: Stanford University Press, 1964), 251.
26. Nyerere, *Ujamaa*, 8.
27. Ibid., 103.
28. Ibid., 84.
29. Cited by Chaliand, *Revolution in the Third World*, 91.
30. F. Fitzgerald, *Fire in the Lake*, (Boston: Little, Brown and Company, 1972).
31. Chaliand, *Revolution in the Third World*, 134, 92.
32. ibid., 133.
33. J. Al-e Ahmad, *Plagued by the West (Gharbzadegi)*, (Delmar: Caravan Books, 1982), 67.
34. Ibid.

35. J. Al-e Ahmad, *Lost in the Crowd*, (Washington, DC: Three Continents Press, 1985).
36. Cited by Robert Young, *Postcolonialism: An Historical Introduction*, (Oxford: Blackwell, 2001), 186.
37. Fanon, *The Wretched of the Earth*, 175, 178.
38. Ibid., 175.
39. Chaliand, *Revolution in the Third World*, 10.
40. Fanon, *The Wretched of the Earth*, 168–9.
41. Chaliand, *Revolution in the Third World*, 8.
42. Ibid., 198.
43. Ibid., 187.
44. Kopytoff, 'Socialism and traditional African societies', 62.
45. F. Fanon, *Black Skin, White Masks*, (London: Pluto, 1986), 133, 135.
46. Fanon, *The Wretched of the Earth*, 252, 28, 254.
47. Ibid., 84.
48. On Fanon's unorthodox communism see William Hansen, 'Another side to Frantz Fanon: reflections on socialism and democracy', *New Political Science*, 19, 3, (1997).
49. Two further points are relevant:

1. That at Bandung Conference in 1955, the founding moment of Third World anti-colonialism, a debate did take place on Soviet colonial domination. The final communiqué which condemned all colonialism was seen as a vindication of non-aligned communism and a challenge to the Soviet Union.
2. Many countries have territories in which independence movements seek to gain legitimacy for their cause by describing themselves as subject to colonial domination. From Tibet in China to Biafra in Nigeria anti-colonialism exceeds and complicates the concerns of anti-capitalism and anti-Westernism. Once colonialism is opened up beyond the confines of 'the West and the rest' a mosaic of colonial projects and anti-colonialism starts to come into view. We can get a sense of this multiplicity by reference to the choices open to Georgians in the face of Russian colonial ambitions. Hélène Carrère d'Encausse notes,

> For many people subjugated by Russia, the choice had not between colonization or freedom, but between two colonlizations. For instance, Georgia had been threatened on the one hand by Turkey and Iran, which would have destroyed its culture, and on the other by Russia, which had preserved the culture and opened the way to socialism. (*The Nationality Question in the Soviet Union and Russia*, Oslo: Scandinavian University Press, 1995, 26)

See also H. Carey and R. Raciborski, 'Postcolonialism: a valid paradigm for the Former Sovietized states and Yugoslavia?', *East European Politics and Societies*, 18, 2, (2004).
50. W. Kulski, 'Soviet colonialism and anti-colonialism', *Russian Review*, 18, 2, (1959), 114.
51. V. Lenin, *Selected Works, Volume 5*, (London: Lawrence & Wishart, 1935), 270.
52. K. Račevskis, 'Toward a postcolonial perspective on the Baltic states', *Journal of Baltic Studies*, 33, 1, (2002), 45.
53. For information on the Hrushevsky Translation Porkect see http://www.ualberta.ca/CIUS/jacykcentre/HTP-main.htm. Also Serhii Plokhy, *Unmaking Imperial Russia: Mykhailo*

Hrushevsky and the Writing of Ukrainian history, (Toronto: University of Toronto Press, 2005).

54. Serhii Mazlakh and Vasyl' Shakhrai, *On the Current Situation in the Ukraine* (Ann Arbor: University of Michigan Press 1970).

55. Cited by Plokhy, *Unmaking Imperial Russia*, 224.

56. Kulski, 'Soviet colonialism and anti-colonialism', 119.

57. Raymond Pearson, *The Rise and Fall of the Soviet Empire*, (London: Palgrave Macmillan, 1998).

58. Edmund Gaspar, ' Nationalism vs. internationalism: Hungarian history in the re-making', *RFE/RL Collection; Background Reports*, (1969), available at: http://www.osaarchivum.org/files/holdings/3000/8/3text_da/34–4-255.shtml, accessed 29.06.2009.

59. D. Moore, 'Is the post- in postcolonial the post- in post-Soviet? Toward a global postcolonial critique', *PMLA*, 116, 1, (2001), 111.

60. Berger, 'After the Third World?', 27.

61. L. Yew, *From Third World to First: The Singapore Story, 1965–2000*, (New York: HarperCollins, 2000).

62. A. Dirlik, *The Postcolonial Aura: Third World Criticism in the Age of Global Capitalism*, (Boulder: Westview, 1997), 147.

63. S. Chandra and N. Larsen, 'Postcolonial pedigrees: *Postcolonialism: An Historical Introduction*', *Cultural Critique*, 62, (2006), 201.

64. Ibid.

65. Scott, *Conscripts of Modernity*, 207.

66. H. Gill, 'Hegemony and ambiguity: discourses, counter-discourses and hidden meanings in French depictions of the conquest and settlement of Algeria', *Modern and Contemporary France*, 14, 2, (2006)', 171, 157–72.

67. L. Gordon, 'Fanon's tragic revolutionary violence', in L. Gordon, T. Sharpley-Whiting and R. White (Eds), *Fanon: A Critical Reader*, (Oxford: Blackwell, 1996), 304.

68. Scott, *Refashioning Futures*, 204.

69. David Chioni Moore has provided some of the most acute observations on the need to break open the political bonds that shackle discussion of anti-colonialism. Rather than seeking to 'perpetuate the already superannuated centrality of the Western or Anglo-Franco world. It is time, I think, to break with that tradition.' For Moore 'every human being and every literature on the planet today stands in relation' to colonialism. Moore, 'Is the post- in postcolonial the post- in post-Soviet?, 123, 124.

70. Ibid., 43. The relationship between the left and communist colonialism is more complicated than Račevskis's polemical remarks imply. A consistent, if marginal, history of identifying the Soviet Union as a colonial power can be identified within the non-communist left in the West, notably within the anarchist left and the socialist democratic and liberal left. Moreover, the idea of complicity has often worked in the opposite direction to the one he identifies. To give attention to communist or other non-Western forms of colonialism was seen, by many on the left, as a way of distracting attention from, or offering a kind of apology for, Western colonialism. Frank Füredi has identified this kind of displacement as an 'official line', made in response to accusations of colonial racism. Drawing on British government and UNESCO material from the 1950s, he finds a 'compulsive . . . desire to transform racism into a transcendental curse that afflicted all societies throughout history'. F. Füredi, *The Silent War*, (London: Pluto, 1998), 228.

71. Račevskis, 'Toward a postcolonial perspective on the Baltic states', 42.

72. Edward Said, *Culture and Imperialism*, (London: Chatto and Windus, 1993), 9.
73. Moore, 'Is the post- in postcolonial the post- in post-Soviet?, 119.
74. Edward Said, *Culture and Imperialism*, 9.
75. Ibid., 292. Other references to the Soviet Union are found on pages 54 and 286.
76. E. Shohat, 'Notes of the "post-colonial"', *Social Text*, 31/32 (1992), 111, 99–113.
77. Moore, 'Is the post- in postcolonial the post- in post-Soviet?', 116–17.
78. O. Baddeley, 'Nostalgia for a new world', *Third Text*, 6, 21, (1992), 29, 29–34.
79. Young, *Postcolonialism*, 218.
80. The outlines of the debate are discussed in Alastair Bonnett, *Radicalism, Anti-Racism and Representation*, (London: Routledge, 1993).
81. E. San Juan, *Beyond Postcolonial Theory*, (New York: St. Martin's Press, 1998).
82. D. Scott, *Refashioning Futures: Criticism after Postcoloniality*, (Princeton: Princeton University Press, 1999).
83. See, for example, Divya Tolia-Kelly, 'Investigations into diasporic "cosmopolitanism": beyond mythologies of the "non-native"', in C. Wyer and C. Bressey (Eds), *New Geographies of Race and Racism*, (Aldershot: Ashgate, 2008); Homi Bhabha, 'Unsatisfied: notes on vernacular cosmopolitanism', in G. Castle (Ed.), *Postcolonial Discourses: An Anthology*, (Oxford: Blackwell, 2001).
84. M. Nada, 'We are all hybrids now: the dangerous epistemology of post-colonial populism', *Journal of Peasant Studies*, 28, 2, (2001), 166, 162–86.
85. W. Mignolo, *Local Histories/Global Designs*, (Princeton: Princeton University Press, 2000), 310; W. Mignolo, 'The many faces of cosmopolis: border thinking and critical cosmopolitanism', *Public Culture*, 12, 3, (2000), 745.
86. Ibid., 302, 149.
87. Ibid., 299.
88. B. de Sousa Santos, 'Beyond abyssal thinking: from global lines to ecologies of knowledges', (2007), available at: www.eurozine.com, accessed 29.09.2009.
89. Nanda, 'We are all hybrids now', 163.
90. Kwame Appiah, 'The postcolonial and the postmodern', in B. Ashcroft, G. Griffiths and H. Tiffin (Eds), *The Post-Colonial Studies Reader*, (London: Routledge, 1995), 123.
91. Scott, *Conscripts of Modernity*, 3.
92. A. Gupta, *Postcolonial Developments: Agriculture in the Making of Modern India*, (Durham, NC: Duke University Press, 1998), 238.
93. Nanda, 'We are all hybrids now', 164.
94. Gill, 'Hegemony and ambiguity', 171.
95. Nanda, 'We are all hybrids now', 165.
96. Robert Young, *Postcolonialism: An Historical Introduction*, (Oxford: Blackwell, 2001).
97. P. Morey and J. Procter, 'Colonial discourse, postcolonial theory', *Year's Work Critical and Cultural Theory*, 11, 1, (2003), 43.
98. Young, *Postcolonialism*, 124.
99. Ibid., 123.
100. Ibid., 124.
101. Ibid., 123.
102. The less faithful might look upon the Tricontinental Conference of 3–15 January, 1966, as a move in the geopolitics of communism. Although the conference was endorsed by the Soviet Union, Castro used the event to wrest some degree of leadership over Third World revolutionary forces away from the Soviet Union and exploit the schism between

the Soviet Union and China. The event also offered him an opportunity to denounce the lively challenge from Trotskyism (that 'repugnant thing' as Castro called it in his closing speech) in the Americas and to affirm the necessity of armed struggle ('all people will have to take up arms to liberate themselves' in Latin America said Castro). Fidel Castro, 'At the closing session of the Tricontinental Conference', speech delivered to Tricontinental Conference, Chaplin Theatre, Havana, 15 January, 1966, available at: www.marxists.org/history/cuba/archive/castro/1966/01/15.htm, accessed 12.07.2009.
103. Young, *Postcolonialism*, 5.
104. Ibid., 169.
105. Ibid., 428.
106. Ibid., 175.
107. Ibid., 61, 218.
108. Ibid., 212.
109. Ibid., 5 (also 194), 125, 65.
110. Ibid., 418.
111. Ibid., 169.
112. Ibid., 334.
113. Ibid., 338.
114. Ibid., 413.
115. Ibid.
116. Ibid., 425.
117. Ibid., 412.
118. Chandra and Larsen, 'Postcolonial pedigrees', 204.
119. Ibid., 201.
120. Young, *Postcolonialism*, 59.
121. Nandy, 'Modernity and the sense of loss', 42. Also A. Nandy, *The Intimate Enemy: Loss and Recovery of Self under Colonialism*, (Delhi: Oxford University Press, 1983).
122. Ibid., 41.
123. Bhabha, 'Unsatisfied', 39.
124. Young, *Postcolonialism*, 410.

CHAPTER FOUR

The Melancholia of Cosmopolis

Introduction

The past 40 years have seen the emergence of a new form of radicalism centred on the multicultural metropolis. The dream of 'cosmopolis', the world city, have been democratized, culturally pluralized and made real in ordinary streets and neighbourhoods. For the left this is also a political landscape. The multiracial city is cast as an arena of political resistance. In a post-communist era, the celebration of the diverse metropolis has become central to a new kind of left politics. Hostility to nostalgia is a central theme in this new discourse. This chapter looks at how this form of radicalism emerged in Britain and how its antagonism to nostalgia shapes its representation of metropolitan culture. As we shall see, in this radical cosmopolitan vision of urban space, nostalgia is routinely reduced to a racist grunt, an ugly noise made by place-bound primitives. But nostalgia cannot be so easily dispatched. It re-emerges in cosmopolitanism as an awkward and disruptive presence, a discordant sigh of regret; a disconcerting lapse in the up-beat sound track for a tirelessly celebratory narrative.

I look at this process in more detail with the help of an example: Paul Gilroy's resolutely anti-nostalgic *After Empire: Melancholia or Convivial Culture?* (published in 2004; in the United States the book was published a year later retitled as *Postcolonial Melancholia*).[1] Gilroy's *After Empire* is important both because of its author's status (Colin MacCabe calls Gilroy 'the most influential intellectual writing in Britain today') and because it has been presented as the most penetrating anti-racist assessment of British culture.[2] It also brings into focus the nature and limits of the antagonism to nostalgia that still marks the radical imagination. For Gilroy, Britain is in the grip of 'melancholia', a morbid obsession with its own long gone days of glory that creates a dismal culture of regret and fear. This 'pathological formation' is contrasted with the 'vibrant, ordinary multiculture' emerging within the 'convivial metropolitan cultures of the country's young people'.[3]

My critique of *After Empire* is in two parts. First, I look at the stereotyping and repression of themes of loss that sustain Gilroy's account. Secondly, I address *After Empire* as a nostalgic text, burdened with a yearning for lost political potency. Thus we shall see, once again, how, even among those who profess to despise it, nostalgia creeps in and makes its presence known. However, before we get to Gilroy's book it is necessary to introduce the two key debates that have fed into it. The first turns on aspirations towards cosmopolitanism. The vision of a cosmopolitan future of continuously fluid culturally attachments and detachments is introduced as a re-envisioning of the anti-nostalgic tradition. However, it is also noted that left cosmopolitanism contains its own nostalgic agendas, organized around the hope of recreating left political community. The chapter then turns to the national context of British anti-racism, in the 1980s and 1990s, that provides the local setting for Gilroy's work. More specifically, it addresses the ways anti-nostalgia and nostalgia were mapped onto radical anti-racism in Britain in these decades. It is suggested that the stereotype of the young black rebel concealed and cohered the tensions between a declining socialist movement and the politics of loss.

Cosmopolitan Attachments

A cosmopolitan is a citizen of the world. Richard Hakluyt's definition from 1598, which appears to be the first English use of the term, depicts 'Cosmopolites' as 'a citizen and member of the whole and onely one mysticall citie universal'.[4] In one of the major texts of the Enlightenment, Diderot and d'Alembert's *Encyclopédie*, the cosmopolite is identified as, 'a man who is a stranger nowhere' and a denizen of 'the world city'.[5] These meanings remain familiar to us today. The quest to escape the confines of the merely local is as old as modernity itself. The postnational political claim that usually follows is also familiar. Thomas Paine framed it thus: 'my country is the world, my religion is to do good to mankind.'[6]

However, these recognizable desires have become connected to a wider set of social process, creating a debate on the political meaning of cosmopolitanism. Marx and Engels saw cosmopolitanism as the emancipated product of capital's power to uproot traditional attachments.

> The need of a constantly expanding market for its products chases the bourgeoisie over the whole surface of the globe. It must nestle everywhere, settle everywhere, establish connexions everywhere. The bourgeoisie has through its exploitation of the world market given a cosmopolitan character to production and consumption. To the great chagrin of Reactionists, it has drawn from under the feet of industry the national ground on which it stood. . . . In place of the old local and national seclusion and self-sufficiency, we have intercourse in every direction, universal inter-dependence of nations. . . . National one-sidedness and narrow-mindedness become more and more impossible, and from the numerous and local literatures, there arises a world literature.[7]

Although Marx looked forward to the coming of unalienated 'man', he clearly envisaged communism not as a return to 'narrow-mindedness' but as a completion of the cosmopolitan condition. In the second half of the twentieth century, the accelerated pace of globalization has established an even more central place for cosmopolitanism within the political narratives of the left. At the same time, cosmopolitanism has become the site of an increasingly complex set of dilemmas. In part this is because globalization has ensured that, far from withering away, cosmopolitanism's 'bourgeois' roots in the 'world market', have become ever more obvious and influential. But it is also due to the fact that, cosmopolitanism, like post-colonialism (with which it is often associated), is another example of a resurgent form of anti-nostalgia that exhibits its own backward-looking tendencies. We can observe this momentum in more detail by looking at two particular paradoxes exhibited in the work of academic advocates of the cosmopolitan condition. The first paradox arises from the fact that, as the early definitions of the cosmopolite offered above suggest, although cosmopolitanism appears to raise us above local, insular cultures, it also represents an attempt to *connect* with others. This is a tendency not restricted to radical or left cosmopolitanism but found across the spectrum of those who look forward to a new cosmopolitan order of human 'openness' and generosity. It is not surprising, therefore, that the vision of a postnational, post-essentialist, world offered by many of the recent proponents of cosmopolitanism is dependent upon a politics of sentiment. What is, perhaps, of more interest is the way this vision also evokes a retrieval or reanimation of emotions of fellowship and love. The nostalgic moment becomes a moment of release: freed from the past we rediscover the well-springs of humanity. Once the barriers and invented identities that divide us fall away, cosmopolis emerges as a city of care and creativity.

The beneficent quality of this particular cosmopolitan vision contrasts with the prosaic reality of cosmopolitan sharedness and negotiation offered by many authors on the left. However, my second example of yearning and redemption in cosmopolitanism locates a nostalgic imperative in the portrayal of its everyday forms. For what appears to be occurring in these benign and inclusive portraits of ordinary cosmopolitans, is that a left community is being reimagined and resurrected. To put it more crudely, it seems that, in a post-socialist era, cosmopolitanism has been fashioned into a discourse of attachment and solidarity.

The Return of Love

Cosmopolitanism appears to offer detachment, a cooling of local and intimate relationships of loyalty and affection, and the development of more distant, reasoned and intellectual connections. Yet when we listen to those who advocate cosmopolitanism, who identify it as a positive project, we often hear an insistent sense that it reveals and opens emotional resources of love and care. Martha Nussbaum advises that,

> Becoming a citizen of the world is often a lonely business. It is, in effect, a kind of exile from the comfort of local truths, from the warm nestling feelings of patriotism, from the absorbing pride in oneself and one's own . . . Cosmopolitanism offers no such refuge; it offers only reason and the love of humanity.[8]

Cosmopolitanism, it seems, is a kind of offering up of oneself, a willingness towards others. Nussbaum calls it love. Others shy away from the word but it seems to surface nevertheless. For Walter Mignolo, cosmopolitanism 'demands yielding generously'.[9] Even Sheldon Pollock and Homi Bhabha seem to find a kind of tough romance in cosmopolitanism, for them it is the ability 'to learn to live tenaciously'.[10]

In *Empire*, Hardt and Negri try to put their finger on the nature of the new, postnational, post-capitalist, society they seek. It is a society that has rid itself of ethnic and national loyalties and in which open attachments and creativity are the guiding spirits. It is a vision, they explain, that 'makes rebellion into an act of love', and where 'communism, cooperation and revolution remain together, in love, simplicity, and also innocence'.[11] Ronald Niezen comments that this shimmering prospect 'falls almost accidentally, into an anarchistic idealism that rejects permanent power while upholding a form of powerless permanence'.[12] Yet, perhaps, the most striking aspect of Hardt and Negri's vision is its belief in innocence and its faith in love. After the false barriers that divide people have crumbled away, cosmopolis emerges as a redemptive post-community; a site of pure humanity. In *The Coming Community* Giorgio Agamben, also premises his argument against fixed identities on the ideal of 'the loveable'. And what is love?

> Seeing something simply in its being-thus – irreparable, but not for that reason necessary; thus, but not for that reason contingent – is love.[13]

Love is rarely to the fore in debates on cosmopolitanism. But the terms of the debate often suggest that it is precisely a *faith* in people's capacity for emotional connection and release that makes the cosmopolitan condition so alluring and plausible. Consider the case made by Don Flynn, in a piece called 'Beyond boundaries' for the British socialist magazine *Chartist*. Arguing against the fear of immigration, Flynn writes that 'engagement with otherness is, for a significant proportion of people, the very essence of adventure and personal liberation'.[14] There is a promise of freedom here, as well as the promise of what Flynn calls 'the joyous crowd'. But this promise does not rely on any political or economic transformation but, rather, on a willingness, an openness, towards 'otherness'. Flynn is telling us that once all the false insularities and blinkered attachments have fallen away, people's capacity for 'engagement', the 'essence' of liberation, stands revealed. The association of cosmopolitanism with exploration and creativity is also suggested by Ulf Hannerz for whom 'genuine cosmopolitanism' may be defined as 'an orientation, a willingness to engage with the Other. It is an intellectual and aesthetic stance of openness'.[15] Samuel Scheffler argues that cosmopolitanism emphases the value of fluid identities, of 'peoples remarkable capacity to forge new identities using material from diverse cultural sources'. Based on this 'remarkable capacity' Scheffler concludes that,

> [I]ndividuals have the capacity to flourish by forging idiosyncratic identities from heterogeneous cultural sources and are not to be thought of as constituted or defined by ascriptive ties to a particular culture, community or tradition.[16]

Ulrich Beck has emphasized that cosmopolitanism is a difficult encounter, a compromised and imperfect negotiation between people coming together in the new spaces of a globalizing world. He wryly observes that '[t]he everyday experience of cosmopolitanism is not a love affair of everyone with everyone.'[17] Nevertheless, it is surely significant that recent academic evaluations of cosmopolitanism have turned repeatedly to the idea that cosmopolitanism involves the development and reanimation of basic emotional resources. It is precisely because the human 'capacity' for 'openness', 'engagement' and 'adventure' is understood to be penned in by borders and barriers – and because it is imagined that it will be unleashed once the artifice of identity and territory is exposed – that cosmopolitanism is celebrated as a path towards freedom.

Developing the geopolitical implications of the cosmopolitan order, David Held looks forward to a world where sovereignty is 'stripped away from the idea of fixed borders'.[18] When this aspiration is allied to an emphasis on 'forging idiosyncratic identities', we arrive at a post-modern political vision which associates fragmentation and impermanence with liberation. It is a project that may be contrasted with the Eurocentrism of traditional communism but also with communism's desire for human wholeness and completeness. Sennett makes the distinction explicit when he writes that an 'Openness to the needs of others comes from ceasing to dream of the world made whole.'[19] Yet although these examples of contemporary cosmopolitanism may not 'dream of a world made whole', they are still recognizable as dreams of the 'return of man into himself' (to use Marx's phrase). The conception of a more open, more generous, world, inhabited by people who are able to look beyond local attachments and loyalties, promises to overcome the compartmentalizing logic of modernity. But it is also a moment of innocence, reaffirmation and return.

Remaking Left Community

The term 'cosmopolitan left' denotes a political identity in which themes of diversity, tolerance and internationalism complement but also, to some extent, displace, the traditional socialist focus on public ownership and class struggle. However, when we approach this attachment to the signs and symbols of cultural difference in the context of an interest in radical nostalgia yet another paradox comes into view. For, despite the avowed inclination to 'radical openness', cosmopolitanism has been employed to reconstruct a community of the left. This process can be seen at work in a variety of ways. One of the most common is by representing a 'cosmopolitan community' which continues to sustain the traditions of solidarity and struggle abandoned in the capitalist West. An influential, if much criticized, example of this way of thinking is Frederick Jameson's essay 'Third-World literature in an era of multinational capitalism'.[20] Jameson offered 'Third World literature' as a site of redemption and renewal. In Jennifer Wenzel's critical view, for Jameson, 'the contemporary Third World becomes the mirror for the irrecoverable past of the "American scene"'.[21] Wenzel adds that Jameson 'dramatize[s]' his sense of 'loss by showing the constitutive presence of those things . . . in other parts of the world'.[22]

However, the central terrain of left cosmopolitanism is not the 'Third World' but the multicultural city in the West. Doreen Massey's 1993 essay 'A global sense of place' remains a touchstone for this geographical agenda. Massey's concern is to identify what she calls an 'adequately progressive sense of place'; that is, a sense of place that is not 'reactionary' or defensive but open and diverse. Massey offers, then, a defence of the cosmopolitan local. She proceeds, appropriately enough, with a celebration of her own neighbourhood. To get a flavour of the kind of attachments and representations that Massey values, her portrait is worth quoting at length:

> [A] walk down Kilburn High Road, my local shopping centre. It is a pretty ordinary place, north-west of the centre of London. Under the railway bridge the newspaper stand sells papers from every county of what my neighbours, many of whom come from there, still often call the Irish Free State. The postboxes down the High Road, and many an empty space on a wall, are adorned with the letters IRA. Other available spaces are plastered this week with posters for a special meeting in remembrance: Ten Years after the Hunger Strike. At the local theatre Eamon Morrissey has a one-man show; the National Club has the Wolfe Tones on, and at the Black Lion there's Finnegan's Wake. In two shops I notice this week's lottery ticket winners: in one the name is Teresa Gleeson, in the other, Chouman Hassan.

> Thread your way through the often almost stationary traffic diagonally across the road from the newsstand and there's a shop which as long as I can remember has displayed saris in the window. Four life-sized models of Indian women, and reams of cloth. On the door a notice announces a forthcoming concert at Wembley Arena: Anand Miland presents Rekha, life, with Aamir Khan, Salman Khan, Jahi Chawla and Raveena Tandon. On another ad, for the end of the month, is written, 'All Hindus are cordially invited'. In another newsagents I chat with the man who keeps it, a Muslim unutterably depressed by events in the Gulf, silently chafing at having to sell the *Sun*.[23]

What is going on in this description of what Massey calls an 'ordinary place'? I would argue that one of the things that this passage illustrates is the attempt to construct a new community for the left. Despite its prosaic trappings, this is not, after all, pure description. The signs and symbols that might jar with a liberal-left reading of Kilburn High Road are notable by their absence. The multiple reactionary essentialisms, the isolated lives, the deep sense of loss . . . all *that* kind of diversity is not there. The landscape we are presented with is populated by the kind of people and things that those on the left might hope to find, or at least that they could rub along with. Massey's rather touching relationship with this imagined place is not coldly instrumental: it seeks out friendship and hope. In an era in which the left seems so friendless Massey constructs a streetscape characterized by a combination of radicalism with innocent sympathy and kindness. Massey's account might also suggest that one of the appeals of the idea of fluid, permanently unsettled, communities to the left, is that they can be imaginatively appropriated and absorbed into a discourse of resistance far more easily than communities with relatively fixed and clear local identities.

Massey presents us with a simple stroll and a simple set of observations. Her politics of representation are unmarked. It seems that even the most subtle of theorists can become oddly innocent when constructing the story of the cosmopolitan city. Other examples of this unreflexive disposition can be found in Homi Bhabha's influential article 'Unsatisfied: Notes on Vernacular Cosmopolitanism'. Bhabha's essay is also notable for its insistence on a critical relationship between cosmopolitanism and the local. He is interested in,

> a cosmopolitan community envisaged in a *marginality*, even metonymy . . . of a certain postcolonial translation of the relation between the patriotic and the cosmopolitan, the home and world.[24]

Bhabha's emphasis on the marginal and mixed is a refusal of closed identities and metanarratives. He wishes to give attention to the irreducible *singularity* of events and circumstances. Bhabha's essay might seem, then, to be an unlikely place to find a narrative of rekindled left community. That such themes are, in fact, present is suggested by Bhahba's response to a poem that sits at the centre of his essay. The poem is 'Eastern Wartime' by Andrienne Rich. Bhabha cites it as follows:

> I'm a canal in Europe where bodies are floating
> I'm a mass grave I'm the life that returns
> I'm a table set with room for the Stranger
> I'm a field with corners left for the landless
> [. . .]
> I'm a man-child praising God he's a man
> I'm a woman bargaining for a chicken
> I'm a woman who sells for a boat ticket
> I'm an immigrant tailor who says *A coat
> is not a piece of cloth only* I sway
> in the learnings of the master-mystics
> I have dreamed of Zion I've dreamed of world revolution
> [. . .]

I'm a corpse dredged from a canal in Berlin
a river in Mississippi I'm a woman standing
[. . .]
I am standing here in your poem unsatisfied.

The non-reducible singularities that Rich moves through in this work are not its only motif. For these singular points are woven together and emerge from the poet's radical concerns. We are reminded of the dispossessed of Europe, the victims of the West. These images do not overwhelm the poem but drive it forward through a staccato set of intimate and affective moments. However, in Bhabha's account of the work, Rich's attempt 'to maintain the *singularity* of each event and person she inscribes', is rendered into a starkly political list: 'World War, starvation, Indian landless peasants, migrant labor, religious custom, Vietnamese boat people, feminist solidarity'. Thus Bhabha distils the political momentum of the poem into a politically recognizable, left cosmopolitan, discourse; a litany of resistance and struggle.

Rendering transparent the political dynamic that he has just drawn to the surface, Bhabha insists that Rich's images 'are not correlated because they share the same historical "cause" or are mediated by the same sign'.[25] Indeed, he argues that 'there is no easy ethical analogy or historical *parallelism*' in the work:

[A]s for instance, in the deaths by water – Rosa Luxemburg once, now the Turkish *Gastarbeiter* – offered up in the *landwehrkanal* in Berlin, or the lynched body floating in the Mississippi.[26]

Bhabha suggests that Rich's single voices are only 'representative of the cosmopolitan contingency, or the transnational uncertainty'.[27] Yet his own reading of the work ensures that its 'representativeness' goes well beyond contingency. Bhabha's version of Rich's poem offers a familiar left narrative of victimhood. The 'historical "cause"' is unmissable and immediately recognizable. Bhabha is not constructing Massey's cheery multicultural neighbourhood but something equally selective and equally capable of rendering the chaotic flows of contemporary cultural change into a well known and, hence, comforting community of victims and rebels. Indeed, there is a kind of willed innocence to his deployment of themes of non-correlation and singularity. Bhabha tries to flee the hold of radical tradition. Yet he seeks it out in Rich and brings it before us, not as something named or categorized, but as something felt and demanded. Like Massey, Bhabha offers us an empathetic politics. Like Massey, he also seems to have difficulty in being explicit about the politics of his own interpretation. In the left cosmopolitan political reclamation of the fragments of modernity, loss and yearning are present but unacknowledged.

Renewing Resistance: Nostalgia and Anti-nostalgia in British Radical Anti-racism

Anti-racism emerged in Britain in the late 1970s and early 1980s as a radical critique of multiculturalism. The urban riots of 1981 and 1985, combined with the strength of radical left elements in the Labour Party, provoked and provided space for an anti-racist movement that eschewed reformism and compromise with what was portrayed as a racist state.[28]

Although a relatively novel political development, the British anti-racist movement was firmly aligned to the traditional radical ambition of making a new society and sweeping away the past. Indeed, radical anti-racism may be seen as offering a powerful reaffirmation of this disposition. A characteristic of radical anti-racist rhetoric was the charge that the traditional 'white left' were stuck in the past and, hence, unable to grasp the shift towards race as a site of anti-capitalist conflict. The influential formula offered by Stuart Hall asserted that 'Race is the modality in which class is lived . . . the medium in which class relations are experienced.'[29]

The idea that the 'old Left' cannot see the new realities of British society was powerfully developed by Paul Gilroy in his first book, *There Ain't No Black in the Union Jack: The Cultural Politics of Race and Nation*.[30] Paul Gilroy offered a critique of English socialists (notably Tony Benn and E. P. Thompson) for their insular attempts to root socialism in English and/or British tradition. If 'the hold of nationalism on today's socialists is to be broken', Gilroy argued, a new postnational, postnostalgic, radicalism needs to be forged.[31]

However, at the political heart of *There Ain't No Black in the Union Jack* is the representation of the young black man as a site of resistance. This designation reflected a wider trend within the anti-racist left. In 1980s, British socialism was a declining force both as a mass movement and an intellectual agenda. Within this context the assertion, found across a wide range of radical anti-racist discourses, of racialized minorities – specifically, young black men – as a repository of revolutionary hope took on a variety of connotations.[32] A new and youthful social group was being identified as challenging and upsetting an old social formation and auguring the creation of a new one. At the same time, in the context of the apparent loss of the traditional class agent of popular politics, the image of everyday, street-level, black militancy acted as a replacement for, and nostalgic echo of, an earlier, more certain period in political life.

Hence, the construction of migrant communities as 'communities of resistance' meant that they could be slotted into a rhetorical repertoire of struggle.[33] In 1977, Gérard Chaliand had already observed among the French left that 'the final embodiment of Third Worldism may well be found in the recent myth of immigrant workers as representing the potential revolutionary vanguard.'[34] More recently, in his 2006 article, 'Immigrationism, the last utopia of the bien-pensants', Pierre-André Taguieff identified a new left ideology centred on the political and cultural value of immigration.[35] 'Immigrationism', says Taguieff, constructs immigration and immigrants as a kind of final repository of radical hopes. However, if our focus is upon British radical anti-racists in the 1980s, although what might be called 'immigrationism' was becoming ubiquitous, the core political figure was not the immigrant but the black youth. Indeed, the evolution of black Britain from quiescence to rebellion was narrated in terms of the transition from immigrant to second generation. The 'shattered illusions' of the former were understood to provide fertile ground for the militancy of the latter.[36] Thus black youth were represented as the rebellious and dissatisfied children of less politicized parents.

The figure of the 'black rebel' allowed the contradictory relationship of British radicalism to the past to be cohered and concealed. In part, this process was achieved by the assimilation of black history into socialist history. For the anti-racist theorists Bourne and Sivanandan,

> West Indian cultures are, by the very nature of their slave and plantation histories, anti-racist and anti-capitalist.[37]

The obvious implication is that the torch of revolt may be safely passed into the hands of 'West Indians cultures', and more specifically, of 'black youth':

[B]lack youth . . . they take nothing as given, everything is up for question, everything is up for change: capitalist values, capitalist mores, capitalist society.[38]

Ironically Sivanandan also inveighed against the disposition of 'a certain politics on the black Left' to 'romanticise the youth'.[39] In fact, the romance of black rebellion was integral to the radical anti-racist project. For Carby,

[B]lack youth recognise liberal dreamers and the police for what they are and act. They determine the terrain on which the next struggle will be fought – the street, the day.[40]

This new politics of race routinely overlooked the diversity of Britain's minority population. The figure of the 'black youth' was made to carry the weight of a putatively anti-capitalist ethnic culture while also offering a generic, non-ethnically specific, politically defined, location of social revolt. The definition of 'Black' that emerged in Britain at this time – as 'a common term used to describe all people who have experienced and have common history of: imperialism, colonialism, slavery, indentureship and racism' – assisted in this interpretation.[41] Although this British use of 'Black' as a political label was uneven (along with its corollary – that 'White as a political term is a term for the oppressor'), it helped secure the rearticulation of the language of class rebellion into a rhetoric of race rebellion.[42] One of the consequences of the notion that British society is split between rebellious, anti-capitalist blacks and oppressive, conservative whites, was the emergence of a pattern of neglect towards British Asians, other ethnically non-African heritage minority groups, as well as those ethnicities defined around religion.[43] The deployment of 'black youth' as the axial term in a new lexicon of radicalism also had implications for the way the history of African heritage people (and to a lesser extent all majority world heritage people) could be told. By the 1970s and 1980s, the nostalgic retrieval of 'black history' was already well established. In as much as this project relied on the attempt to supply cultural definitions and 'positive images' of racialized minorities and, hence assimilate them into the 'mainstream society', it remained an object of intense suspicion for British radical anti-racists.[44] Far more congruent was the representation of black history as a history of continual struggle and resistance. Gilroy developed this position by tracing the 'oppositional' or 'alternative' modernities formed by intellectuals from the African Diaspora.[45] Indeed, he became an acute commentator on the need for remembrance and the use of myths of the past to contest Eurocentric modernity. Writing about 'modern black art' in 1993 Gilroy's focus was upon its deployment of symbols of the past. Gilroy's vision of dispersed and politicized modernities led him to suggest that,

[T]his remembering is socially and politically organised in part through assertive tactics which accentuate the symbolism of the pre-modern as part of their anti-modern modernism.[46]

Gilroy's interest in counter-modernities as alternative nostalgias opens out the possibility of a break with the conflation of nostalgia with conservatism and racism. Yet, as we shall see in the next section, *After Empire* treats nostalgia as inherently suspect. This may suggest

Gilroy's ambivalence towards the topic. It also indicates that, for Gilroy, the value of attachments to the past, where admitted at all, must be measured in terms of their political utility in fermenting radical political change.

However, the figure of the black rebel remained a largely aspirational presence in British radical anti-racism. Despite the fiery rhetoric, evidence of a socialist or anti-capitalist movement taking hold among black youth was elusive. It is difficult not to conclude that the attempt to find in black youth a substitute for, or development of, militant radical consciousness, tells us more about the aspirations of the British left than British blacks. From the early 1990s, in the context of the receding tide of the worldwide socialist project (eventually made crystal clear in Britain with the birth of 'New Labour'), and a lack of any substantive constituency to defend the gains of the urban left, radical anti-racism in British local government and within non-governmental organizations began to disappear. In organizational terms, radical anti-racism declined throughout the 1990s (indeed, Gilroy announced 'the end of anti-racism' in 1990).[47] Nevertheless, the political aspirations it articulated continued to be heard in a number of areas, perhaps most clearly among radical social scientists. Despite the disappointments of the past (and the present), the desire to locate an agitational and anti-capitalist popular constituency remain powerful. In the 1990s, this aspiration began to be mapped onto notions of diversity, hybridity and diversity. In Britain multiculturalism had initially been rejected by radical anti-racists. In the 1980s it was routinely described as an ideological product of the state's attempts to diffuse and manage black resistance. However, a decade later, by emphasizing the connections between myths of cultural homogeneity and conservatism and, at a theoretical level, between 'essentialism' and conservatism, multiculturalism began to be represented as having a disruptive and critical content. Thus, by construing 'multiculture' as an energetic challenge to racism, and as a facet of internationalism and anti-nationalism, it began to be drawn into the anti-racist and radical project. Yet, as we shall see in the company of Paul Gilroy's *After Empire*, the dilemmas of nostalgia are not necessarily lessened or avoided by installing new agents of revolt (whether hybrid multicultures or black youth) within the radical project.

Nostalgia Strikes Back: Paul Gilroy's *After Empire*

In *After Empire* Paul Gilroy diagnoses British culture as afflicted with yearning. In Gilroy's Britain loss has metastasized and requires urgent treatment. His remedy is 'convivial culture'; a 'radical openness'; a way of being that 'makes a nonsense of closed, fixed, and reified identity'.[48] The conviviality Gilroy offers in opposition to melancholia is defined as 'the processes of cohabitation and interaction that have made multiculture an ordinary feature of social life in Britain's urban areas and in postcolonial cities elsewhere'.[49] Gilroy sets 'convivial culture' against an insular and reactionary culture of 'multiple anxieties': the former is cast as insurgent and full of a youthful, rascally charm; the latter is understood to be dominant but aged, decrepit and contemptible.[50] It generates the,

> guilt-ridden loathing and depression that have come to characterise Britain's xenophobic responses to the strangers who have intruded upon it more recently.[51]

How could anyone object to conviviality? Yet it is the *ingratiating* nature of the concept that first provoked my unease with *After Empire*. The smooth agreeability of the idea seems designed to construct nostalgia as misanthropic and monstrous. Yet, this deployment of the term provokes something of a double take, for the idea of 'conviviality' has many nostalgic resonances. The friendly, cheery disposition that Gilroy offers as a slogan of the new, echoes the most ubiquitous and familiar discourse of longing: for a time when people were nicer, kinder, happier; when doors were left unlocked and neighbours greeted each other in the street. Indeed, within early English socialism 'the joy of conviviality' was once firmly associated with the patriotic socialism offered by the Clarion movement.[52] However, as we shall see later, the limits of Gilroy's own conviviality are often stark. *After Empire* displays unlimited enthusiasm for those who are young, male, black or white, urban and situate themselves within a mid-Atlantic racialized cultural politics. But Gilroy often becomes terse and sarcastic when his eye falls upon those unfortunate enough to fall outside this circle.

Gilroy's critical focus is on emotional attachments to empire and memories of the Second World War. The following passage is also illustrative of his disdain for 'melancholic' patriots.

> For about three decades, the brash motto of true-Brit sporting nationalism was supplied by the curious boast: 'Two world wars and one World Cup, doo dah, doo dah'. Future historians will doubtless puzzle over this odd phrase, which, as it echoed around many British sports venues, became an ugly chant. They will probably struggle to make sense of the strange symbolic system in which the words circulated and grasp the warped patriotism to which they gave disturbing expression.[53]

Gilroy's 'future historians' will contrast this sorry scene with the 'convivial metropolitan cultures of the country's young people'.[54]

Before proceeding a note is needed on Gilroy's use of the terms 'melancholia' and 'cosmopolitanism'. In an article on Gilroy's use of the latter term, Sam Knowles tracks both his suspicions ('simply one more imperialistic particularism dressed up in seductive universal garb'), alternative ('planetary humanism') but also his uncritical deployment (e.g. his uncritical use of the term 'cosmopolitan conviviality').[55] Knowles concludes that Gilroy's hostility to cosmopolitanism is not consistent nor are his objections to the idea developed. In sum, it seems reasonable to refer to Gilroy's vision of conviviality as 'cosmopolitan conviviality'. Gilroy's attitude to melancholia is more intriguing. *After Empire* is, after all, ostensibly an engagement with this concept (a fact made more prominent in the title of the US version, *Postcolonial Melancholia*). Gilroy borrows his definition of the term from Alexander and Margarete Mitscherlich, who applied melancholia to the inability to 'mourn' and, hence, come to terms with, the Nazi past, they identified in post-Second World War Germany.[56] Gilroy translates this idea across to post-imperial Britain, a country unable to mourn (and, hence, come to terms with) the violence of its imperial past. However, while the Mitscherlichs' account detailed a culture of turning away from the past – what they called 'breaking all affective bridges with the immediate past' – Gilroy's material is very different.[57] The relationship to the past he details is one of yearning, illustrated most forcefully by his numerous references to Briton's desire to relive the national drama of the Second World War. These examples display, not a breaking of 'affective bridges', but an attraction to the past, indeed a revelling in it. Moreover, Gilroy offers little evidence of the kind of contemplative, quiet pleasure in sadness traditionally associated with melancholia. Although the two terms overlap and do much the same work in his book, it is the nostalgic nature of British culture and not simply its melancholia, that Gilroy engages and challenges in *After Empire*.

Gilroy does, though, begin to disentangle the varieties of melancholia. In a tantalizingly short passage he employs Mathew Arnold's (1867) poem 'Dover Beach' to make a distinction between Victorian and contemporary melancholia. Arnold's version of melancholy, Gilroy tells us, offered 'consolation in the private and intimate places where romantic love and fidelity could offset the worst effects of warfare, turbulence, and vanished certitude'.[58] Gilroy contrasts this disposition with the contemporary British scene:

> We can say that Arnold's articulate melancholy was shaped by the culture of that Empire in its emergent phase. It combined with and was complemented by the older melancholy of the poor, the expropriated, the empressed and the abjected which is still remembered in the folk music of England. An altogether different pattern became visible once the imperial system shifted into undeniable decline. Victorian melancholy started to yield to melancholia as soon as the natives and savages began to appear and make demands for recognition in the Empire's metropolitan core.[59]

This passage is the only one I can find in *After Empire* where Gilroy does not equate a sense of loss with political conservatism. The historical shift he proposes – from melancholy to melancholia – recognizes the longevity of emotions of loss and regret while reinforcing the argument that, today, nostalgia is a reactionary and morbid cultural current. However, Gilroy's periodization needs to be questioned. Given the presence of themes of national decadence and decay in late Victorian literature it would be more plausible to argue that melancholia reached its apogee with the rise of Empire.[60] Such a perspective might also usefully draw out the connections between nostalgia and imperial cosmopolitanism. For the imperial project was, in part, one of deracination; a cultural uprooting both for imperialists and their subjects that simultaneously excited sentiments of loss, transgression and progress. These insights are foreclosed, both by Gilroy's historical despatching of 'good melancholia' to a poetic moment in the late 1860s, and by his political categorization of contemporary nostalgia as a right-wing aliment that needs to be treated with a dose of cultural destabilization and transnationalism. Hence, Gilroy's brief concession to the possibility of radical nostalgia is suggestive, not of the utility of arguing that British culture moved from a good sense of loss to a bad sense of loss 'as soon as the natives and savages began to appear', but of the difficulties attendant on any generalization about nostalgia being, at any one time, either progressive or reactionary.

Sick Nostalgia versus Convivial Youth

Nostalgia was first diagnosed as a medical condition so it is appropriate that Gilroy applies a clinical vocabulary to its various symptoms. The contrast he draws between backward-looking Britain and forward-looking conviviality is between a 'neurotic', 'pathological' culture, and a 'restored and healthier Britain'.[61]

Gilroy's target is Briton's unhealthy fascination with romanticized images of the nation's past glories. Yet because his analysis is premised on the opposition of old and new, the ageing and the youthful, melancholia and an 'emergent Britain', his political focus looses precision.[62] It rolls together seeming any and all aspects of British life that do not conform to his vision of the 'convivial metropolitan cultures of the country's young people', into a landscape that is 'anxious, fearful, or violent'.[63] Gilroy's Britain is a diseased and ugly society: the 'arterial system of [its] political body' is 'obstructed'; its attitude to strangers characterized by a 'violence and hostility'.[64]

[A]n anxious melancholy mood has become part of the cultural infrastructure of the place, an immovable ontological counterpart to the nation-defining ramparts of the white cliffs of Dover.[65]

The youthful Britons that will scale these 'ramparts' are not unfamiliar. Gilroy takes an established radical stereotype – that urban youth are the heartland of rebellion – and applies it to 'the chaotic pleasures of the convivial postcolonial urban world'.[66] In this way one of the paradoxes of left-wing hostility to nostalgia is replayed: intimate, organic community is repudiated only to be reinvented in a radical guise.

For Gilroy this is a doubly awkward manoeuvre, for by linking street-level, conviviality to multiculturalism he is connecting it to what, in Britain, is a well-established institutional and municipal ideology. This difficulty may help explain his insistence that, while authentic multiculturalism emerges from 'ordinary' people, politicians, with their 'strategic crocodile tears', traduce such efforts.

There is no governmental interest in the forms of conviviality and intermixture that appear to have evolved spontaneously and organically from the interventions of anti-racists and the ordinary multiculture of the postcolonial metropolis.[67]

This depiction is developed by Gilroy into a vision of popular resistance. The 'spontaneous tolerance and openness evident in the underworld of Britain's convivial culture' becomes a recognizable resource for agitational activity.[68]

The enduring quality of resistance among the young is no trivial matter . . . [I]t communicates something of the irreducibly changed conditions in which factors of identity and solidarity that derive from class, gender, sexuality, and region have made a strong sense of racial difference unthinkable to the point of absurdity.[69]

Gilroy's reference to 'factors of identity and solidarity' reminds us of his broader quest for 'planetary humanism'.[70] However, both phrases have a fugitive quality. They suggest a familiar political paradigm of struggle and transcendence. Yet, apart from their apparent power to overcome 'racial difference', the nature and consequences of the various 'factors' Gilroy lists remain ill-defined. Young people's 'enduring quality of resistance' is evoked but remains frustratingly unclear.

'White or black' young men are Gilroy's vehicle of change and the site of nearly all his depictions of 'conviviality'. One of the striking ironies of the book arises from his minimal concession to the fracturing of notions of blackness, or the rise of religion as an axis of conflict. A one sentence depiction of those 'young black Europeans' who are 'willing to hitch their hopes for a just world to the absurd engine of an Islamic revolution' suffices to dispatch the ambitions of Islamism.[71] Gilroy shows even less interest in Britons of Asian, Chinese, Arab, Scottish, Welsh, Irish or of continental European origin. These groups remain as invisible in *After Empire* as they were in Gilroy's earlier accounts of 'multiracial' Britain.[72] The intellectual task facing us today, Gilroy tells us, is to explain how 'the brutal, dualistic opposition between black and white became entrenched and has retained its grip'.[73] Yet while Gilroy's vision of the 'warring totalities of blackness and whiteness' secures blackness as a location of struggle, it undermines the reach and generosity of Gilroy's own 'convivial' disposition.[74] His attempt to rescue the radical subject clashes with his claims of 'radical openness', leaving readers with the impression that Gilroy's vision of political agency is premised not on 'anti-essentialism', but on ethnic and age particularism.[75]

Gilroy's celebration of the convivial culture of ordinary young people is also weakened by the fact that, although his main argument leads us to expect a detailed depiction of this new social realm, this account never arrives. There is a blankness at the heart of *After Empire*: the vigorous and intimate street-level creativity constantly alluded to remains distant and unreal. The vignettes that Gilroy does offer have a generalizing quality. For example, he suggests that 'many British youth have been delivered to a place, as Nitin Sawhney memorably put it, "beyond skin"'; supporting this idea with the observation that,

> Electronic dance music, almost always without words, has been a dominant form during most of these years. Its technological base and its metropolitan conditions of existence have promoted a spontaneous and ordinary hybridity that has, as The Streets continually remind us, been alloyed with recreational drug use on an extraordinary scale.[76]

Gilroy's reference to pop band The Streets is supplemented by explorations of the television comedy character Ali G and the BBC comedy 'The Office'. This material is used to flesh out the meaning of convivial Britain. Gilroy's focus on television as the locus on conviviality may be said to offer an accessible guide to the book's political journey. However, I would suggest that it also represents a telling absence. The non-appearance of the ordinary, creative youth upon whose shoulders Gilroy has laid such burdens (for they are said to represent the future and are required to overcome the past) creates a phantom presence. Gilroy has sketched the part and set the scene but the stage remains empty. We are left with memories of struggles from earlier periods, when young rebels really did occupy the streets; when books on radical politics in Britain did not dwindle into accounts of television comedies.

Loss in After Empire

After a consideration of Gilroy's 'planetary humanism' Don Robotham concludes that Gilroy's politics have 'nothing to do with notions of a proletarian internationalism springing from the socialist tradition'.[77] Robotham arrives at this judgement in response to Gilroy's earlier book, *Against Race*. However, if one traces Gilroy's work through from his early anti-racist radicalism to the present day, one finds a consistent socialist internationalism. *After Empire* confirms this political location.

'[T]his book', he tells us, 'offers an unorthodox defence of [the] twentieth-century utopia of tolerance, peace, and mutual regard.'[78] Gilroy's portrait of the 'utopia' he wishes to defend – before the 'flight from socialistic principles' – has all the hallmarks of nostalgia. It is soft-edged, regretful and yearning.[79] Once,

> Neither women nor workers were committed to a country. They turned away from the patriotism of national states because they had found larger loyalties.[80]

Back then, 'Socialism and Feminism . . . came into conflict with a merely national focus because they understood political solidarity to require translocal connection.'[81]

The fundamental point is that today, cosmopolitan estrangement and democracy-enriching dissent are not prized as civic assets. They are just routine signs of subversion and degeneration.[82]

Indeed, while Gilroy provides a long list of 'emergent' forms of 'convivial culture' in music and television, it is striking that when he turns towards contemporary *political* allies his enthusiasm dries up. Even the 'tolerant, humane, pluralistic and cosmopolitan' elements within 'black political culture' have deserted the cause.

They are still present in diminishing quantities, but they are muted these days. They have to take a back seat behind simpler, noisier, and for many, more attractive options that are in step if not always in tune with the mainstream sentiment of consumer capitalism.[83]

Thus, ironically, the youthful new culture Gilroy wishes to celebrate becomes a site of regret and loss: in today's individualistic society and 'beleaguered multiculture' Gilroy offers himself as a lost prophet of 'larger loyalties' against a 'currently fashionable' insularity.[84]

Nostalgia is not a minor theme in *After Empire*. The book strains to identify itself with the emergent and forward-looking and, by so doing, allows a hostility to nostalgia to shape its political and intellectual structure. At the same time, *After Empire* is shot through with a sense of loss. The past is deployed as a place of certainty, of community and of morality, and used to critique the present. The presence of loss in *After Empire* may be tied to the specific contemporary context in which the book was written, a time when socialists of many different stripes are turning to the past for compensation and inspiration. However, Gilroy's antagonism to nostalgia is indicative of the fact that the presence of loss is still an unacknowledged feature of the modern radical imagination.

Conclusion: Sharing Loss

The past that looms largest in *After Empire* is not that of the British empire but of socialism. 'Multiculture' is made to do the work of popular solidarity and resistance; it is fashioned into a vehicle of resistance which both challenges and somehow renews the socialist lineage. The clichés of youthful resistance, the anachronistic insistence on 'warring totalities', combine with Gilroy's melodramatic vignettes of the sins of melancholia, to create a pressing sense of nostalgia's unacknowledged presence.

This chapter has approached *After Empire* not as a unique intervention but as emerging from two current on the left, cosmopolitanism and anti-racism. The latter was introduced in its British form while the former was approached as a term in an international academic debate. However, in both we found processes of recreation in which tropes of community and militancy were recast and reimagined in new forms. It is not my argument that this process may be reduced to nostalgia. My intention, rather, has been to pull out the nostalgic threads within these projects.

There are a number of implications that flow from this analysis. Many turn on the way radical anti-racism politically characterizes the past and present. The framing of radicalism as necessarily focused upon 'emergent' and youthful groups and the related association of capitalism and authoritarianism with the nostalgic and the old is a central trope of twentieth-century socialism. Yet this approach relies on a set of questionable stereotypes.

Over the past decade, a variety of survey evidence has suggested that young people may, in fact, be more politically conservative than their parents.[85] The figures of the 'young rebel', the 'black rebel', of 'communities of resistance' fighting for a 'new society', as well as the more recent notion of anti-authoritarian hybrid 'everyday multicultures', provide radicals with a set of assumptions and expectations through which to make sense of social change and the political character of different ethnic and age groups. However, the conflation of nostalgia with conservatism, and the related hostility to all signs of yearning and loss, creates a myopic and, ultimately, self-defeating, view of contemporary political and emotional landscapes.

The political identity of both multiculturalism and cosmopolitanism is far from settled. The attempt to cast cosmopolitanism as vernacular, everyday or working class marks many recent interventions on the topic. James Clifford points out that 'the project of comparing and translating different traveling cultures need not be class or ethno-centric'.[86] Uma Kothari's research on migrant peddlers suggest that '[t]heir lived realities disrupt the predominately elitist and Eurocentric characterizations of cosmopolitanism'.[87] Yet these bottom-up visions have to work hard to counter the fact that it is elites who provide the most well-developed examples of international knowledge and ease of mobility. The insistence that such things need not be *only* associated with the wealthy takes on a wishful quality when set in the context of the jet-setting image cultivated by the rich and the relative parochialism of so many 'traditional' societies. For Craig Calhoun,

> Cosmopolitanism – though not necessarily cosmopolitan democracy – is now largely the project of capitalism, and it flourishes in the top management of multinational corporations and even more in the consulting firms that serve them. Such cosmopolitanism often joins elites across national borders while ordinary people live in local communities.[88]

Even Massey, who allies Gilroy's perspective to her own interest in creating an anti-essentialist senses of place is perplexed by his insistence on the dominance in Britain of a gloomy, backward-looking sense of loss. Massey points out that,

> [T]he financial City [in London] and the constellation of interests and social forces that surround it are by no means melancholic. Those who are at the heart of (this aspect of) London's claim to global citydom are triumphant and celebratory, as they pick up and build upon the threads of an older imperial order.[89]

Massey's point could be extended further. Until the financial crisis of late 2008, the political and economic life of 'New Labour' (and 'New Conservative') Britain was aggressively forward-looking. This neo-liberal and multicultural success story drew in 'young exiles' from abroad attracted by the competitive and meritocratic 'Anglo model'; exiles who found something 'dynamic and cosmopolitan' in the United Kingdom's (or at least London's) brash multiculture of consumption.[90]

Left cosmopolitanism is a paradoxical political form. Its attempts to dispatch notions of settled community and welcome a new dawn of flexibility and instability suggest it has given up the struggle against capitalism. These ideas become even more questionable when we observe the powerful yet unacknowledged flows of nostalgia that wash through the work of many cosmopolitan authors. Cosmopolitanism is a convincingly modern political ideology. But its appropriation by the left is far less plausible. Calhoun argues that,

> A through going cosmopolitanism might indeed bring concern for the fate of all humanity to the fore, but a more attenuated cosmopolitanism is likely to leave us lacking the old sources of solidarity without adequate new ones.[91]

As we saw in Chapter Two, in his historical work Calhoun made the case that traditional attachments and solidarities are a necessary resource for the poor. He connected this argument with another, that nostalgia can enable political radicalism. We do not have to accept every aspect of Calhoun's interpretation of the development of political consciousness among radical artisans in the early nineteenth century, to appreciate that his work is part of an important reassessment of the assumption that deracination creates the conditions for militancy. Calhoun's turn towards the critical interrogation of cosmopolitanism continues his interest in opening up this orthodoxy.

Left cosmopolitanism is, in part, a restatement of a long-standing set of radical suspicions of nostalgia. Yet it also takes these suspicions further, into a post-modern utopia of the kaleidoscopic 'multitude'. To end this chapter I will probe a little further the popular constituency and consequences of this vision in Britain.

Recent years have witnessed the experience of immigration and exile being discussed in terms that suggest that, far from being a problem to be overcome, nostalgia is an inevitable component of emotional responses to modern population mobility.[92] Drawing up battle lines between racist nostalgics and the anti-racist proponents of a 'new society' may make sense in certain circumstances and certain places. But it seems to be an inadequate paradigm through which to understand 'street-level' responses to globalization. In Britain the need to acknowledge nostalgia has also emerged in explorations of 'progressive patriotism' and, even more controversially, in wide-ranging attacks on the left's supposed contempt for the fear and sense of loss experienced by the 'indigenous' working class.[93] Some of the seeds of this latter approach may be detected in the work of Jeremy Seabrook. In the 1970s Seabrook produced a set of ethnographic studies on a generation of working-class people who, to judge by his interviews, felt displaced and devalued.[94] The result is that,

> [P]eople talk as though they were under siege; victims of some universal and impenetrable conspiracy. A fictive sense of shared values evolve ad hoc to fill the vacuum which ought to be occupied by a shared sense of social purpose. These values are reductive and inconsistent; often vengeful and cruel.[95]

More recently, Dench and Gavron ignited opprobrium from sections of the left, and praise from the British press, for their account of the way a left-wing 'urban elite' has stereotyped English heritage working-class Londoners as a nostalgic and, hence, reactionary social force:

> [T]he old Bethnal Greeners have been condemned for their 'irrational' attachment to locality . . . Whites resentful of loss of local rights have been discredited politically by being represented as pathologically inadequate, not capable of living alongside people different from themselves.[96]

Although identifying such locally 'attached' groups as 'white' may be misleading (both in terms of contemporary patterns of immigration and indigenous identity, which has often turned on attachment to Englishness) Dench and Gavron appear to have hit upon a rich seam of class resentment.[97] Without an understanding of the chronic nature of nostalgia within the modern imagination, of the inextricable ties between resistance to uprooting and resistance to capitalism, the radical anti-racist response to such fears is inevitably dismissive. Certainly, the temptation to suggest that these concerns can be easily resolved – that the yearning for intimacy and roots will go away as population mobility increases – needs to be resisted. The more difficult but, I think, necessary response is to admit that nostalgia is a shared and inevitable emotion in an era of rapid and enforced change. Across different ethnic, age and political groups, displacement and uprooting are painful processes (especially for the least affluent, for whom locality, community and attachment are not dispensable aspirations). Being 'bandied about from pillar to post' is the modern experience. Yet so too is nostalgia. A sense of loss is a necessary burden. The cosmopolitan left carry this burden, as do the critics of cosmopolitanism. The challenge is not to discard or embrace it but to recognize it.

Notes

1. P. Gilroy, *After Empire: Melancholia or Convivial Culture?*, (London: Routledge, 2004); P. Gilroy, *Postcolonial Melancholia*, (New York: Columbia University Press, 2005)
2. C. MacCabe, 'Paul Gilroy: against the grain', http://www.opendemocracy.net/globaliza-tion-Literature/gilroy_3465.jsp, accessed 20.09.2009; A. Beckett, 'History lessons: British multiculturalism is under attack. Andy Beckett assesses Paul Gilroy's timely analysis, After Empire' *The Guardian*, (Saturday, 11 December, 2004); J. Ford, 'Paul Gilroy, *After Empire* (London: Routledge, 2004) and Huey P Newton & V I Lenin (ed. Amy Gdala), *Revolutionary Intercommunalism & the Right of Nations to Self-Determination* (London: Superscript, 2004)'.
3. Gilroy, *After Empire*, 107, 131.
4. R. Hakluyt, *The Principal Navigations, Voyages, Traffiques and Discoveries of the English Nation*, Volume 1, (Whitefish: Kessinger Publishing, 2004), 54.
5. J. Diderot and D. d'Alembert, *Encyclopédie* (1751–1772), available at: http://encyclope-die.uchicago.edu/, accessed 29.09.2009.

    The French original indicates that the ambitious claims of the cosmopolite are being offered with a wry smile:

    COSMOPOLITE, (*Gram. & Philosoph.*) On se sert quelquefois de ce nom en plaisant-ant, pour signifier *un homme qui n'a point de demeure fixe*, ou bien *un homme qui n'est étranger nulle part*. Il vient de χόσμος, *monde*, & πόλις, *ville*.

6. Cited by Lasch, *The True and Only Heaven*, 123.
7. K. Marx and F. Engels, *The Communist Manifesto*, (Harmondsworth: Penguin, 1967), 83–4.
8. M. Nussbaum, 'Patriotism and cosmopolitanism', in J. Cohen (Ed.), *For the Love of Country*, (Boston: Beacon, 1996), 15.
9. Mignolo, 'The many faces of cosmopolis', 744.

10. 'S. Pollock, H. Bhabha, C. Breckenridge and D. Chakrabarty, 'Cosmopolitanisms', *Public Culture*, 12, 3, (2000), 580.
11. M. Hardt and A. Negri, *Empire*, (Cambridge: Harvard University Press, 2000), 413.
12. R. Niezen, 'Postcolonialism and the utopian imagination', *Israel Affairs*, 13, 4, (2007), 721.
13. G. Agamben, *The Coming Community*, (Minneapolis: University of Minnesota, 1993).
14. D. Flynn, 'Beyond boundaries', *Chartist*, (January/February, 2008), 30.
15. U. Hannerz, 'Cosmopolitans and locals in world culture', in M. Featherstone (Ed.), *World Cultures*, (London: Sage, 1990), 239.
16. S. Scheffler, 'Conceptions of cosmopolitanism', *Utilitas*, 11, 3, (1999), 257–8.
17. U. Beck, *The Cosmopolitan Vision*, (Cambridge: Polity Press, 2006), 23.
18. D. Held, *Democracy and the Global Order*, (Stanford, CA: Stanford University Press, 1995), 234.
19. Cited by Bhabha, 'Notes on vernacular cosmopolitanism', 43.
20. F. Jameson, 'Third-World literature in the era of multinational capitalism', *Social Text*, 15, (Autumn, 1986).
21. J. Wenzel, 'Remembering the past's future: anti-imperialist nostalgia and some versions of the Third World', *Cultural Critique*, 62, (2006), 15.
22. Ibid.
23. D. Massey, 'A global sense of place', in T. Oakes and P. Price (Eds), *The Cultural Geography Reader*, (London: Routledge, 2008), 261.
24. Bhabha, 'Notes on vernacular cosmopolitanism', 42.
25. Ibid., 46.
26. Ibid., 44.
27. Ibid., 46.
28. See Bonnett, *Radicalism, Anti-Racism and Representation*.
29. S. Hall, C. Critcher, T. Jefferson, J. Clarke and B. Roberts, *Policing the Crisis: Mugging, the State and Law and Order*, (London: Macmillan, 1978), 394.
30. P. Gilroy, *There Ain't No Black in the Union Jack: The Cultural Politics of Race and Nation*, (London: Hutchinson, 1987).
31. Ibid., 69.
32. A. Sivanandan, *Communities of Resistance: Writings on Black Struggles for Socialism*, (London, Verso, 1990); Centre for Contemporary Cultural Studies, *The Empire Strikes Back: Race and Racism in 70s Britain*, (London: Hutchinson/Centre for Contemporary Cultural Studies, 1982).
33. ALTARF [All London Teachers Against Racism and Fascism] (Ed.), *Challenging Racism*, (London: ALTARF, 1984); K. Ebbutt and B. Pearce (Eds), *Racism and Schools: Contributions to a Discussion*, (London: Communist Party of Great Britain, undated); C. Mullard, *Race, Power and Resistance*, (London: Routledge and Kegan Paul, 1985); F. Dhondy, 'Teaching young blacks', in F. Dhondy, B. Besse and L. Hassan (Eds), *The Black Explosion in British Schools*, (London: Race Today Publications, 1982).
34. Chaliand, *Revolution in the Third World*, xv.
35. P-A. Taguieff, 'L'immigrationnisme, ou la dernière utopie des bien-pensants', available at: http://www.communautarisme.net/L-immigrationnisme,-ou-la-derniere-utopie-des-bien-pensants_a754.html, accessed 28.07.2009. Taguieff's analysis is developed in *Les contre-réactionnaires: Le progressisme entre illusion et imposture* (Paris: Denoel, 2007).
36. See Trevor Carter, *Shattering Illusions: West Indians in British politics*, (London: Lawrence & Wishart, 1986).

37. J. Bourne and A. Sivanandan, 'Cheerleaders and ombudsmen: the sociology of race relations in Britain', *Race and Class*, 21, 4, (1980), 345.

38. Sivanandan, *Communities of Resistance*, 70.

39. Ibid., 67.

40. H. Carby, 'Schooling in Babylon', in *The Empire Strikes Back: Race and Racism in 70s Britain*, (London: Hutchinson/Centre for Contemporary Cultural Studies, 1982), 208.

41. G. Clark and N. Subhan, 'Some definitions', in K. Ebbutt and B. Pearce (Eds), *Racism and Schools: Contributions to a Discussion*, (London: Communist Party of Great Britain, undated), 33.

42. Ibid.

43. T. Modood, ' "Black", racial equality and Asian identity', *New Community*, 14, 3, (1989).

44. For example, P. Dodgson and D. Stewart, 'Multiculturalism or anti-racist teaching: a question of alternatives', *Multiracial Education*, 9, 3, (1981).

45. P. Gilroy, *The Black Atlantic*, (London: Verso, 1993).

46. P. Gilroy, *Small Acts: Thoughts on the Politics of Black Cultures*, (London: Serpent's Tail, 1993), 164.

47. P. Gilroy, 'The end of anti-racism', W. Ball and J. Solomos (Eds), *Race and Local Politics*, (London: Macmillan, 1990).

48. Gilroy, *After Empire*, xi.

49. Ibid.

50. Ibid.

51. Ibid., 98.

52. Deborah Mutch, 'The *Merrie England* Triptych: Robert Blatchford, Edward Fay and the didactic use of Clarion fiction', *Victorian Periodicals Review*, 38, 1, (2005), 97. In another interesting historical echo, Andrew Blake depicts what he calls 'Gilroy's hybrid utopia' as 'a post-post-colonial version of the Blitz mentality' (A. Blake, 'From nostalgia to postalgia: hybridity and its discontents in the work of Paul Gilroy and the Wachowski brothers', in J. Kuortti and J. Nyman (Eds), *Reconstructing Hybridity: Post-Colonial Studies in Transition*, (Amsterdam: Rodopi, 2007), 129.

53. Gilroy, *After Empire*, 17. A tone of dismissal and condescension seems to be habitual within radical critiques of post-imperial nostalgia. 'Mournful histories: narratives of postimperial melancholy', a paper by Ian Baucom (*Modern Fiction Studies*, 42, 2, 1996), that prefigures *After Empire*, drips with sarcasm. For Baucom the nostalgic is a risible and mediocre figure, with a 'teary eye towards the image of a vanishing England' (271) and a sad fetish for 'chewing England's picturesque cud' (286).

54. Gilroy, *After Empire*, 131.

55. S. Knowles, 'Macrocosm-opolitanism? Gilroy, Appiah, and Bhabha: the unsettling generality of cosmopolitan ideas', *Postcolonial Text*, 3, 4 (2007); Gilroy, *After Empire*, 4, 9.

56. A. Mitscherlich and M. Mitscherlich, *The Inability to Mourn: Principles of Collective Behaviour*, (New York: Grove Press, 1967).

57. Gilroy, *After Empire*, 26.

58. Ibid., 99.

59. Ibid.

60. For example, M. Nordau, *Degeneration*, (Lincoln: University of Nebraska Press, 1993). See also J. Chamberlain, and S. Gilman (Eds), *Degeneration: The Dark Side of Progress*, (New York: Colombia University Press, 1985).

61. Gilroy, *After Empire*, 97, 107, 166.

62. Ibid., 104.
63. Ibid., 131, 13.
64. Ibid., 98, 166.
65. Ibid., 15.
66. Ibid., 167.
67. Ibid., 136.
68. Ibid., 144.
69. Ibid., 132.
70. See also P. Gilroy, *Against Race: Imagining Political Culture beyond the Color Line,* (Cambridge: Harvard University Press, 2000).
71. Gilroy, *After Empire,* 144.
72. Gilroy, *There Ain't No Black in the Union Jack.*
73. Gilroy, *After Empire,* 31.
74. Ibid., 39.
75. Ibid., xi.
76. Ibid., 132. Another statement of Gilroy's interest in a street-level and anti-authoritarian scrabbling of fixed images of racial and national identity, also refers to the pop band The Streets,

    In The Streets' playful ontology, race is not an identity that can fix or contain individuals; it is a practice that can be understood through a comparison with the strategic choice of drug that a variety of person opts for in a particular situation: 'whether you're white or black; smoke weed, chase brown, toot rock'. (105)

77. D. Robotham, 'Cosmopolitanism and planetary humanism: the strategic essentialism of Paul Gilroy', *The South Atlantic Quarterly,* 104, 3, (2005), 576.
78. Gilroy, *After Empire,* 2.
79. Ibid., 135.
80. Ibid., 5.
81. Ibid., 5.
82. Ibid., 27.
83. Ibid., 61.
84. Ibid., xi, 27. In *The Black Atlantic* Gilroy also refers to 'the tragic popularity of ideas about the integrity and purity of cultures' (7). In a similar reference later in the book he makes a call 'to embrace the fragmentation of the self (doubling and spitting) which modernity seems to promote', but again suggests that 'this option is less fashionable these days. Appeals to the notion of purity as the basis of racial solidarity are more popular' (188).
85. E. Noe and M. Gannon, 'Younger voters are more conservative, but less likely to vote on election day', available at: http://www.siue.edu/ALESTLE/library/FALL2000/november2/yvoters.html, accessed 29.05.06; R. Allison, 'Teenagers react against "anything goes" society', *The Guardian* (11 March, 2004); J. Glassman, 'U.S. youths turning normal and conservative', available at: http://findarticles.com/p/articles/mi_qn4188/is_20040706/ai_n11464766, accessed 05.05.08.
86. J. Clifford, 'Travelling cultures', in L. Grossberg, C. Nelson and P. Treichler (Eds), *Cultural Studies,* (London: Routledge, 1992).
87. U. Kothari, 'Global peddlers and local networks: migrant cosmopolitanisms', *Society and Space,* 26, (2008), 500. See also Pnina Werbner, 'Global pathways: working class

cosmopolitans and the creation of transnational ethnic worlds', *Social Anthropology*, 7, 1, (1999).

88. C. Calhoun, 'The class consciousness of frequent travellers: toward a critique of actually existing cosmopolitanism', *The South Atlantic Quarterly*, 101, 4, (2002), 890.

89. D. Massey, *World City*, (Cambridge: Polity Press, 2006), 175–6.

90. Quotes from A. Seager and A. Balakrishnan, 'Young exiles embrace the Anglo model', *The Guardian*, (Saturday, 8 April, 2006).

91. Calhoun, 'The class consciousness of frequent travelers', 873.

92. S. Akhtar, 'The immigrant, the exile, and the experience of nostalgia', *Journal of Applied Psychoanalytic Studies*, 1, 2, (1999); V. Volkan, 'Nostalgia as a linking phenomenon', *Journal of Applied Psychoanalytic Studies*, 1, 2, (1999); A. Ritivoi, *Yesterday's Self: Nostalgia and the Immigrant Identity*, (Oxford: Rowman and Littlefield, 2002). See also P. Geschiere, *The Perils of Belonging: Autochthony, Citizenship, and Exclusion in Africa and Europe*, (Chicago: Chicago University Press, 2009).

93. B. Bragg, *The Progressive Patriot: A Search for Belonging*, (London: Bantam Press, 2006); David Goodhart, *Progressive Nationalism: Citizenship and the Left*, (London: Demos, 2006).

94. J. Seabrook, *City Close-Up*, (London: Allen Lane, 1971); J. Seabrook, *What went Wrong? Working People and the Ideals of the Labour Movement?*, (London: Victor Gollancz, 1978). See L. Spencer, 'British working class fiction: the sense of loss and the potential for transformation', *Socialist Register*, 24, (1988).

95. Seabrook, *What went Wrong?*, 71.

96. G. Dench and K. Gavron, *The New East End: Kinship, Race and Conflict*, (London: Profile Books, 2006), 212–13.

97. See also M. Collins, *The Likes of Us: A Biography of the White Working Class*, (London: Granta Books, 2004). Gilroy accused Collins of being an 'intellectual outrider of the BNP [British National Party]' cited by L. Taylor 'Low blows of a class warrior', *The Independent*, (Friday, 16 July, 2004).

PART THREE

CHAPTER FIVE

Yearning at the Extremes: Situationist Nostalgia

Introduction

The Situationist International (1957–1972: hereafter 'SI') presented itself as 'the most danger-ous subversion there ever was'.[1] A central component of the situationists' provocation was their desire to extend Marx's message and apply it to both the Stalinist and Trotskyist left. In *De la misère en milieu étudiant*, an SI declaration issued in 1966, they announce,

> This revolution must definitively break with its own prehistory and derive all its poetry from the future. Little groups of 'militants' claiming to represent the authentic Bolshevik heritage are voices from beyond the grave; in no way do they herald the future.[2]

The first page of the second issue of *Internationale Situationniste* is given over to an arti-cle whose title expresses what has come to be regarded as a traditional revolutionary hos-tility: 'Les souvenirs au-dessous de tout'.[3] The SI positioned themselves as 'the partisans of forgetting'.[4]

Today the situationists' nostalgia is almost as stark as their revolutionary zeal.[5] Yet this increasingly unavoidable aspect of their project remains difficult territory. The situationists' nostalgia is no sooner noted as it is explained away as further testament to their quixotic genius. It has been consigned to the status of strategy, reflecting the situationists' understand-ing of the politically disruptive, 'uncanny' qualities of the outmoded for David Pinder and the role of the past as 'a poisoned weapon to be used against the existing order of things' for Michael Löwy.[6]

This chapter offers a closer, and more sceptical, reading of the place of nostalgia within this group of postwar avant-garde Marxist revolutionaries. By doing so it offers a case-study of the intimate yet contradictory relationship between, on the one hand, an attachment to the past and, on the other, an ultra-radical desire to commence a new society. I shall argue that nostalgia had both a productive and disruptive role in situationist thought; that it enabled some of their key insights yet also introduced incoherence and tensions into their political project (in part, because it was unacknowledged). This productive and disruptive relation-ship will be explored through two central situationist themes, the idea of the spectacle and the critique of urbanism. These two examples also allow me to show how the form and object of nostalgia can be identified in two distinct (if interconnected) ways within situationism. The idea of the spectacle contains what I describe as an 'unrooted' nostalgia; a free-floating sense of loss that presents permanent marginality and 'the alienated life' as a political identity (and there are few who claimed a greater sense of alienation than the group's principal theorist, Guy Debord, 1931–1994). The SI's concern for the demise of the city in the wake of modern-izing bulldozers, suggests a different tendency of nostalgic form and object, a tendency that evokes specific places and particular experiences and memories. 'Whoever sees the banks of the Seine', explained Debord in 1989, 'sees our grief'.[7]

The Spectacle as Loss

The situationists have become identified with one central explanatory concept, 'the spectacle'. Debord explained the idea as follows:

> The first phase of the domination of the economy over social life brought into the definition of all human realisation the obvious degradation of being and having. The present phase of total occupation of social life by the accumulated results of the economy leads to a generalised sliding of having into appearing, from which all actual 'having' must draw its immediate prestige and its ultimate function.[8]

The spectacle implies a society of pacified viewers, of consumers of images. Many academic interpretations in the 1980s and 1990s sought to elucidate Debord's notion of the spectacle by claiming that it presaged post-modern ideas of the 'end of the real'.[9] However, such comparisons mislead by drawing attention away from the fact that the SI was above all a political group, engaged in revolutionary activity.

The SI's members were not simply offering a critique of authenticity, they were seeking to re-establish it. For Debord the task of the revolution is to reintroduce history. *Society of the Spectacle* draws deeply on the Hegelian notion of 'historical time' to argue that 'the bourgeoisie made known to society and imposed on it an irreversible historical time'.[10] Within 'spectacular society' historical time has been overturned, masked and distorted by 'frozen time', an anti-historical 'false consciousness of time'.[11] Thus the revolution becomes synonymous with the reawakening of historical time, albeit with the proletarian and libertarian characteristics of unalienated experience:

> In the demand to live the historical time which it makes, the proletariat finds the simple unforgettable centre of its revolutionary project; and every attempt (thwarted until now) to realise this project marks a point of possible departure for new historical life.[12]

Yet this theorization is suffused by another sensibility, namely a sense of absolute loss. This historical melancholia sustains *Society of the Spectacle* and becomes explicit and dominant in Debord's later works.[13] Debord's revolutionary intent required that he identify and place some hope in those processes and social groups able to reintroduce historical time and articulate 'the poetry of the future'. Yet the scale and characterization of loss that Debord depicted undermines this political logic, both in terms of his barely repressed despair with the present and with his tendency to conflate technology and alienation.

Before teasing out these themes in more detail it is necessary to establish that Debord's version of situationist thought was contested both within the SI and by a number of breakaway factions.[14] Recent years have seen a reorientation of interest among some British and other European activists away from the 'authoritarian' Debord and 'French situationism' and towards the more sensuous and irrationalist radicalism of 'Scandinavian situationism'.[15] Something of the appeal of the latter is intimated by the quotation from Christian Dotremont that Asger Jorn, the Danish painter who was Scandinavian situationism's principal theorist, wrote on, and used as a title for, one of his early oil paintings: 'There are more things in the earth of a picture than in the heaven of aesthetic theory' (1947). Jorn and his allies expressed a hostility towards purely abstract theorization, a position that led Jorn to an attempt to extricate the idea of 'value' from Marxist suspicion and imagine it as a revolutionary attribute rooted in the human capacity for creativity.[16] In Jens Jorgen Thorsen's terms, 'situationism is art'.[17] Thorsen went on to explain that, unlike the 'Parisian Situationists' who believe 'human beings are produced by their environment', in fact 'the continuous realisation of new possibilities of inter-human activity are the source of life'. Through such notions, the so-called Second Situationist International, distanced themselves from the bleak rationalism of Debord's concept of the spectacle. However, the nostalgic content of the 'Jornist' project is both more obvious and, I would suggest, less intriguing than the dominant 'Debordist' line. The 'Scandinavians'' cultural reference points – which are typically exotic and permeated with an interest in folk and shamanic traditions that contain 'the rhythm of life' – place them within a well-established avant-garde primitivist tradition.[18]

The writings of Guy Debord and the idea of a society of near total commodity-based reification – the 'society of the spectacle' – are likely to remain the most influential legacies of situationist thought. This status derives from their ability to give rhetorical shape to widely held concerns about the deepening of social alienation in late capitalism. The nostalgic content of the concept of the spectacle is not prominent, at least at first glance. My argument suggests that it has both a productive and disruptive presence, tendencies which worked themselves out within a nostalgic form that is characterized by a rootless melancholy, a revolutionary poetry of alienation. Further, this rootless melancholy forms an identity, a sense of the situationist as a sage yet uneasy spirit, a wise onlooker adrift in this 'present age'.

Nostalgia in and against the Idea of the Spectacle

'We are bored in the city, there is no longer any Temple of the Sun.' The opening lines of Chtcheglov's classic prototext of the situationist enterprise, 'Formulaire pour un urbanisme nouveau', evoke the romantic and surrealist heritage of the situationists.[19] This epigram also suggests how a longing for the marvellous can be structured round narratives of loss and dissatisfaction and, by implication, that a rhetoric of yearning is a central situationist resource. An absolute aversion to the present, a contempt for those who settle for less than an end to all forms of alienation: each are archetypal situationist themes and each is driven by a powerful sense of humanity's fall from both its potential and its mythic past.

The 'potlatch', 'lazy liberty without content' and 'festivals' that are 'the moment of a community's participation in the luxurious expenditure of life' were associated by Debord with a pre-historical, pre-political era.[20] Yet they are also evoked throughout situationist literature as (a) images of the kind of society that the situationists wished to create; and (b) the inverse of the spectacle, which is portrayed as a society without real festival, without real life and without real liberty. As this implies, 'primitive communism' for the situationists was more than just a prosaic, base form of communism (as it is within orthodox Marxism). It was a site of fantasy and wistful longing. Moreover, the spectacle, for Debord, is produced within and through modern technology. Although Debord's formal concern is with the co-option of technology by capitalism, he implies a much stronger critique.

From the automobile to television, all the goods selected by the spectacular system are also its weapons for a constant reinforcement of the conditions of isolation of 'lonely crowds'.[21]

Debord's analysis wraps technology so closely around the spectacle as to make it impossible to disentangle the two. It is hard not to read passages, such as the one cited above, without being 'reminded' of a simpler, more authentic era. A similar dynamic may be observed in respect to Debord's critique of the ahistoricism of the spectacle. For, although the desire to escape the spectacle as a 'frozen' society and to re-enter history is explained by Debord as a revolutionary process of supercession, he binds his glimpses of non-spectacular society tightly to a childlike Arcadia, creating a privileged place for the politics of loss. In *Society of the Spectacle* Debord argued that within the spectacle the 'reality of time has been replaced by the advertisement of time', a pseudo-experience based on consumerism and fashion.[22] Debord's *Comments on the Society on the Spectacle* sets both this yearning for real history and its connection to a sense of loss for the past into sharper relief:

> The precious advantage which the spectacle has acquired through the outlawing of history, from having driven the recent past into hiding, and from having made everyone forget the spirit of history within society, is above all the ability to cover its own tracks.[23]

The value of nostalgia is beginning to nudge its way to the fore in Debord's later works. However, the difficulty of admitting or acknowledging its presence remains immense. This awkwardness introduces us to the disruptive role of nostalgia within situationism. Nostalgia is something unnamed and, hence, untheorized; a desire which goes unchecked and that ultimately works against the coherence of the theory of the spectacle.

Situationist texts are littered with collisions between nostalgia and anti-nostalgia. Rapture with technological liberation and dreams of sparkling 'situationist cities' of the future tussled with critiques of the technological mediation of the spectacle. As I have already implied, the latter tendency showed a persistent tendency towards, what is, from a Marxist perspective, a reactionary repudiation of technology:

> [A]ll aspects of technological development of the present and, above all, the means of so-called communication, are designed to produce the greatest possible passive isolation of individuals.[24]

It is revealing that the historical figure Debord cited in *Society of the Spectacle* to symbolize the revolutionary hopes of his day is General Ludd, the phantom leader of a famously 'backward-looking' resistance movement. Those rebellious currents of the 1960s that 'are the portents' of revolution, Debord tells us, 'follow a new "General Ludd" who, this time, urges them to destroy the machines of permitted consumption'.[25]

In fact, Debord's evocation of 'a critique which does not compromise with any form of separate power anywhere in the world' sets its itself against so many aspects of modern life as to make an engagement with progressive change virtually impossible.[26] The 'totalism' of situationist thought, in which even anti-capitalist resistance is seen as another part of the spectacle, has often been attacked as a political dead-end.[27] Consideration of the presence of nostalgia in situationism may help us to grasp how this impasse arose. For while a sense of loss may have enabled much of the emotion and excitement we find in situationist rhetoric, it also resulted in a despairing sensibility. It is not coincidental that Debord's suicide in 1994 is represented in later sympathetic treatise on the movement as a culmination of situationist praxis.[28] The creation of a personal identity revolving round an attitude of political despair is etched deeply into Debord's intellectual journey. *Society of the Spectacle* offered precious few glimmers of hope, *Comments on the Society of the Spectacle* offers none. In a passage that brings together a technological and social pessimism, Debord tells us,

> There is no place left where people can discuss the realities which concern them, because they can never lastingly free themselves from the crushing forces organised to relay it. Nothing remains of the relatively independent judgement of those who once made up the world of learning . . . There is no longer even any incontestable bibliographical truth, and the computerised catalogues of national libraries are well-equipped to remove any residual traces. It is disorienting to consider what it meant to be a judge, a doctor or a historian not so long ago, and to recall that obligations and imperatives they often accepted, within the limits of their competence: men resemble their times more than their fathers.[29]

Debord concludes this paragraph with a medieval Arab aphorism. However, he uses the preceding sentences to load it with some tendentious baggage. It would be better, he seems to be saying, for people today to resemble their fathers than their times. It is as an odd conclusion for the archetypal late modern revolutionary. Yet, as we have seen, it flows directly from the presence of a powerful nostalgic tendency within the idea of the spectacle. We have also seen that this tendency has a dual life in Debord's thought: it is both productive, a fertilizing resource and disruptive, a force, unacknowledged and untheorized, that sowed incoherence into the situationist project. We shall address both of these themes through a different example of situationist activity a little later. However, the idea of the spectacle also allows us to explore one of the two forms of situationist nostalgia which I have identified, namely 'unrooted' nostalgia.

Unrooted Nostalgia: The Spectacle and Radical Identity

The situationists were not the first political current to accommodate Marxism with romanticism. The surrealists and the Frankfurt School provide earlier instances. It is not coincidental that both also offer examples of intellectual projects – such as Breton's 'gothic Marxism' of the uncanny or Horkheimer's hunger for social release – which articulate an omnivorous alienation from their times.[30] However, the situationists provide the consummate twentieth-century example of this type of radical identity. And it is an 'identity', for it established a sense of self that structured the situationists' experiences and interpretations.

In excavating the nostalgic content of the idea of the spectacle, what we encounter is rarely an attachment to particular periods or places that have been lost. Rather, we meet with a roving disposition; a restless, seemingly self-sufficient, state of yearning. In his film 'Critique de la séparartion' (1961), Debord provides an elegiac commentary on the 'sphere of loss':

> Everything that concerns the sphere of loss – that is to say, the past time I have lost, as well as disappearance, escape, and more generally the flowing past of things, and even what in the prevalent and therefore most vulgar social sense of the use of time is called wasted time – all this finds in that strangely apt old military expression 'en enfants perdus' its meeting ground [in] the sphere of discovery, adventure, avant-garde.[31]

Although washed through with melancholy, Debord is outlining in this passage a heroic role for the situationists as the most abandoned, the most marginalized, yet bravest of social 'adventurers'. In a society of spectacle, a general assertion of disaffection and loss becomes the only authentic political and personal path. In this way, existing traditions of bohemian nihilism were given a theoretical backbone of communist militancy and hostility to the commodity. What emerges is a politicized way of living: of the 'authentic life' as a series of spontaneous acts of refusal of the spectacle that are simultaneously expressions of revolutionary hope and despair. The SI offered us a way 'to be at war with the entire earth, lightheartedly'.[32]

The SI's romantic extremism encourages a proclivity for personal testaments of excess and marginality. Although Debord's one-time SI and enragé comrade, René Riesel, has dismissed Debord's autobiographical statement *Panegyric* as 'the aestheticisation of his life', there exists a continuity of self-conscious alienation between it and Debord's earlier works.[33] More specifically, it is noticeable from *Panegyric* how drawn Debord is to the idea of his own youth a site of adventure within and against an alienated world:

> In the zone of perdition where my youth went as if to complete its education, one would have said that the portents of an imminent collapse of the whole edifice of civilisation had made an appointment. Permanently ensconced there were people who could be defined only negatively, for the good reason that they had no job, followed no course of study, and practised no art.[34]

The image of Debord's 'tribe' as a 'rogue's gallery of hard drinkers and thinkers', has been centre-stage in contemporary ultra-leftist nostalgia for itself.[35] It is a milieu that, then as now, takes a fierce delight in its lonely iconoclasm; a milieu personified by Debord, who muses in his own *Panegyric* 'I wonder if even one other person has dared to behave like me, in this era.'[36]

'Whoever sees the banks of the Seine sees our grief': Situationist Nostalgia for Place

The situationists had a fascination with the built environment that reflected their interest in revolutionary politics as a struggle that takes place at the level of everyday life. However, this arena also shows us a number of struggles within situationism itself, between technocratic modernism and its repudiation; between the desire for endless disorientation and warm memories of the solidarities of working-class life.

These conflicts were played out at a factional level. The principle split was between the technocratic planners of 'situationist cities' (notably the Dutch member of the SI – up to 1960 – Constant) and the more politically focused approach associated with Debord. The productive and disruptive role of nostalgia within situationist geography took place within these factions as well as between them. Indeed, the avowedly technocratic faction represented by Constant entered situationism through the critical loopholes created by Debord's ambivalent relationship to industrial modernity. However, as I show later, what is, perhaps, most striking about the nostalgic tendencies at work within situationist geography is that this is a rooted nostalgia, tied to specific landscapes and specific cities. The nostalgic form we encounter here is soaked with personal memories and particular attachments, evocations that the situationists struggled to corral within their familiar political lexicon.

The name 'Situationist International' obscures an elementary fact: this was a movement born and bred in one particular place, postwar Paris. The relationship many situationists had with Paris was a passionate one. In part this fire was lit by the perception that 'their' Paris – the Paris of bohemian and working-class community – was under assault.[37] Twenty-four per cent of the surface area of the city was demolished and rebuilt between 1954–1974.[38] Between the same two dates the working-class population of the Ville de Paris fell by 44 per cent.[39] Massive road building programs, housing developments on the city limits, the eradication of ancient markets such as the Halle aux Vins and Les Halles; to the situationists all these things seemed to presage the dawn of a homogenized and historically brainwashed city. The situationists interpreted these changes through Debord's notion that within a society of the spectacle history was 'outlawed', to be replaced by 'frozen time'. Debord established this link in *Society of the Spectacle* through the following example:

> The 'new towns' of the technological pseudo-peasantry clearly inscribe on the landscape their rupture with the historical time on which they are built; their motto could be: 'On this spot nothing will ever happen, and *nothing ever has*'. It is obviously because history, which must be liberated in the cities, has not yet been liberated, that the forces of *historical absence* begin to compose their own exclusive landscape.[40]

In Raoul Vaneigem's terms: 'The new towns will efface every trace of the battles that traditional towns fought against the people they wanted to oppress.'[41] What is being articulated here is a nostalgia for the political memories contained in buildings and streets that have witnessed past conflicts. It is not, ostensibly at least, a mourning for the loss of the picturesque or quaint but for popular memory. The SI and their direct forerunners, the Lettrist International (LI), were conservationists in a strictly political cause: 'beauty, when it is not a promise of happiness, must be destroyed'.[42]

The situationists' favourite illustration of the extinction of popular memory through urban renewal programs was the suppression of the street. Construed as the social and imaginative centre of working-class community, the street was presented as endangered by modern urbanism; more specifically modern urbanism as devised by situationist *bête noire*, Le Corbusier. In 1954, the Lettrist International noted that,

> In these days where everything, across all areas of life, is becoming more and more repressive, there is one man in particular who is repulsive and clearly more of a cop than most . . . Le Corbusier's ambition is the suppression of the street . . . [and] an end to opportunities for insurrection.[43]

This hostility suggested the need to move away from technocratic solutions to social problems and towards the reuse, and political resignification, of the existing environment. Hence, we arrive at the idea of a 'turning aside', or détournement, of environments that are rich with memory and symbol.

> The employment of détournement in architecture for the construction of situations marks the reinvestment of products that it is necessary to protect from the existing socio-economic system, and the rupture with the formalist concern of abstractly creating the unknown.[44]

The situationists celebrated the occupations and street protests of May 1968 as a moment of everyday recreation, a reclaiming of the city that was also a reintroduction of time and, hence, of real life. It was a revolutionary event, says René Viénet, when,

> Capitalized time stopped. Without any trains, metro, cars, or work the strikers recaptured the time so sadly lost in factories, on motorways, in front of the TV. People strolled, dreamed, learned how to live.[45]

The situationists' attachment to the Paris of intimate streets, to a pre-car centred Paris, is reflected in their wandering, footloose (and foot based), geographical praxis, which they called 'psychogeography'. Psychogeography attempts to explore the city politically, identifying spaces and places of intensity and disorientation. Its principal technique was the drift (or dérive), which demands a playful yet militant engagement with the city.[46]

The old market at Les Halles was psychogeographical mapped out following two drifts by Abdelhafid Khatib in 1958. The same area was tenderly observed by Debord a year later in his film 'Sur le passage de quelques personnes a travers une assez courte unite de temps' (1959). The prospect of the demolition and displacement of Les Halles, Khatib noted,

> will be a new blow to popular Paris, which has for a century now been constantly dismissed, as we know, to the suburbs. A solution aimed at creating a new society demands that this space at the centre of Paris be preserved for the manifestations of a liberated collective life.[47]

Debord's own drunken, slightly boorish, drifts, as well as the collaborative cut-up maps (in which zones of intensity are snipped out, separated and connected by arrows) he made with Asger Jorn ('Guide pyscogéographique de Paris' of 1956 and 'Naked City' of 1957), can be read as typical avant-garde transgressions.[48] Yet they are propelled by a deep sadness. McDonough suggests that Debord's maps 'stand as the last articulations of a city which is irretrievable, a Paris now lost to us'.[49] For Simon Sadler, Debord's cut-up maps may be seen as

> guides to areas of central Paris threatened by development, retaining those parts that were still worth visiting and disposing of all those bits that they felt had been spoiled by capitalism and bureaucracy.[50]

In *The Situationist City* Sadler goes on to discuss the 'drift' as a form of heritage survey. The drifters, he explains, gravitated towards old working-class streets and spaces: 'recording them for posterity, fastidiously avoiding the fluid traffic of the boulevards in favour of the still pools and backwaters of the city'.[51]

The productive role of nostalgia in situationist geography lies in its capacity to provoke a critical historical sensibility. This was nostalgia that acted, not as a retreat from time, but as a challenge to 'frozen time'; not a desire for all things gone but for landscape as an arena of struggle and popular memory. However, as we saw in respect to the idea of the spectacle, nostalgia could also be a disruptive force within situationism, creating incoherence and introducing theoretically undigested elements. One of the most glaring manifestations of this disruption is the ease with which the situationists allowed their avant-garde conceits to follow the pattern of Dada and surrealism and slip into an aristocratic dandyness. The drifter, once transmuted into the flâneur, may remain a cultural transgressor but is no longer recognizable as a communist revolutionary. Debord, Wolman and Bernstein's foppish, jokey protest letter to *The Times* in 1955, complaining about plans to demolish 'the Chinese quarter in London', retains its snobbishness despite its satire of the English:

> The only pageants you have left are a coronation from time to time, an occasional royal marriage which seldom bears fruit; nothing else. The disappearance of pretty girls, of good family especially, will become rarer and rarer after the razing of Limehouse. Do you honestly believe that a gentleman can amuse himself in Soho?[52]

Sadler pointedly compares the situationist drifters to aristocratic 'gentlemen of leisure':

> Situationists mythologised the poor as fellow travellers on the urban margins, treating the ghetto as an urban asset rather than an urban ill . . . Like new gentlemen of leisure, promoting their 'revolutionary' motto of *Ne travaillez jamais* (Never work), they reserved a sort of *ancien* disdain for the petit-bourgeois areas of Paris.[53]

Nostalgia, unrecognized, undiscussed, was allowed to create spaces of condescension and contradiction in situationist thought. The ambiguities of the situationists' heady mixture of utopianism and wistful regret for the Paris of yesteryear opened up inconsistencies that acerbated the SI's factionalism. As this implies, the SI's schisms were a product of deeply entrenched and unrecognized intellectual fissures. Indeed, even years after the technocratic situationists, personified by Constant, had left the SI, Debord was still articulating a confusing combination of futuristic utopianism and pathos soaked anti-modernism. Through the theoretical slight of hand of fetishizing 'endless play' as a revolutionary goal, these aspirations were welded into uncomfortable union. Debord connects ludic solipsism with class history by claiming the culmination of the latter can give birth to the former. Yet this association relies on a potentially endless deferment of authentic revolution as well as a doctrinaire reliance on a single form, 'the game', as its utopian conclusion. Debord's rhetorical flair only exacerbates the political thinness of the vision:

> History, which threatens this twilight world, is also the force which could subject space to lived time. Proletarian revolution is the critique of human geography through which individuals and communities have to create places and events suitable for the appropriation, no longer just of their labor, but of their total history. In this game's changing space, and in the freely chosen variation in this game's rules, the autonomy of places can be rediscovered without the reintroduction of an exclusive attachment to the land, thus bringing back the reality of the voyage and of life understood as a voyage which contains its entire meaning within itself.[54]

Given the ambiguities within Debord's ludic vision is not surprising that some radicals looked to the situationists as a movement committed to the creation of new cities of endless play. It is a little more surprising, perhaps, that so much contemporary academic commentary on situationist urbanism should concentrate on this tendency. Indeed, it is a perverse tribute to the SI's influence that Constant now finds his entire career celebrated and narrated as a contribution to so-called situationist architecture.[55]

The effort required to imagine a coherent political project that includes Constant, Jorn and Debord is considerable (and, I believe, misjudged).[56] It has demanded a variety of contortions, most notably the interpretation of Constant's fantastical models of situationist cities (most famously, New Babylon, 1974) as not really models at all but merely 'critical provocations'.[57] A more realistic assessment is to admit the discordant role of technocratic situationism within and against Debord's (and Jorn's) situationist vision.[58] Constant plugged into a utopian urge within the situationist movement and wider avant-garde to imagine a new, modernist, Eden. His spectacular models and futuristic sketches depicted cities on stilts that hover over existing landscapes like vast, invading space-ships:

> In such huge constrictions we envisage the possibility of conquering nature and subjugating to our will the climate, the lighting and the sounds in these different spaces.[59]

During one of the fractious meetings that precipitated his departure Constant gave voice to his hostility to any 'romanticised notion of a past reality'.[60] However, once gone, the SI lost no time in denouncing Constant's 'technocratic concept of a situationist profession' as 'deviationist'. Constant, it was said, was a 'cunning operator' who,

> frankly offers himself, along with two or three plagiarised and badly understood situationist ideas, as a public relations man for the integration of the masses into capitalist technological civilisation.[61]

Yet Constant was responding to aspects of the situationist project which were maintained long after his departure. We have seen how nostalgia produced a variety of critical interventions for the situationists. However, it remained an undigested force, colliding queasily with a thirst for utopian new beginnings. Both Debord and Khatib mourned the passing of Les Halles as a centre of working-class community. Yet it is telling that just one sentence after calling for the area to be 'preserved' Khatib demands that it be gutted and replaced with 'situationist architectural complexes' and 'perpetually changing labyrinths'.[62]

The idea of the spectacle contains an abstract nostalgia, an unspecified sense of loss and alienation. By contrast, the ruination of Paris is different nostalgic territory: for here we encounter a set of specific, placeable, memories and attachments. Although what I am calling 'rooted' and 'unrooted' nostalgias are not discrete forms, they do contain identifiable and distinct tendencies. Rooted nostalgias (which, we must not forget, are not necessarily for one's own roots) evoke intricate and emotional reactions which are often bound up with feelings of loss associated with childhood (and, by implication, of revolution as a way of rediscovering childhood). They carry a sense of being wounded and of bewilderment, emotions which are compounded by the difficulty of articulating just what is at stake – especially politically – for those who have seen 'their city taken away from them'. This is not comfortable territory for revolutionaries. That the SI, and Debord in particular, broached it at all, is indicative of an openness that reminds us of the daring nature of the situationists' amalgam of militancy and passion.

In tracing the passage of these emotions through Debord's work, we can identify three stages, which also describe an age-line for the situationist generation. First, a youthful phase in the 1950s, characterized by a dandyish and solipsistic anarchist conservationism; second, a middle stage, characterized by a more doctrinaire, and sharply politicized, critique of urbanism; third and last, a late stage, characterized by mournful reverie for the loss of authentic city life. Although each of these stages has already been illustrated in this chapter, the last requires further discussion. In *Panegyric* Debord repeatedly employs a geography of loss to depict not only a general shift in the nature of French society but a personal journey, from hopeful radical to pessimist. After outlining in detailed terms the small area of Paris where he once lived,[63] Debord says

> I never, or hardly ever, would have left this area, which suited me perfectly . . . Always briefly in my youth, when I had to risk some forays abroad in order to further extend disruption; but later for much longer, when the city had been sacked and the kind of life that had been led there had been completely destroyed – which is what happened from 1970 onwards . . . Whoever sees the banks of the Seine sees our grief: nothing is found there now save the bustling columns of an anthill of motorized slaves.[64]

This nostalgia clearly sustains the alienated identity discussed earlier in this essay. However, it also disturbs and threatens it: for the securely political and aloof world vision associated with critique of the spectacle is here dragged down to earth. Debord, the avant-garde revolutionary, is revealed to be a lost soul, made homeless by the changes that have occurred in his lifetime. Debord's rage at what has happened to Paris could, perhaps, be explained as a matter of strategy. But Debord's intimate nostalgia suggests a less cerebral, if no less political, explanation, one which points to the memories and pleasures Debord once found within, now lost, Parisian streets. Indeed, Debord, who often spoke of his comrades coldly, articulated a vulnerability, a forlorn love, for Paris. He was drawn back, in spite of everything:

> when the tide of destruction, pollution and falsification had conquered the whole surface of the planet . . . I could return to the ruins of Paris, for then nothing better remained anywhere else. One cannot go into exile in a unified world.[65]

Conclusions and New Departures

It is no surprise that nostalgia was an object of contempt for the situationists. Debord and Wolman's gnomic declaration that 'Life can never be too disorienting' is merely an extreme expression of the status accorded to deracination found across Marxist revolutionary movements.[66] This chapter has questioned the coherence of this claim by (a) identifying the productive and disruptive role of nostalgia and (b) distinguishing two forms of nostalgia within the situationist project, what I have called the rooted and the unrooted. This latter distinction has been illustrated by, respectively, the idea of the spectacle and situationist geography. Inevitably, these forms are not discrete but rather represent intercutting tendencies. Yet they do provide a sense of the multiplicity of nostalgia, its diverse scales and intellectual range.

The situationists have also emerged as the subject of nostalgia. In 'thinking about Debord today', argues Chamsy el-Ojeili, 'is not nostalgia the dominating modality, the reason we are so reluctant to forget what is, and should be, forgettable in Debord'.[67] Reviewing the 'reverential' tone of the exhibitions that launched the SI into mainstream art criticism, hosted in London, Paris and Boston in 1989, Peter Smith remarked that 'We have seen a shift from the utopianism of the 1960s to a culture of nostalgia.'[68] Smith bluntly contends that 'the exhibition and the books which accompany it look backward in a search for appearances as if they were compensatory fantasies for a forgotten dream'.[69] The surge of interest in the situationists in a period dominated by conservatism is certainly telling. Nevertheless, as we have seen,

Smith is mistaken in his implication that the subversions of the past were free from nostalgia or, indeed, that the politics of nostalgia are inevitably non-revolutionary.

The situationists are gone. But the dilemmas of their nostalgic radicalism remain. Moreover, there are signs that these dilemmas are beginning to be actively engaged. I am not referring to the kind of punk and 'culture-jamming' cultural politics of the past 30 years that is sometimes classed as neo-situationist.[70] Far more interesting, I would suggest, are those rather less prominent trajectories that have sought to learn from, but also escape, the confines of the situationist project.

Perhaps the most important example is the attempt to fully combine the critique of 'industrial society', with which the situationists wrestled, into ecological radicalism. These influences have been drawn together by René Riesel. Riesel, one-time member of the SI and personification of enragé 'attitude', is now a campaigner against GM crops.[71] In 2001 he explained to *Libération* his journey 'from situationism to the Farmers' Confederation':

> I left for the Eastern Pyrénées and became a [sheep] breeder, a way of life that suited me and allowed me to reconstruct a 'rear base', not in military terms, but in terms of relearning practices that in many respects make up the genuine riches of humanity. In the present state of our societies' decay, we need to re-endow a certain number of lost savoir-faires.

Riesel goes on to explain that 'Since the "industrial revolution" in England, industrialisation has been an absolutely fundamental rupture with the essence of the progress of humanisation.'[72] Riesel's vision is a break from situationism but it also emerges from it and represents a kind of resolution of some of its central tensions. What is striking about Riesel's combination of revolutionary and agricultural traditionalist is how it has moved on with and from situationism. Another striking development may be witnessed in the evolution of psychogeography which we shall explore in the next chapter.

Notes

1. G. Debord, 'On wild architecture', in E. Sussman (Ed.), *On the Passage of a Few People through a Rather Brief Moment of Time: The Situationist International 1957–1972*, (Cambridge, MA: MIT Press, 1989), 175.
2. Situationist International, 'On the poverty of student life', in K. Knabb (Ed.), *Situationist International Anthology*, (Berkeley: Bureau of Public Secrets, 1981), 333.
3. Situationist International, 'Les souvenirs au-dessous de tout', *Internationale Situationniste*, 2, (1958), 3. The phrase is translated as 'Nostalgia beneath contempt' by 'International Situationist Online'. Citations from *Internationale Situationniste* derive from the compendium published by Editions Champ Libre in 1975. However, those English-language readers interested in the situationists now have the most comprehensive set of English translations that is available for any avant-garde group. 'Situationist International Online' (http://www.cddc.vt.edu/sionline/si/situ.html) provides full translations of all issues of Internationale Situationniste, as well as a vast range of other situationist texts (e.g. a full translation of the journal of the Lettrist International, Potlatch). Further material can be found at 'The Situationist International Text Library' (http://library.nothingness.org/articles/SI/all/). I have consulted these translations, and sometimes used them, in making my own translations from the French.

4. Ibid., 4. Cf. the phrase used by Vincent Kaufman, in his biography of Debord, to depict his milieu: 'specialists in loss' (*Guy Debord: Revolution in the Service of Poetry*, Minneapolis: University of Minnesota Press, 2006, 50).

5. M. Löwy, 'Consumed by night's fire: the dark romanticism of Guy Debord', *Radical Philosophy*, 87, (1988); D. Pinder, '"Old Paris is no more": geographies of spectacle and anti-spectacle', *Antipode* 32, 4, (2000). See also D. Pinder, *Visions of the City: Utopianism, Power and Politics in Twentieth-Century Urbanism*, Edinburgh: Edinburgh University Press, 2005.

6. Pinder, 'Old Paris is no more'; Löwy, 'Consumed by night's fire', 33.

7. G. Debord, *Panegyric*, (London: Verso, 1991), 45.

8. G. Debord, *Society of the Spectacle*, (Detroit: Black and Red, 1983), thesis 17. Citations from *Society of the Spectacle* are from the 1977 revised translation of the first English translation of 1971. Readers have the opportunity of cross-checking a number of translations of the book against each other and against the French original (Debord, 1967). The latter is available at: 'The Situationist International Text Library' (http:/library.nothing-ness.org.articles/SI/all/), while the 1977, 1994 and 2002 English translations are available at: 'Situationist International Online' (http://www.cddc.vt.edu/sionline/si/situ.html).

9. S. Plant, *The Most Radical Gesture: The Situationist International in a Postmodern Age*, (London: Routledge, 1992); 1992; A. Bonnett, 'Situationism, geography and poststructuralism', *Environment and Planning D: Society and Space*, 7, (1989).

10. Debord, *Society of the Spectacle*, thesis 143.

11. Ibid., thesis 200, thesis 158.

12. Ibid., thesis 143.

13. G. Debord, *Panégyrique 2*, (Paris: Arthème Fayard, 1997); G. Debord, *Comments on the Society of the Spectacle*, (London: Verso, 1990); Debord, *Panegyric*.

14. A concern with the SI's exclusions and splits often dominates activist, non-academic, forms of situationist history. Suffice to record that the SI had 72 members throughout its life-span (1957–1972), and only three when it dissolved itself 1972. In 1969 the SI declared that it 'worked hard to make it almost impossible to join the SI' (Situationist International, 'L'élite et le retard', *Internationale Situationniste*, 12, (1969), 93).

15. H. Slater, *Divided We Stand: An Outline of Scandinavian Situationism*, (London: Infopool, 2001); S. Home, *The Assault on Culture: Utopian Currents from Lettrisme to Class War*, (Stirling: AK Press 1991); F. Tompsett, 'Preface to the English edition', in A. Jorn, *Open Creation and Its Enemies with Originality and Magnitude (On the System of Isou)*, (London: Unpopular Books, 1994).

16. A. Jorn, 'La fin de l'économie et la réalisation de l'art', *Internationale Situationniste*, 4, (1960); A. Jorn, 'La création ouverte et ses ennemis', *Internationale Situationniste*, 5, (1960).

17. J. Thorsen, 'Co-ritus interview with Jorgen Nash and Jens Jorgen Thorsen', available at: http:///www.infopool.org.uk/6304.html, accessed 21/04.2005.

18. See S. Crook, 'Moving mountains: "shamanic" rock art and the International of Experimental Artists', *Transgressions*, 4, (1998).

19. G. Ivain (pseudonym), 'Formulaire pour un urbanisme nouveau', *Internationale Situationniste*, 1, (1958), 15.

20. Debord, *Society of the Spectacle*, thesis 127; thesis 154.

21. Ibid., thesis 28.

22. Ibid., thesis 154.

23. Debord, *Comments*, 15–6.

24. Situationist International, 'La technique de l'isolement', *Internationale Situationniste*, 9, (1964), 66.
25. Debord, *Society of the Spectacle*, thesis 115.
26. Ibid., thesis 121.
27. For example, Bonnett, 'Situationism, geography and postructuralism'.
28. For example, S. Home, 'The perfection of suicide is in its ambiguity', *Transgressions*, 1, (1994), 82.
29. Debord, *Comments*, 19–20.
30. M. Cohen, *Profane Illumination: Walter Benjamin and the Paris of Surrealist Revolution*, (Berkeley: University of California Press, 1993); B. Shaw, 'Reason, nostalgia, and eschatology in the critical theory of Max Horkheimer', *The Journal of Politics*, 47, 1, (1985).
31. G. Debord, *Society of the Spectacle and Other Films*, (London: Rebel Press, 1992), 49–50.
32. G. Debord, 'In girum imus nocte et consumimur igni', Simar Films, (1979).
33. (2005); *Panegyric* (1991; first published 1989; also Debord, 1997).
34. Debord, *Panegyric*, 23.
35. J-M. Mension, *The Tribe*, (San Francisco: City Lights Books, 2001), back cover; R. Rumney, *The Consul*, (San Francisco: City Lights Books, 2002).
36. (1991: 17). This judgement seems to be supported by Vincent Kaufman in *Guy Debord: Revolution in the Service of Poetry*, (Minneapolis: University of Minnesota Press, 2006): 'It is not easy to live like Debord. It is not easy to think like him or even with him. Which is why it is not easy to forget him' (275).
37. L. Chevalier, *The Assassination of Paris*, (Chicago: University of Chicago Press, 1994).
38. Pinder, 'Old Paris is no more'.
39. S. Sadler, *The Situationist City*, Cambridge, MA: MIT Press, 1998.
40. Debord, *Society of the Spectacle*, thesis 177.
41. R. Vaneigem, 'Commentaires contre l'urbanisme', *Internationale Situationniste*, 6, (1961), 36.
42. Lettrist International, *Potlatch 1954–1957*, (Editions Gérard Lebovici, 1985), 178.
43. Ibid., 34–5.
44. Situationist International, 'La frontiere situationniste', *Internationale Situationniste*, 5, (1960), 9.
45. R. Viénet, *Enragés and Situationists in the Occupation Movement, France, May '68*, (New York: Autonomedia, 1992), 77.
46. Cf. the surrealists' Parisian wanderings, in which the aim was to give oneself up to chance. A comparison between the two forms of avant-garde geography is developed by A. Bonnett ('Art, ideology and everyday space: subversive tendencies from Dada to postmodernism', *Environment and Planning D: Society and Space*, 10, 1992) and M. Bandini ('Surrealist references in the notions of derive and psychogeography of the situationist urban environment', in L. Andreotti and X. Costa (Eds), *Situacionistas: Arte, Politica, Urbanismo/ Situationists: Art, Politics, Urbanism*, Barcelona: Museu d'Art Contemporani de Barcelona, 1996).
47. A. Khatib, 'Essai de description psychogéographique des Halles', *Internationale Situationniste*, 2, (1958), 17.
48. G. Debord, 'Two accounts of the derive', in E. Sussman (Ed.), *On the Passage of a Few People through a Rather Brief Moment of Time: The Situationist International 1957–1972*, (Cambridge, MA: MIT Press, 1989).

49. T. McDonough, 'The derive and situationist Paris', in L. Andreotti and X. Costa (Eds), *Situacionistas: Arte, Politica, Urbanismo/Situationists: Art, Politics, Urbanism*, (Barcelona: Museu d'Art Contemporani de Barcelona, 1996), 65.

50. Sadler, *The Situationist City*, 61.

51. Ibid., 56.

52. Lettrist International, *Potlatch 1954–1957*, 171.

53. Sadler, *The Situationist City*, 56–7.

54. Debord, *Society of the Spectacle*, thesis 178.

55. Sadler, *The Situationist City*; C. de Zegher and M. Wigley (Eds), *The Activist Drawing: Retracing Situationist Architecture from Constant's New Babylon to Beyond*, (Cambridge, MA: MIT Press, 2001); I. Borden and S. McCreery (Eds), *New Babylonians*, (London: Architectural Design, 2001); L. Andreotti and X. Costa (Eds), *Situacionistas: Arte, Politica, Urbanismo/ Situationists: Art, Politics, Urbanism*, (Barcelona: Museu d'Art Contemporani de Barcelona, 1996).

56. The Italian situationist Giuseppe Pinot-Gallizio, who produced large rolls of 'industrial painting', sought to combine some of the primitivist and technocratic tensions within the movement when he extolled the role of the modern revolutionary artist in 1959: 'we are close to the primitive state but equipped with modern means: the promised land, paradise, eden can only be the air we breath, eat, touch, invade' (cited by Bandini, 'Surrealist references in the notions of derive and psychogeography', 51). However, Pinot-Gallizio's pieces, despite their 'industrial' label, were craft-based, and certainly far easier to assimilate into the situationist milieu than the megastructures modelled by Constant.

57. D. Pinder, 'Utopian transfiguration: the other spaces of New Babylon', in I. Borden and S. McCreery (Eds), *New Babylonians*, (London: Architectural Design, 2001), 18.

58. Jorn scholar Graham Birtwistle explores the split between Constant's technocratic and Jorn's primitivist vision of landscape in his essay 'Old Gotland, New Babylon' (*Transgressions*, 2/3, 1996).

59. Constant, 'Une autre ville pour une autre vie', *Internationale Situationniste*, 3, (1959), 38.

60. Constant cited by Situationist International, 'Discussion sur un appel aux intellectuels et artistes revolutionnaires', *Internationale Situationniste*, 3, (1959), 23. Constant has spoken of his own resignation from the SI in terms of his dislike of the fact that there were 'too many painters' (Constant, 'A conversation with Constant', in C. de Zegher and M. Wigley (Eds), *The Activist Drawing: Retracing Situationist Architecture from Constant's New Babylon to Beyond*, (Cambridge, MA: MIT Press, 2001), 23.

61. Situationist International, 'Critique de l'urbanisme', *Internationale Situationniste*, 6, (1961), 6.

62. Khatib, 'Essai de description psychogéographique des Halles', 17.

63. '[E]xactly in the triangle defined by the intersections of the rue Saint-Jacques and the rue Royer-Colard, rue Saint Martin and rue Greneta, and the rue du Bac and rue de Comailles' (Debord, *Panegyric*, 43–4).

64. Debord, *Panegyric*, 44–5.

65. Ibid., 47.

66. G. Debord and G. Wolman, 'Methods of detournement', in K. Knabb (Ed.), *Situationist International Anthology*, (Berkeley: Bureau of Public Secrets, 1981), 13.

67. C. el-Ojeili, 'Forget Debord?', *Thesis Eleven*, 89, (2007), 124.

68. P. Smith, 'On the passage of a few people: situationist nostalgia', *Oxford Art Journal*, 14, 1, (1989), 124.

69. Ibid. Another exhibition on the situationists held in London tripped itself up on nostalgia almost before visitors were through the door. To enter the exhibition of situationist material at The Aquarium gallery in London in August 2003 one had to step over an unlikely message, artfully sprayed on the entrance floor, 'Nostalgia ends here'.

70. G. Marcus, *Lipstick Traces: A Secret History of the Twentieth Century*, (London: Secker & Warburg, 1989).

71. See R. Riesel, *Remarques sur l'agriculture genetiquement modifiee et la degradation des especes*, (Paris: Editions de l'Encyclopedie des nuisances, 1999); R. Riesel, 'Biotechnology: public and private', available at: http://www.notbored.org/biotechnology.html, accessed 11.05.2005.

72. Cited by A. Léauthier, 'Submission is advancing at a frightful speed', *Libération* (3–4 February, 2001), available at: http://www.cddc.vt.edu/sionline/postsi/submission.html, accessed 22.04.2005.

CHAPTER SIX

The Psychogeography of Loss

'You walked?' said Ballard, incredulously. 'We do have buses in Shepperton.'

Iain Sinclair[1]

Introduction

During his walk around the byways of London's outer ring road, the British novelist, film-maker and poet Iain Sinclair called in at J. G. Ballard's house in Shepperton. In *London Orbital*, Sinclair explains that he wanted to 'pay homage . . . to the man who has defined the psychic climate through which we are travelling'.[2] But instead of a blessing Sinclair receives a polite but bemused welcome. Ballard is clearly at a loss to understand what Sinclair is up to, including his perverse refusal of modern transport.

Sinclair's ramble around the M25's noisy margins was a journey in and against the contemporary landscape. It was an act of retrieval of radical histories now bypassed. But it was also a kind of romantic tribute to the brute energy of a technocentric, dehumanized environment. In either guise, *London Orbital* is one of the central examples of the 'psychogeographical turn' that can be identified in British literary culture and avant-garde activity in the 1990s.[3] This body of work explores and reimagines the forgotten nooks and crannies of ordinary landscapes. It seeks to re-enchant and remythologize prosaic geographies. The resultant effect is disorientating; funny yet melancholic; utterly of our time but ill at ease with modern Britain.

Critical reaction has tended to locate this strange new subgenre of travel writing as a post-modern incarnation of a longer tradition of ludic *flânerie*.[4] A smooth and largely biographical (indeed, often hagiographic) history has been constructed. This lineage usually starts with literary walkers. In Britain the assembled cast includes Defoe, De Quincy and Arther Machen. Twentieth-century psychogeography is offered as the next step: an avant-garde radicalization of earlier forays. However, Sinclair's pilgrimage to Shepperton, along with his awkward reception, implies the need for a more analytical and less deferential approach: for what is most intriguing about Sinclair's travel narratives is their *ambivalence*. Robert Macfarlane, noticing the presence in Sinclair's work of a mood and style 'usually associated with the *Daily Telegraph* [rather] than with avant-garde psychogeographers', highlights the *unresolved* nature of his project.[5] He goes on to categorize Sinclair's approach as 'nostalgic radicalism'. In this chapter I will be developing this interpretation and arguing that contemporary British psychogeography should be understood as a site of struggle over the politics of loss within the radical imagination. More specifically, I will show that British psychogeography is an arena of conflict between two important strands within British radicalism: the use of the past to critique industrial modernity and the suppression of nostalgia. It will also be shown how these tendencies, though they remain discordant presences are, in fact, partially resolved into novel forms of creative praxis.

The term 'psychogeography' derives from the Lettrist and Situationist Internationals. For these groups it referred to spatial practices designed to confuse and reimagine everyday space. The most important of these techniques was a politically purposeful 'drifting'; a transgressive wandering around and through the many barriers, forbidden zones and distinct atmospheres of the city. I have discussed the relationship between situationist nostalgia and psychogeography in Chapter Five. In fact this phase of psychogeography has received a considerable amount of attention in recent years. What is less often acknowledged is that, over the past two decades, psychogeography has re-emerged and been reworked. It has not simply been inherited and continued but reimagined in ways that reflect the changing nature of the relationship between radicalism, history and geography.

This chapter has two sections, which are used to explore two different types of British psychogeography. The first and most well known of these forms is the travel narratives of Iain Sinclair. The second form is less well known but is shown to be an original response to the crises of the left. Revolutionary psychogeographical groups sprang up in a number of British cities in the mid-1990s (a phenomenon also witnessed in the United States and Italy; as seen, for example, in the New York Psychogeographical Association and the Associazione Psicogeografica di Bologna). These groups shared with Sinclair a quixotic, love-hate relationship with the past. Like Sinclair, they emphasized historical re-readings of the everyday landscape and exhibited an uneasy combination of deracinating modernism and folksy localism. However, the reason I have chosen to distinguish these two forms of the psychogeographical turn is because they work through their fraught relationship with nostalgia in distinct ways. Within Sinclair's travel books, the modern landscape becomes a site of creative purgatory, a necessary violence that simultaneously anchors the writer in modernism while establishing marginal spaces and histories discovered on foot as expressions of a profound cultural and social loss. This double mapping of modernity and nostalgia is then used to imagine a community of creative and other cultural workers who have found a way of being 'at home' and finding friendship in and against an alienating landscape.

In what I call 'revolutionary psychogeography' nostalgia is also simultaneously refused and deployed. However, this process is enacted in a different way and to different ends. The use of a self-consciously exaggerated and, hence, self-subverting rhetoric of class war enabled these activists to evoke and ironize orthodox revolutionary politics. The development within this resolutely 'underground' community of so-called magico-Marxism encapsulates the novelty but also the folk-historical inclinations of their project. I also show that a newly confident politics of nostalgia can be glimpsed within this milieu: at the counter-cultural margins of society radicalism is (once again) becoming tied to a popular politics of loss. Hence, it will, hopefully, be clear that this chapter has wider ambitions than the provision of a more nuanced account of an often wilfully *outré* cultural current in late modern Britain. It is a contribution to ongoing attempts to re-examine the relationship between radicalism and the politics of loss.

Purgatory and Redemption around the M25: The Radical Nostalgia of Iain Sinclair

The nostalgic content of Iain Sinclair's walks in and around London has not been lost on his reviewers. Corralling his work together with other contemporary writers who excavate London's hidden past (notably Peter Ackroyd and Michael Moorcock), James Heartfield identifies Sinclair's work as part of a genre of 'Londonnostalgia'. Among 'Londonnostalgics' he argues,

> Against the superficial trend towards modernity – millennium bridge and riverside apartments – the stronger current is for a gloomy nostalgia. The London imagined by Ackroyd, Sinclair and Moorcock is, above all, a backward-looking one. The Londonnostalgics adore everything arcane and archaic about the city.[6]

For Heartfield, Sinclair is 'backward-looking' and, hence, a misguided and conservative commentator on London. There is much to dispute in this dismissal. We might first note that Sinclair's attitude towards the past is more ambivalent than Heartfield allows. After all, what kind of nostalgic would insist on a pilgrimage to J. G. Ballard's house? Indeed, Sinclair cites Ballard's creed with approval: 'Rather than fearing alienation . . . people should embrace it. It may be the doorway to something more interesting.'[7] Moreover, we must ask, if Sinclair 'adore[s] everything arcane', why does he write books about the M25? In fact what we might call Sinclair's *double mapping* of modernity and loss has long provided an example and a point of connection between experimental poets (notably Ginsburg), and the resurgent interest among counter-cultural radicals with environmental sustainability and visions of the pre-industrial, folk past. The DIY localism of the small press Sinclair helped found in 1970 in Dalston, London (the Albion Village Press), wove together avant-garde and folkish themes. Sinclair's first books, published by the Albion Village Press, such as *The Kodak Mantra Diaries* (1971) and *Muscat's Würm* (1972), are resolutely disorientating and anti-traditional.[8] Yet the political ethos of Albion Village Press is reminiscent of a long aesthetic folk-radical tradition, reaching back to Morrisian socialism. As Sinclair recalls,

> It was all that stuff of the previous era – making your own bread, and yoghurt, and living very simply, in a pleasant area where things were cheap, and producing your own books, and walking into the Whitechapel gallery and putting on an exhibition.[9]

In his later book Sinclair's double mapping of modernity and loss is narrated as an engagement with alienating, often brutally instrumental, landscapes. These places (or non-places) offer disorientation and disharmony while establishing the possibility and the necessity of resistance and human solidarity. Later in this section I consider how Sinclair creates a fragile resolution of these tensions by evoking a community of like-minded wanderers. I start though with the opening passage of the book from which I shall be drawing most of my examples, *London Orbital*.

> It started with the Dome, the Millennium Dome. An urge to walk away from the Teflon meteorite on Bugsby's Marshes. A white thing had dropped in the mud of the Greenwich peninsula. The ripples had to stop somewhere. The city turned inside-out. Rubbish blown against the perimeter fence. A journey, a provocation. An escape. Keep moving, I told myself, until you hit tarmac, the outer circle. The point where London loses it, gives us its ghosts. I have to admit it: I was developing an unhealthy obsession with the M25, London's orbital motorway. The dull silvertop that acts as a prophylactic between driver and landscape. Was this grim necklace, opened by Margaret Thatcher on 29 October 1986, the true perimeter fence?[10]

Sinclair suggests that Thatcher's speech, celebrating the opening of this 'grim necklace', also inaugurated 'the introduction of US mall-viruses, landscape consumerism, retail land-fill' (2003: 4).

Thus, from the start of *London Orbital*, it is clear that there is something determinedly perverse about Sinclair's 'escape'. His desire to 'walk away' from one symbol of modern Britain, the Millennium Dome, to another even more depressing destination, is an act of confrontation. Further, to walk around the M25 – 'a legendary presence that nobody wants to confront or confirm' – is a deliberate entry into hell.[11] Sinclair describes his mission as 'Exorcism, the only game worth the candle'.[12]

Sinclair's attitude to the M25 is not simple. He both repudiates and welcomes its dis-turbance, its capacity to dehumanize and deracinate. The ceaseless motorway provides the kind of hostile terrain and antagonism to sentiment required by Sinclair, both to explore the creativity born of disorientation and his own profound sense of loss. The road and its sur-rounding 'retail landfill' are used to experience the violence of modernity. It is a violence that lures those who find themselves in and against their era: the experimental modernist turned into a walker of unusable pathways, 'an antiquated lifeform'.[13] This intellectual structure has been echoed in Sinclair's other travel books. In *Edge of the Orison* (2005) the A1, another huge road, along with various homogeneous commuter hotels along its edges, performs the same function as the M25. Rampant bureaucracy and the urban scars of Thatcherite capitalism do the same in *Lights Out for the Territory* (1997).[14]

However, *London Orbital* is, to date, Sinclair's most revealing and edgy confrontation with the dilemmas of radical nostalgia. The M25's power to reduce landscapes and individuals to a weary smudge gives Sinclair's attempts to accommodate it, to feed off its virile destructive-ness, a desperate and unlikely quality. His 'Ballardian' assertion that the motorway's droning tarmac may provide soil for new creativity – 'that this nowhere, this edge, is the place that will offer fresh narratives' – has the ring of grim satire.[15] Furthermore, Sinclair's determination to take pleasure in the futuristic business parks that lie alongside the motorway is too staged and eager to be convincing. For example, the transformation of Theobalds Park into the home for the 'Abbey National Centre of Excellence', elicits the comment: 'A surveillance checkpoint and voice box to interrogate unlicensed visitors. I loved it. This was the true territory for the fiction that is England.'[16]

A similarly unlikely reaction occurs when Sinclair wanders into one of his top 'attractions' on the motorway periphery, a company building for Siebel.[17] Sinclair goes to some lengths to make the elusive presence of this 'Solutions provider' appear alluring. This 'beautiful bird of a building', he writes, 'appeared, fully formed from nowhere':

> You can't date it . . . The building doesn't impose, it insinuates: no sweat, today is your first tomorrow. A metal arm, a gesture that divides Siebel-world from the Egham underpass, creaks. The only sound in a perfectly smooth acoustic environment. A car arrives, the arm cranks up. A man in a lightweight suit, no papers, no case, saunters to the entrance, the green world of indoor tree shadows and underwater light.[18]

Unsurprisingly, the soft-tinted pleasures of the Siebel building (or indeed, the Abbey National Centre of Excellence) soon pall. Like the motorway that sweeps past them, they are explored – and temporarily valued – as territories in which memory and place have been eradicated. It is an extinction which fascinates Sinclair but which appals him. After ambling around 'Siebel-world' he abruptly declares, 'I've had enough . . . If we believe in the Siebel world, we might as well give up the walk now.'[19] With this turn of the heel, Sinclair's nostalgia comes into definition as social criticism produced, not by a flight from the modern but through engagement with it. Despite Sinclair's hostility to 'heritage and development scams' and the 'false memory' of attempts to conserve redundant landscapes, there is no mistaking his underlying contempt for instant landscapes 'with no memory'.[20] Describing a new residential park (called 'Crest Homes'), he tells us that it is:

> A stylish no-place that is every place. No attachment to the local, an easy commute to the centre. The ideal Crest Homes estate defies history and computer-enhances geography.[21]

Wandering slightly off-course in Kent, Sinclair also reminds us that the violence of modernism can find its mirror in a Betjemanesque rage. He offers no rhapsodies on the theme of sleek efficiency for the Bluewater Shopping Centre. It is simply a 'Wellsian pit', a 'retail quarry'.[22] The Dartford Bridge, a nearby motorway bridge crossing the Thames, provides the occasion for a similar grimace of despair:

> [T]he Dartford Bridge (with its necklace of slow-moving traffic) is our horizon. Smeared headlights spit their short beams into the wet night. The bridge spells civilisation. And spells it loud: FUCK OFF. Liminal graffiti. A mess of letters sprayed on grey stone windbreaks. FUCK OFF.[23]

There is an apocalyptic edge to Sinclair's work. Thus, although, as we shall see, he attempts to resolve the tensions I have been outlining in a redemptive fashion, it is necessary to acknowledge that he also sometimes coheres and conceals them by way of visions of the coming collapse of industrial society. The 'slow-mo apocalypse' he sees around him in London augers the final triumph of nature over a vile city which 'snorts human meat through metalled tubes. And later exhales the de-energised husks, its wage slaves'.[24] After a conversation with an artist-seer in Bethnal Green, he writes,

> It was only a matter of time, in his opinion, before all this trash, dirt and dust was swept away. We were amphibians in remission. On good mornings, looking out on the wet street, I was sure that he was right.[25]

Visions of the doom of Western civilization combine the violence of modernity with a violence towards modernity. They are a familiar avant-garde trope. However, Sinclair's work offers other, less cataclysmic resolutions. Indeed, his wanderings may be represented as a search for restorative and redemptive community. In the film *London Orbital* (2002) he describes his journey as a 'project of restitution'.[26] This restitutive impulse forges bonds of solidarity and empathy with earlier generations of radicals. The most developed instance is Sinclair's *Edge of the Orison*, which lovingly traces a journey made by the 'peasant poet' John Clare. Tying the knot between his own life and Clare's, Sinclair's walk interweaves places associated with his wife's family with points along Clare's *Journey Out of Essex* (1841). Sinclair places himself in the trusted company of Clare's account. But he is far more dislocated than the earlier poet. 'The birds knew him, knew John Clare', Sinclair writes, 'a wanderer in fields and woods; they recognised him and he belonged'.[27] Sinclair never belongs. Indeed, he implies that belonging is now impossible. But this only intensifies his hunger for company, for a community of the dispossessed. In *London Orbital* Sinclair searches out the landscapes and locales of other predecessors. His most diligent efforts are focused upon the mid-Victorian mystic and artist Samuel Palmer and his fraternity of 'Ancients'. Seeking out the exact spot (near Shoreham in Kent) where Palmer painted *The Golden Valley, or Harvesting with Distant Prospect,* Sinclair admits that he is participating in 'a self-conscious restatement of Samuel Palmer's gang'.[28]

Sinclair's reference to his 'gang' reminds us that his 'project of restitution' is not a solitary one. One of the notable characteristics of Sinclair's travel books is that they are accounts of journeys made with friends. Within and against territories of extreme banality and disconnection, Sinclair draws together a circle of fellow travellers: writers, film-makers and artists whose eccentricities are mined for comic effect and whose names the reader soon comes to recognize (including, Lee Drummond, Marc Atkins, Chris Petit, Renchi). Indeed, despite Sinclair's austere claim to delight in the 'warm glow in not belonging', his accounts are saturated with a very English chumminess.[29] The sense of bonhomie is heightened by Sinclair's fondness for in-jokes and fabrication. The fact that his friends seem delighted to be 'cruelly caricatured' in his books only adds to the impression of fellowship; a bond formed, in part, by the act of walking together through landscapes that produce atomization.[30]

It is in *Edge of the Orison* that Sinclair comes closest to the kind of heartfelt sense of remembrance that one always suspects lies just below the rather glassy façade of *London Orbital.* Exploring places and pathways associated with his wife's family in north Essex Sinclair sunders all ties to his ostensible magus, J. G. Ballard. Instead, he offers a straightforward plea for remembering: 'They live in us, the old ones', Sinclair writes, 'and we have a duty to honour their presence. There are no clean slates.'[31]

> Our walk made something happen, happen to us. Nothing changed out there, in the drift of the motorists and their suspended lives; in my conceit, we were transformed. On a molecular level. Very gradually, and with considerable reluctance (on their part), forgotten ancestors acknowledged our feeble interventions. We relived their histories and remade our own.[32]

Fired against the 'virtual landscapes . . . laid down over something drowsy but not quite dead', Sinclair seems ready in *Edge of the Orison* to be explicit about the intrinsic importance of recovering 'our own drowned memories'.[33]

Like William Morris, whose 'fragmentary consciousness' has long perplexed more orthodox critics, Sinclair's politics have been pronounced 'curious and inconsistent'.[34] However, unlike Morris, Sinclair is writing in an era when communist revolution is understood to have come and gone, a failed project of yesteryear. Indeed, Sinclair does not conceal his disaffection with twentieth-century revolutionaries, noting that 'even by the mid-sixties' he 'was getting very dubious' about these kind of political agendas.[35] Reading Sinclair one may wonder how his melancholic concerns could ever be compatible with the rhetoric of class struggle. Such an incongruous mix is precisely what can be witnessed within the agitational psychogeographical groups to which I now turn. In *Lights Out for the Territory* (1997) Sinclair records coming across the newsletter of the London Psychogeographical Association (LPA). It is 'the most useful of all London's neighbourhood tabloids', he writes, despite (or because) it is 'mysterious and fugitive'.[36] He adds: 'If you need it, it finds you. It writes itself.' I have a more prosaic analysis to offer.

My argument addresses the way revolutionary psychogeographers negotiate the politics of loss in a post-revolutionary era.

Radical Re-enchantments: Magic, Preservationism and Nostalgia in Revolutionary Psychogeography

The early 1990s witnessed the birth of an intriguing political subculture. Across Europe and the United States local psychogeography groups sprang into existence.[37] Although, in part, inspired by situationist antecedents, these groups charted novel, idiosyncratic, trajectories. From the late 1990s activity among these revolutionary groups diminished and interest in psychogeography passed to the arts community[38] and related 'urban explorers'.[39] However, although the work of the British agitational groups which I shall discuss here ceased some years ago, they remain one of the most provocative recent reinventions of the radical tradition. They also represent the most explicitly activist example of the turn in the 1990s towards the politics of 'everyday space' and, hence, of the wider 'spatial turn' within intellectual life.

The originality of these groups arises from their willingness to play with notions of revolutionary intent and folkish anti-modernism. Out of this intersection came a highly self-conscious deployment of the rhetoric of class struggle. Indeed, they aestheticized and ironized communism so heavily as to make it appear more akin to a cultural provocation than a political project. This process was also bound up with two other novel ideas, both of which turned on the way the past connects to the present within the landscape. The first concerns a so-called magico-Marxist reading of the landscape; the second an assertion of the radical role of landscape preservation. I shall address both in turn.

However, before going further I should mention that my knowledge of this community is, in part, derived from having been part of it. I once edited a magazine that sought to be, among other things, a repository of the new revolutionary psychogeography. It was called *Transgressions: A Journal of Urban Exploration* and ran for five issues between 1995 and 2000 (published and created by Fabian Tompsett, the leading figure within the London Psychogeographical Association). I soon came to regret the title. The concept of 'transgression' captured a partial truth and had, in the early 1990s, a lively ring. Yet I already suspected that to conflate psychogeography with transgression was misleading; that it obscured something fundamental about the nature of the enthusiasms and influences I saw about me. Thus, in a rather bewildering editorial for issue one of *Transgressions*, I announced that it was not 'a journal dedicated to the celebration of transgression'. Indeed, that we were 'as interested in acts of conformism as we are in acts of transgression'.[40] It was a confusing message. I was grappling with the odd amalgam of preservationism and radicalism, modernism and anti-modernism, that I saw propelling psychogeographical activity. Thankfully, others were working through the same tension with more flair and a greater sensitivity to the range of influences upon the new psychogeography.

Among the most important of these influences were the sensuous, irrationalist situationism of Asger Jorn and a politicized version of New Age notions of sacred landscape. The influence of Iain Sinclair's London novels (such as *Lud Heat*, which offers a 'high occulting' mapping of the city) may also be discerned.[41] The main thesis of the LPA and, somewhat less explicitly, the Manchester Area Psychogeographic (MAP) group, was that class power relies on and demands the analysis of hidden knowledge and undisclosed networks and traditions. It was argued that the nature of power can be disclosed through an understanding of the way these concealed forces have been deployed and imposed upon the landscape. It is important to stress that this analysis does not accept or offer occultism. Rather it seeks to scurrilously construct and imagine occultism (along with other hidden forms and sources of power) as a class strategy, a technique of control in the management of the spectacle. These ideas came to be categorized as 'magico-Marxism'.[42] As with many avant-garde interventions magico-Marxism is determinedly disorientating: it is evasive, infuriating, constantly asking that we see the city in new, unexpected, ways. However, I would also argue that the disorientating game played by these psychogeographical groups acted to conceal and cohere the tension between nostalgia and anti-nostalgia, modernist and anti-modernist politics, that animated their project.

Magico-Marxism and its kindred re-enchantments combined communist militancy with a romanticization of landscape and memory. The most outrageous examples derive from the LPA, which was 'brought back into being in the Rosicrucian Cave at Royston Herts' in 1992.[43] The LPA's characteristic style was an ingratiating amalgam of class struggle rhetoric and antiquarian dottiness.

The numerous trips it organized to ancient and otherwise mystic sites were frequently turned into excuses for nostalgic regression. Participants were advised to 'bring stout shoes in case of rain'.[44] The 'motor car' became an object of affected fascination: 'This device, little more than a box with wheels and an internal combustion engine, enabled [psychogeographers] to roam around at high speed.'[45] The LPA's report on a visit to the ancient earth figure, the Cerne Giant (on the day that its 'penis is directly oriented towards the sunrise'), recalls that 'as we sat eating our sandwiches, two comrades emerged from the swirling mist. They were using a map of Canada to guide their way.'[46]

The LPA made use of humour both for its own sake and in an effort to disorientate and denaturalize authority. Their account of the London Marathon in 1996 provides a helpful and typically startling example. The LPA *Newsletter* mapped the run onto a set of ley-lines. It claimed that the route 'snakes around a conflux of ley lines' and, hence, would induce 'mass psychological processing' among participants. For reasons too obscure to detail, this ruse of ruling-class power is claimed to be 'part of the preparation of a site for ritual murder' (replacing Prince Charles with a monarch more to the liking of 'the establishment').

> [T]he essence of our approach is that we seek to prevent that which we predict from happening. If our goal is achieved, and it is impossible for the ritual murder to take place, we will have substantially weakened the psychogeographcal subjugation of the proletariat.[47]

It is pointless interrogating the validity of such assertions, or even whether they are seriously meant. What is of interest is how a revolutionary rhetoric can be spliced with an overt rejection of modernist rationality. It is a combination that is genuinely unsettling. Yet it also has the unintended consequence of satirizing class politics. The use of the term 'the proletariat' in the passage above elicits a smile; it has a self-consciously anachronistic quality that topples into farce by virtue of the framing discussion of 'ley lines' and other esoteric mysteries. Another illustration of this same process came with the LPA's decision to abandon the Christian calendar, and adopt an ancient Egyptian alternative. 'How can we expect the working class to take us seriously', the LPA explained, 'when we still use the superstitious calendar of the Christians imposed by the bosses?'[48] Such playful ideas absorb class within an aesthetics of provocation. They rely on a sense of nostalgia for 'real' class politics but exhibit a brazen confidence that revolutionary rhetoric is today so hollow that it can be scripted as a kind of elaborate joke.

The determinedly eccentric nature of the LPA's activities attracted a small amount of media attention. *The Observer* published 'A Psychogeographical Gazetteer' in 1994, in which the LPA was described as at the 'outer edges of reality'.[49] Another militant group that courted this label was the MAP. The MAP members' desire to 'to walk unregulated, unrepaired, atmospheric streets' was first provoked by urban gentrification.[50] This concern was soon aligned to an interest in the rites of capitalism, for only those who 'open their mindset to invisible forces can comprehend the mental, imaginary fields where the post-industrial land-scape is being mapped'.[51] Like the LPA, MAP's effort to 'disorientate the public and destabi-lise the scientifically-enforced version of the present' reached back to pre-modern sources not simply to engage the modern landscape but in order to find a radical rhetoric that uses the past to supersede the present.[52]

This leads us to the second of the two original themes within British revolutionary psy-chogeography, namely the linking of preservationism with radicalism. Reviewing the work of the Nottingham Psychogeographical Unit (NPU) and two American groups (the New York Psychogeographical Association and the Washington Psychogeography Association), one critic observed that a 'conservationist instinct is something one can detect' in the SI. However,

> [I]t was a hesitant emotion, something often masked by other claims, such as the notion that the old bits of cities are inhabited by the working class (and, hence, are the locations of dissent). The contemporary psychogeographical associations . . . by contrast, are much clearer and bolder in their preservationism. They belong to a new generation of radicals that are convinced that clearing away the landscapes of the past is a reactionary rather than a revolutionary activity. If their declarations have a conservative, traditionalist sound to them (and, of course, they do), it is partly because so many socialists and communists remain unable to reimagine social liberation as something that grows from within an existing society rather than as something imposed by a modernist elite.[53]

Both the MAP and the NPU offered explicit attempts to reconnect radicalism and nos-talgia. This was done in two ways: through a romanticization of decayed and abandoned landscapes and through a hostility to the destruction of old buildings. The first attitude has the flavour of a punk version of William Morris's 'anti-scrape' campaign of the late 1870s. It is equally Morrisian in its horror of commercial civilization. A MAP-organized walk around a derelict churchyard in September 1996 illustrates the point. The trip is said to have allowed an encounter with a graveyard that is,

> magnificent in a way no well-kept churchyard could be. From the vandalised vaults to the used condoms, the overgrown lawns and trees, the graffiti, the remnants of the Church and the weathered gargoyles, the atmosphere and emotional responses generated were absolutely overwhelming. And to think Aldi are going to destroy it and turn it into a buck cheap supermarket.[54]

The NPU offered even bolder statements of preservationism. Not unrelatedly, and in con-trast to the other groups mentioned, the NPU arrived at a form of psychogeography which jettisons avant-garde iconoclasm. For the NPU psychogeography is a form of community cri-tique of the contemporary landscape, a critique based unapologetically on memories of past landscapes. The following account of one of their projects, from 1997, exemplifies the group's methodology and central concerns.

> Set in the inner city area of Sneinton, the Salvation Army charity shop doubles up as a drop-in centre for local people of all ages and walks of life. We asked them to sit down and draw their own map of Nottingham out of memory alone . . . A sad journey for most as for years they helplessly watched their hometown being systematically destroyed and rebuilt . . . At dawn, I wandered around for an hour following the mental maps we collected. People were also able to blindly guide me through the Internet. Aimlessly strolling around the waking city I found myself making my way towards Sneinton windmill. I reached it as the sun rose, a rage for building sites building up inside me.[55]

The emotions of both the elderly and the psychogeographer described in this passage were later developed into a polemic on the relationship between memory and environment, titled 'An Appeal to Stop Building Altogether'.[56] Hostility to new buildings is not uncommon in Britain. But to hear it expressed by psychogeographers, former denizens of the wildest shore of the avant-garde, putative transgressors of all things conventional, is significant. It tells us that the relationship between radicalism and nostalgia is changing. The hostility to the past that shaped the socialist tradition from the late nineteenth century onwards is no longer the force it was. This weakening may also be witnessed in the convoluted creativity of the magico-Marxists. However, unlike those psychogeographical groups, who stage an ironic redemption of modernism by way of a hollowed out class rhetoric, the NPU appears to have lost interest in the spectacle of modernist revolution. The explorations of the London and Manchester groups are stranger and more ludic than the NPU's engagements with ordinary people in ordinary places. But they are also more easily slotted into a familiar lineage of avant-garde provocation. The Nottingham group is less familiar. Perhaps it must be classified as post-avant-garde. More productively, the NPU may be represented as having overcome the anxiety towards the past that has played such a large part in shaping twentieth-century radicalism. Ironically, in doing so they surrender some of their claims to originality. For they offer a moment of reconnection with earlier traditions of British radicalism. The NPU's undiluted and unblinking antagonism towards the violence of modernity reminds us of a time when popular attachment to the past was treated as an inevitable component of radical culture.

Conclusion

> The point of the day, the walk, was to lift that grey lid, the miasma of depression that hangs over the city and its inhabitants. To wait for the moment when the sun breaks through, evening beams cartwheeling over an heroic landscape. You have to be there all day to be sure of getting it. The remission. The pay-off that makes urban life worth enduring.[57]

Modernity turns the past into an arena of provocation and danger. Attachments to the past and feelings of loss become sites of repression and potent resources for resistance and critique. These processes can be seen at work across many political projects. However, they appear to have a uniquely troubled relationship with that set of ideas and ideals associated with the pursuit of equality and the critique of commercialization that we can, perhaps, still call radicalism.

I have argued in this book that the transformation of the politics of loss from a prominent part of the radical tradition to a site of anxiety and dilemma began in earnest in the late nineteenth century. It is not coincidental that this period also witnessed the birth of the avant-garde, a cultural and political margin within which myths of the past (and future) could be deployed. The examples of British psychogeography I have explored in this chapter may be approached as part of the avant-garde tradition. However, I have also suggested that they have a querulous, uncomfortable relationship with this lineage.

The psychogeographies discussed in this chapter illustrate different ways the dilemmas of radical nostalgia have been negotiated. Across all these examples we can identify the balancing of anti-modern and modernist impulses. In the travel books of Iain Sinclair the non-place urban realm becomes a site of creative purgatory, a necessary violence that simultaneously positions the writer as dependent upon and antagonistic to deracination and alienation. This double mapping of modernity and nostalgia is also used to imagine an alternative community of cultural workers who have found a way of being 'at home' and finding friendship in and against a backdrop of noise, flux and dissociation.

In what I have called 'revolutionary psychogeography' we also find the simultaneous evocation and refusal of modernity. However, in this tradition this tension is organized around themes of communism, occultism and preservationism. The development of 'magico-Marxism' encapsulates the novelty, but also the folk-radical inclinations, of the most startling (and self-consciously baffling) aspects of this work. Magico-Marxism glories in its own scurrilous obscurity. Its principal thesis – that class power relies on and can be disrupted through occultism and ritualism – is offered as a kind of creative game of disorientation. Yet the end result mocks and ironizes proletarian identity as much as it mocks and ironizes ruling-class power. Magico-Marxism pursues and explores the most outrageous reaches of radical nostalgia. Yet it also has a rather desperate quality: it wants to be communist but it no longer believes; it wants to articulate the sense of loss that sustains it, but it does not know how. However, we can also identify a preservationist tendency within revolutionary psychogeography capable of offering a confident articulation of the politics of loss. This tendency will appear to many as more culturally conservative, more attuned to the concerns of the old than the iconoclastic energies of the young, and more querulous about the point and possibility of industrial civilization. These concerns are all well founded. Yet they also reflect a political paradigm that, although dominant, no longer inspires the automatic loyalty of creative radicals. With the collapse of communism and the widespread questioning of the sustainability of industrial modernity, the radical imagination has been profoundly challenged. Old assumptions and prejudices can be overturned. And not the least of these concern the role of past in the politics of the present.

For many years, William Morris's exhortation to 'cling to the love of the past and the love of the day to be', has curled many a radical toe.[58] It has been cast as an embarrassing relic of the incoherent and immature naivety of early British radicalism. Yet today the shame of nostalgia is fading. It is perhaps fitting that it is radicals at the most iconoclastic edges of political and cultural life who are beginning to grapple with the fact that the poetry of the future is no longer enough.

Notes

1. I. Sinclair, *London Orbital*, (London: Penguin, 2003), 266.
2. Ibid., 268.

3. See, for example, P. Ackroyd, *London: The Biography*, (London: Chatto and Windus, 2000); P. Ackroyd, *Thames: Sacred River*, (London: Chatto and Windus, 2007); P. Keiller, 'London', Koninck/Channel 4, 82 minutes, (1994); P. Keiller, 'Robinson in Space', BBC/Koninck, 78 minutes, (1997); E. Ho, 'Postimperial Landscapes: "Psychogeography" and Englishness in Alan Moore's Graphic Novel *From Hell: A Melodrama in Sixteen Parts*', *Cultural Critique*, 63, (2006); S. Home (Ed.), *Mind Invaders: A Reader in Psychic Warfare, Cultural Sabotage and Semiotic Terrorism*, (London: Serpent's Tail, 1997); M. Moorcock, *Mother London*, (London: Secker & Warburg, 1988). The term 'avant-garde' remains a necessary anachronism. With the collapse of socialist and communist movements, and the absorption of the tactics of disorientation into an ever bolder commercial culture (notably within the realms of advertising and design), the avant-garde has lost definition, along with its social and political role. However, the term continues to be inevitable shorthand for transgressive and experimental cultural provocations.

4. M. Coverley, *Psychogeography*, (Harpenden: Pocket Essentials, 2006).

5. R. Macfarlane, 'A road of one's own: past and present artists of the randomly motivated walk', *Times Literary Supplement*, (7 October, 2005), 4.

6. J. Heartfield, 'Londonostalgia', *Blueprint*, (September, 2004), available at: http://www.design4design.com/artucles/artcles_story.asp?STORYID=5765, accessed 05.04.2005.

7. Sinclair, *London Orbital*, 269.

8. I. Sinclair, *The Kodak Mantra Diaries*, (London: Albion Village Press, 1971); I. Sinclair, *Muscat's Würm*, (London: Albion Village Press, 1972).

9. Cited by K. Jackson, *The Verbals: Kevin Jackson in Conversation with Iain Sinclair*, (Tonbridge: Worple Press, 2003), 68.

10. Sinclair, *London Orbital*, 3.

11. Ibid., 375.

12. Ibid., 44.

13. Ibid., 343.

14. I. Sinclair, *Lights Out for the Territory*, (London: Granta Books, 1997); I. Sinclair, *Edge of the Orison: In the Traces of John Clare's 'Journey out of Essex'*, (London: Penguin, 2005). See also I. Sinclair (Ed.), *London: City of Disappearances*, (London: Penguin, 2006); I. Sinclair, *Hackney, That Rose-Red Empire: A Confidential Report*, (London: Penguin, 2009); M. Atkins and I. Sinclair, *Liquid City*, (London: Reaktion Books, 1999).

15. Sinclair, *London Orbital*, 16.

16. Ibid., 15.

17. Ibid., 318.

18. Ibid., 260–1.

19. Ibid., 262.

20. Ibid., 11, 166.

21. Ibid., 168.

22. Ibid., 467, 454.

23. Ibid., 453.

24. Sinclair, *Edge of the Orison*, 189, 133.

25. Sinclair, *London Orbital*, 8–9.

26. I. Sinclair, *London Orbital*, Illuminations Films, (2002).

27. Sinclair, *Edge of the Orison*, 79.

28. Sinclair, *London Orbital*, 410.

29. Ibid., 19.

30. Jackson, *The Verbals*, back cover.
31. Sinclair, *Edge of the Orison*, 332.
32. Ibid., 6–7.
33. Ibid., 262, 326.
34. Macfarlane, 'A road of one's own', 4.
35. In Jackson, *The Verbals*, 29.
36. Sinclair, *Lights Out for the Territory*, 25. The LPA reappears in Sinclair's *Hackney, That Rose-Red Empire*, as part of the ultra-left London scene narrated by Stewart Home (399–400).
37. British groups active in the 1990s and their associated journals/newsletters and web-sites (where still up in some form at the time of writing) include Manchester Area Psychogeographic (*Manchester Area Psychogeographic*; http://map. twentythree.us/index.html); London Psychogeographical Association (*London Psychogeographical Association Newsletter*; http://www.unpopular.demon.co.uk/lpa/organisations/lpa.html); Nottingham Psychogeographical Unit (*Nottingham Psychogeographical Unit Stories*; http://www.geocities.com/Paris/Rue/5383/index.htm and http://www.corinna.it/qui/); North East Essex Psychogeographical Project (*Outer Space Wayz*). See also *Vague* (undated a, undated b, 1997, 1998); *Transgressions: A Journal of Urban Exploration*; *Network News* (http://www.earthlydelights.co.uk). Outside the United Kingdom, revolutionary psychogeography groups and/or publications include the Washington Psychogeographical Association; New York Psychogeographical Association (http://www.notbored.org/the-nypa.html); *Oblivion: A Journal of Urban Semioclasm and Spatial Practices*; *Days between Stations*; Associazione Psicogeografica di Bologna (*Luther Blissett: Bollettino della Associazione Psicogeografica di Bologna*); Associazione Psicogeografica di Milano; *Luther Blissett: Revista di Guerra Psichica e Adunate Sediziose.*
38. For discussion, see D. Pinder, 'Arts of urban exploration', *Cultural Geographies* 12, (2005); for examples, see Conflux, http://www.glowlab.com/christina-ray/conflux-2007/, accessed 09.09.2007 (updated link: http://confluxfestival.org/2009/); J. Hart, 'A new way of walking: artist-explorers called psychogeographers are changing the way we experience the city', available at: http://www.utne.com/2004–07-01/a-new-way-of-walking.aspx, accessed 07.07.2009; CAA, 'Psychogeography: a selection of maps', available at: http://www.cca-glasgow.com/index.cfm?page=236B7D10–868E-4F86-A306909B378E5655&eventid=139D893C-6477-EE84-DC9C916421E56FAA, accessed 29.09.2009.
39. See L. Deyo and D. Leibowitz, *Invisible Frontier: Exploring the Tunnels, Ruins, and Rooftops of Hidden New York*, (New York: Three Rivers Press, 2003); Ninjalicious, *Access All Areas: A User's Guide to the Art of Urban Exploration*, (Toronto: Infiltration, 2005). See also R. Solnit, *A Field Guide to Getting Lost*, (Edinburgh: Canongate, 2006), 3. The line between arts and agitational psychogeography is disputed territory. Both types of activity, as well as a mingling of the two, were in evidence at TRIP, a 'psychogeography festival' and con-ference held in Manchester, 19–21 June, 2008. See http://trip2008.wordpress.com/
40. A. Bonnett, 'Editorial', *Transgressions: A Journal of Urban Exploration*, 1, (1995), 7.
41. I. Sinclair, *Lud Heat and Suicide Bridge*, (London: Vintage, 1995), 113.
42. The first usage of this term appears to be D. Bin, 'Three psychogeographical groups: activities, websites, publications', *Transgressions*, 5, (no date), 4. Stewart Home describes the same field of activity as 'avant-bard'. It should also be noted that Home has offered an explicitly anti-nostalgic version of this kind of 'psychic warfare', contrasting 'mate-rial science in the form of proletarian postmodernism' with 'pastoralism [which] stands

for stasis and death' (S. Home, *How I Discovered America: Infopool* 6, London: Infopool, 2002, 1).

43. F. Tompsett, 'East London: portal to the land of unbelief', *Infotainment*, 1, (1998), 2. The original LPA was an organization in name only. It was 'a pure invention, a mirage' devised by Ralph Rumney in order to make the groups that merged in 1957 to form the SI sound 'more international' (Rumney, *The Consul*, 37). By contrast the reformed LPA was highly active, splitting into a number of subgroups. As well as publishing 18 *Newsletters* between 1993 and 1997, the LPA hosted numerous events.

44. London Psychogeographical Association, 'Future trips of the LPA', *London Psychogeographical Association Newsletter*, 8, (1994), 4.

45. London Psychogeographical Association, 'Oxford triangulation by the night patrol', *London Psychogeographical Association Newsletter*, 2, (1993), 2.

46. London Psychogeographical Association, 'Cerne Abbas, MayDay 1993', *London Psychogeographical Association Newsletter*, 3, (1993), 3.

47. London Psychogeographical Association, 'Run up to ritual murder', *London Psychogeographical Association Newsletter*, 14, (1996; dated Beltaine 397), 4.

48. London Psychogeographical Association, 'Say no to the millennium', *London Psychogeographical Association Newsletter*, 18, (1997; dated Beltaine 398), 4.

49. B. Hugill, 'Cultists go round in circles', *The Observer*, (28 August, 1994), 3; D. Gill, 'It's a game of three halves when anarchists hit the soccer pitch', *The Observer*, (11 August, 1996).

50. Manchester Area Psychogeographic, 'An interview with: Manchester Area Psychogeographic', available at: http://www.uncarved.org/turb/articles/map-int.html, accessed 30.09.2009.

51. Ibid.

52. Ibid.

53. D. Bin, 'Three psychogeographical groups', 97.

54. Manchester Area Psychogeographic, 'From temple to fairy hill', *Manchester Area Psychogeographic*, 5, (1996), 4.

55. Nottingham Psychogeographical Unit, 'Think of Nottingham: a mental mapping workshop', http://www.corinna.it/qui/npu/mental/think.htm, now available at: http://fasica.altervista.org/npu/mental/think.htm, accessed 29.09.2009.

56. Nottingham Psychogeographical Unit, 'An appeal to stop building altogether', *Nottingham Psychogeographical Unit Stories*, 3, (1998).

57. Sinclair, *London Orbital*, 29.

58. Morris, *The Pilgrims of Hope*, 57.

Conclusion: Acknowledging Nostalgia

In the early twenty-first century the left is often represented as a political tradition from the past of uncertain relevance to the future. Yet one of the dominant themes within left-wing thought is contempt for nostalgia. Thus a paradox appears. This book has explored this and other paradoxes of radical nostalgia within three particular areas (early English radicalism; anti-colonialism and post-colonialism; situationism and its afterlives). I said at the start of this book that I was not going to be offering a guide on how to 'do nostalgia'. Nostalgia has been presented as a field of acknowledgement, an integral aspect of the modern condition, something that is present whether or not we identify and engage it or repress and deny it. The contemporary crisis of the left is helping to bring the nature and importance of loss and longing into the light. Yet it remains a fraught encounter. Resistance to nostalgia is hard-wired into modernity. But so too, it seems, is the possibility of counter-modernity. And with that possibility we find others, such as the idea that nostalgia works within and against the present, that it reconstitutes modernity, that it is not just reactive but reaches out and down to shape our hopes for the past and the future.

From Spence to Sinclair, Marx to Gilroy, radicalism has also been in and against its times. It was never simply modern. Of course, an awkward relationship to contemporary society is not unique to radicalism. Nor does it necessarily represent a point of weakness. The capacity to transcend modernity enables narratives of tradition and attachment, narratives around which political projects can cohere. However, as we have seen, radicalism has a particularly uncomfortable alliance with the past. The two challenges for the left that I will conclude with will not resolve this discomfort. They offer an encounter with it; a reflexive trajectory that is also a necessary moment of critique. The two challenges are, first, the need to reclaim the idea of loss and, second, the need to acknowledge alienation. I will also be returning to a theme that has hovered in the background behind much of the material in this book, the greening of radical politics. I know I have not written enough on this topic. I meant to when I started this book. But it always seemed to slip away (along with many other ideas; I also have a pile of notes on radical nostalgia in folk and world music squatting angrily at my elbow). So it is something of a redemptive act that I finish this book, perhaps, where I should have begun it, with a green vision of the radical tradition.

Acknowledging Loss

The bourgeois viewpoint has never advanced beyond the antithesis between itself and the romantic viewpoint, and the latter will accompany it as its legitimate antithesis up to its blessed end.

Karl Marx[1]

I have returned to Marx many times in this book. He identified more clearly than any other radical thinker how capitalism detaches people from the past. However, by representing a sense of loss as a kind of failure of the will, something that could be conquered and overcome, his analysis also exemplifies the lack of attention given to the inescapable nature of nostalgia that marks all progressivist ideologies. By the turn of the twentieth century, with the 'blessed end' of Marxism as an active and important part of the global political landscape, its own 'romantic viewpoint' was becoming stark. Yet the desire to define the left as an attack on the past and a statement of faith in the future remains tenacious. There is a powerful allure to this narrative. Nostalgia and hope are still commonly offered as antithetical ideas. In 2009 the British liberal-left journalist Polly Toynbee was asked how she defined the left. Her answer reminds just how powerful and persuasive the traditional rhetoric of hostility to nostalgia still is.

> To live on the left is to live optimistically, believing in progress despite set backs, hoping despite frequent disappointment, urging progress against right wing nostalgia for illusory 'better yesterdays'.[2]

Yet Toynbee's clarion is not *as* powerful and persuasive as it once would have been. It is full of too many memories and too much yearning. And too much anguish . . . 'despite set backs' . . . 'despite frequent disappointment' . . . the great tradition soldiers on. Stories of struggle thrive on such brave resolve. Perhaps the marginalization of the left is creating new opportunities for discourses of heroic determination against the odds. Yet, if we wish to talk honestly about the British left in 2009, Toynbee's use of the term 'set backs' appears as something of an understatement, for the left had long since ceased to exist as a mainstream political force.

An intriguing prospect opens up. It is of a small and insular political community being sustained well into the future on images of itself as 'urging progress', while the rest of the world either ignores it or views it with bemused interest as an anachronism.

To seriously engage with the role of loss in modern life demands a fundamental revision of the way the story of the left is told. Most obviously, it suggests that we begin to look at the flows of nostalgia and anti-nostalgia in the making of the left, not as an ascent but as a series of dilemmas, of difficult negotiations and awkward combinations. The history of the left that emerges is more interesting, more human and more vulnerable. It also flies in the face of the idea that radicalism must be defended against accusations of contradiction or uncertainty. Ironically, it often seems as if those who want to defend the old order are also those who are the most resistant to nostalgia.

Acknowledging nostalgia will not necessarily make the left more successful or popular. But it might, to use Fanon's phrase, help 'cut off those wings' and reconnect it with ordinary people. This perspective also implies that the defensive attempts of workers and residents to save occupations, communities and valued landscapes might be looked at more sympathetically or, at least, without a presumption of suspicion. We are all trying to save, to preserve, to protect, against the acids of modernity. The idea that society can be divided between tear-streaked reactionaries besotted with the past and flint-eyed radicals staring into the future, has run its time.

Reclaiming Alienation

Today the idea of alienation (along with its associated concept, authenticity) has a double life. Within popular culture the attempt to consume real food, go to real places, be in real relationships, is ubiquitous. Although often part and parcel of the consumer experience, such ideas have become part of an everyday and wide-ranging critique of unsustainable modernity. Yet over the past 30 years, a deep suspicion of ideas of alienation has grown up within intellectual circles. The notion that forms of thought that are not reactionary are, by definition, against claims to human wholeness and authenticity, has settled into a critical orthodoxy. Although often described as a form of deconstruction, this position substitutes Derrida's notion of the deferral of essences with a transcendental ethic of 'anti-essentialism'. The rupture between the popular deployment of references to 'the real' and the attempt by intellectuals to escape essentialism, is also a schism within radicalism: for both those in pursuit of authenticity and 'anti-essentialists' think of themselves as engaged in a politics of liberation. This book has suggested that the distinction between the two positions is a false one. In large part this is due to the fact that themes of alienation and authenticity are integral components of the modern condition. They cannot be dispatched, treated as a kind of contagion against which healthy minds may be inoculated. In acknowledging nostalgia we also acknowledge alienation and authenticity. We encounter the fact that, even the most radical of us, relies on these tropes to narrate our journey through modernity.

In developing this argument we meet with many other questions. Perhaps the most significant concerns the relationship between loss and liberation. Without loss, what is liberation? What is it for? How do we know it is needed? It is, after all, in our attachments to the past that the possibility and the limits of such hopes are most readily found. To frame loss as an error to be overcome, or a primitive early stage in humanity's rise out of the mire of traditionalism, is to turn liberation itself into an object of suspicion. We see something of this in Michel Foucault's statement, from 1984, that, he

is a little distrustful of the general theme of liberation, to the extent, that, if one does not treat it with a certain number of safeguards and within certain limits, there is the danger that it will refer back to the idea that there does exist a nature or a human foundation which, as a result of a certain number of historical, social, or economic processes, found itself concealed, alienated or imprisoned in and by some repressive mechanism.[3]

One of the doubts this passage creates turns on the point of why Foucault is only a *little* suspicious of liberation? For if the 'danger' of evoking 'a natural or human foundation' is our main concern then ideas of liberation appear as unnecessarily risky. Foucault is offering us an unrelenting scepticism. Yet to be politically meaningful scepticism needs to be sceptical about its own limits. If it is rendered as an idealized category it becomes a form of evasion, untroubled and unsceptical about its ability to either flee the logic of resistance to modernity or escape the political consequences of dispatching one of the central narratives of radicalism.

There are a number of reasons why alienation and authenticity should be acknowledged in sympathetic terms by radicals. I have argued that these themes are embedded in the possibility of political life. Without them virtually the entire set of other aspirations associated with the left – autonomy, freedom, equality – become suspect. It may also be pointed out that authenticity and alienation are presupposed in everyday communication. It is not clear that dialogue could occur at all in a situation in which no distinction was made between simulacra and the real or between something that is whole and complete and something that is not. However, the best reason why alienation and authenticity are so important takes us back to the material on the left's attempts to escape them that I have provided in the preceding chapters. For as we have seen, these attempts have been beset by difficulties. Moreover, we have also seen more popular radical movements (such as anti-colonialism and early English socialism) place such ideas, albeit often unacknowledged and undigested, at the core of their ambitions. What I conclude from this situation is that alienation and authenticity are brought into being as radical ideas at the same time, and in intimate relationship with, the idea of nostalgia. These neologisms of modernity that can appear to be far older than the modern, provide the language of freedom that radicals require.

It is modernity that fragments society into atomized, lonely crowds. In the process, dreams of wholeness, of coherence and the 'return of man', come to gain a new prominence. These aspirations emerge from within real social processes. They may be called necessary myths. Yet it is not clear that the inevitably judgmental and aloof terminology of 'myth' – which pre-supposes and relies on the non-mythical but is rarely able to identify it – is helpful here (nor, indeed, its sociological cognate, 'social construction'). It is more useful to talk of our *relationship* to these ideas within particular historical and geographical contexts. Nostalgia, aliena-tion and authenticity appear before us as ancient cries and the creations of modernity and we are all bound to them. Today, despite the continuing addiction of a lot of critical scholarship to tropes of rootless reverie, nostalgia is being reconsidered across a variety of disciplines. It is, perhaps, significant that at least one of the putative founders of post-modern thought should be among those who have signalled their desire to challenge it, by finding new value in themes of continuance and preservation.[4] And swirling over this academic scene, of argu-ments and counter-arguments, we find the most pressing issue of the twenty-first century, discussed in terms that constantly evoke alienation and authenticity and are often brazenly nostalgic, the environment.

Green Past: Green Future

The spectre of environmental crisis is stalking the world. We are increasingly aware of nature not just as a local, immediate, environment but as a global and interconnected system. The consequences and sudden nature of human incursions into the environment have caught up with industrial societies and are forcing a response. One of the most obvious things about this response is that it seeks to take us *back in order to take us forward*: to lower levels of emissions; to a more sustainable relationship with the earth; to protected biodiversity; perhaps, eventu-ally, to a smaller human population.

The green challenge to the ideology of progress is profound. It is not simply a challenge to capitalism but to modernity as such. Thus it is a challenge to all the different political forms nurtured within modernity: to socialism and communism just as much as to capitalism and liberal democracy. The idea that nature must be conquered and pushed aside, that we can 'do anything', has come to appear unsustainable and old-fashioned. The themes of authenticity and alienation have thus returned in new and more pressing ways. The shift from an anthro-pocentric view of the Earth to a more sustainable and holistic sense of life means that we must expand our ideas of the 'good past', of yearning and loss, of the authentic and the fake, into new realms. This is also a process of rediscovery and, inevitably, romanticization, of nature-human relationships from other times and places. We can find it presaged in the kind of radi-cal nostalgic traditions rediscovered within anti-colonialism, as well as in the early English socialism discussed in Chapter Two. The green agenda is not novel. Nor does it derive from one intellectual source or one part of the world. It has been given voice and been marginalized and ignored many times. What is different is that, today, the technocentric and anthropocen-tric ideologies that have long drowned out these concerns in the name of progress, are them-selves on the defensive. And with this transition comes the possibility of a new appreciation of roots, as a process, a politics and a metaphor. It will be recalled that the word 'radical' is derived from the Latin for 'root'. One of the fundamental dilemmas introduced in this book has centred on the relationship between radicalism and roots. Does radicalism demand that roots are pulled up or does it ask that roots are nurtured? In an era of environmental crisis, the balance between these options appears to have tilted decisively to the latter. The aspiration to plough up the past and cover the world in shining new cities of tomorrow has lost its appeal. The skylines of East Asia may still be sprouting glass and metal towers but they point to the utopias of yesterday. The weary play of post-modernism appears even more distant and uninviting. So we turn away and back to things that remain worth fighting for and which sustain. The longing for human wholeness, for lives not blighted by isolation and alienation, for a green earth: these are the ordinary aspirations that define the limits of modernity and the nature of our loss. In acknowledging nostalgia we are also acknowledging hope.

Notes

1. Marx, *Grundrisse*, 162.
2. P. Toynbee, Interview with Polly Toynbee, available at: http://www.openleft. co.uk/2009/07/20/polly-toynbee/, accessed 20.09.2009.
3. M. Foucault, 'The ethic of care for the self as a practice of freedom', *Philosophy and Social Criticism*, 12, 2/3, (1987), 113, 112–31.
4. Derrida, *Spectres of Marx*; also J. Derrida, *On Cosmopolitanism and Forgiveness*, (London: Routledge, 2001).

References

Ackroyd, P. *London: The Biography*, London: Chatto and Windus, 2000.

Ackroyd, P. *Thames: Sacred River*, London: Chatto and Windus, 2007.

Adorno, T. *Aesthetic Theory*, Minneapolis: University of Minnesota Press, 1998.

Adorno, T. and Horkheimer, M. *Dialectic of Enlightenment*, London: Verso, 1979.

Agacinski, S. *Time Passing: Modernity and Nostalgia*, New York: Columbia University Press, 2003.

Agamben, G. *The Coming Community*, Minneapolis: University of Minnesota, 1993.

Akhtar, S. 'The immigrant, the exile, and the experience of nostalgia', *Journal of Applied Psychoanalytic Studies*, 1, 2, 1999, 123–30.

Al-e Ahmad, J. *Lost in the Crowd*, Washington, DC: Three Continents Press, 1985.

Al-e Ahmad, J. *Plagued by the West (Gharbzadegi)*, Delmar: Caravan Books, 1992.

ALTARF [All London Teachers Against Racism and Fascism] (Ed.) *Challenging Racism*, London: ALTARF, 1984.

Anderson, P. 'The river of time', *New Left Review*, 26, 2004, 67–77.

Antliff, A. *Anarchist Modernism: Art, Politics, and the First American Avant-Garde*, Chicago: University of Chicago Press, 2001.

Antze, P. 'The other side: memory as a metaphor in psychoanalysis', in *Regimes of Memory*, Radstone, S. and Hodgkin, K. (Eds), London: Routledge, 2003.

Appiah, K. 'The postcolonial and the postmodern', in Ashcroft, B., Griffiths, G.and Tiffin, H. (Eds), *The Post-Colonial Studies Reader*, London: Routledge, 1995.

Ashraf, P. *The Life and Times of Thomas Spence*, Newcastle: Frank Graham, 1983.

Atkins, M. and Sinclair, I. *Liquid City*, London: Reaktion Books, 1999.

Auge, M. *Non-Places: Introduction to an Anthropology of Supermodernity*, Verso: London, 1995.

Austin, L. *Nostalgia in Transition: 1780–1917*, Charlottesville: University of Virginia Press, 2007.

Baddeley, O. 'Nostalgia for a new world', *Third Text*, 6, 21, 1992, 29–34.

Bakunin, M. 'The reaction in Germany: from the notebooks of a Frenchman', available at: www.marxists.org/reference/archive/bakunin/works/1842/reaction-germany.htm, accessed 09.09.2009.

Bandini, M. 'Surrealist references in the notions of derive and psychogeography of the situationist urban environment', in Andreotti, L. and Costa, X. (Eds), *Situacionistas: arte, politica, urbanismo/ situationists: art, politics, urbanism*, Barcelona: Museu d'Art Contemporani de Barcelona, 1996.

Baucom, I. 'Mournful histories: narratives of postimperial melancholy', *Modern Fiction Studies*, 42, 2, 1996, 259–88.

Beckett, A. 'History lessons: British multiculturalism is under attack. Andy Beckett assesses Paul Gilroy's timely analysis, *After Empire*', *The Guardian*, Saturday, 11 December, 2004.

Beer, M. *Social Struggles and Thought (1750–1860)*, London: Leonard Parsons, 1925.

Beer, M. *A History of British Socialism*, New York: Ayer Publishing, 1979.

Benn, T. 'Foreword', in F. Brockway, *Britain's First Socialists: The Levellers, Agitators and Diggers of the English Revolution*, London: Quartet Books, 1980.

Berger, M. 'After the Third World? History, destiny and the fate of Third Worldism', *Third World Quarterly*, 25, 1, 2004, 9–39.

Bellamy, E. *Looking Backward 2000–1887*, Oxford: Oxford University Press, 2009.

Benjamin, W. *One-Way Street and Other Writings*, London: New Left Books, 1979.

Benjamin, W. 'Left-Wing melancholy', in Kaes, A., Jay, M. and Dimendberg, E. (Eds), *The Weimar Republic Sourcebook*, Berkeley and Los Angeles: University of California Press, 1994.

Bergson, H. *Henri Bergson: Key Writings*, London: Continuum, 2002.

Berman, M. *All That is Solid Melts into Air: The Experience of Modernity*, London: Verso, 1983.

Bevan, R. *The Destruction of Memory: Architecture at War*, London: Reaktion Books, 2006.

Bhabha, H. 'Unsatisfied: notes on vernacular cosmopolitanism', in Castle, G. (Ed.), *Postcolonial Discourses: An Anthology*, Oxford: Blackwell, 2001.

Bin, D. 'Three pyschogeographical groups: activities, websites, publications', *Transgressions: A Journal of Urban Exploration*, 5, (no date), 95–8.

Birtwistle, G. 'Old Gotland, New Babylon: peoples and places in the work of Jorn and Constant', *Transgressions: A Journal of Urban Exploration*, 2/3, 1996, 55–67.

Blackwell, T. and Seabrook, J. *The Revolt against Change: Towards a Conserving Radicalism*, London: Vintage, 1993.

Blake, A. 'From nostalgia to postalgia: hybridity and its discontents in the work of Paul Gilroy and the Wachowski brothers', in Kuortti, J. and Nyman, J. (Eds), *Reconstructing Hybridity: Post-Colonial Studies in Transition*, Amsterdam: Rodopi, 2007.

Blatchford, R. *God and My Neighbour*, London: Clarion Press, 1903.

Blatchford, R. *Not Guilty: A Defence of the Bottom Dog*, London: Clarion Press, 1906.

Blatchford, R. *Merrie England*, London: Clarion Press, 1908.

Blatchford, R. *As I Lay A-Thinking: Some Memories and Reflections of an Ancient and Quiet Watchman*, London: Hodder and Stoughton, 1926.

Bloch, E. *Heritage of Our Times*, Oxford: Polity Press, 1991.

Blunt, A. 'Collective memory and productive nostalgia: Anglo-Indian homemaking at McCluskieganj', *Environment and Planning D: Society and Space*, 21, 2003, 717–38.

Bolus-Reichert, C. 'Aestheticism in the late romances of William Morris', *English Literature in Transition, 1880–1920*, 50, 1, 2007, 73–95.

Bonnett, A. 'Situationism, geography and poststructuralism', *Environment and Planning D: Society and Space*, 7, 1989, 131–46.

Bonnett, A. 'Art, ideology and everyday space: subversive tendencies from Dada to postmodernism', *Environment and Planning D: Society and Space*, 10, 1992, 69–86.

Bonnett, A. *Radicalism, Anti-Racism and Representation*, London: Routledge, 1993.

Bonnett, A. 'Editorial', *Transgressions: A Journal of Urban Exploration*, 1, 1995, 5–8.

Bonnett, A. *White Identities: Historical and International Perspectives*, Harlow: Pearson, 2000.

Bonnett, A. 'Thomas Spence, *Property in Land Every One's Right* (1775)', *Labour History Review*, 74, 1, 2009, 134–6.

Borden, I. and McCreery, S. (Eds), *New Babylonians*, London: Architectural Design, 2001.

Bourne, J. and Sivanandan, A. 'Cheerleaders and ombudsmen: the sociology of race relations in Britain', *Race and Class*, 21, 4, 1980, 331–52.

Boym, S. *The Future of Nostalgia*, New York: Basic Books, 2001.

Bragg, B. *The Progressive Patriot: A Search for Belonging*, London: Bantam Press, 2006.

Brantlinger, P. 'A postindustrial prelude to postcolonialism: John Ruskin, William Morris, and Gandhism', *Critical Inquiry*, 22, 3, 1996, 466–85.

Brocken, M. *The British Folk Revival 1944–2002*, Aldershot: Ashgate, 2003.

Brockman, S. *Literature and German Reunification*, Cambridge: Cambridge University Press, 1999.

Buck-Morss, S. *Dreamworld and Catastrophe: The Passing of Mass Utopia in East and West*, Cambridge, MA: MIT Press, 2000.

CAA. 'Psychogeography: a selection of maps', available at: www.cca-glasgow.com/index.cfm?page=236B7D10–868E-4F86-A306909B378E5655&eventid=139D893C-6477-EE84-DC9-C916421E56FAA, accessed 29.09.2009.

Calhoun, C. *The Question of Class Struggle: Social Foundations of Popular Radicalism during the Industrial Revolution*, Chicago: University of Chicago Press, 1982.

Calhoun, C. 'The radicalism of tradition: community strength or venerable disguise and borrowed language?', *American Journal of Sociology*, 88, 5, 1983, 886–914.

Calhoun, C. 'The class consciousness of frequent travelers: toward a critique of actually existing cosmopolitanism', *The South Atlantic Quarterly*, 101, 4, 2002, 869–97.

Carby, H. 'Schooling in Babylon', in *The Empire Strikes Back: Race and Racism in 70s Britain*, London: Hutchinson/Centre for Contemporary Cultural Studies, 1982.

Carey, H. and Raciborski, R. 'Postcolonialism: a valid paradigm for the Former Sovietized states and Yugoslavia?', *East European Politics and Societies*, 18, 2, 2004, 5–21.

Carlyle, T. 'Signs of the Times', *Edinburgh Review*, 49, June, 1829, 439–59.

Carson, R. *Silent Spring*, Harmondsworth: Penguin, 1965.

Castro, F. 'At the closing session of the Tricontinental Conference', speech delivered to Tricontinental Conference, Chaplin Theatre, Havana, 15 January, 1966, available at: www.marxists.org/history/cuba/archive/castro/1966/01/15.htm, accessed 12.07.2009.

Centre for Contemporary Cultural Studies, *The Empire Strikes Back: Race and Racism in 70s Britain*, London: Hutchinson/Centre for Contemporary Cultural Studies, 1982.

Chaliand, G. *Revolution in the Third World: Myths and Prospects*, Hassocks: Harvester Press, 1977.

Chamberlain, J. *The Radical Programme*, London: Chapman and Hall, 1885.

Chamberlain, J. and Gilman, S. (Eds) *Degeneration: The Dark Side of Progress*, New York: Colombia University Press, 1985.

Chandra, S. and Larsen, N. 'Postcolonial pedigrees: *Postcolonialism: An Historical Introduction*', *Cultural Critique*, 62, 2006, 197–206.

Chang, A. *The Melancholy of Race: Psychoanalysis, Assimilation, and Hidden Grief*, New York: Oxford University Press, 2001.

Chang, J. and Halliday, J. *Mao: The Unknown Story*, London: Random House, 2006.

Chase, M. *The People's Farm: English Radical Agrarianism 1775–1840*, Oxford: Clarendon Press, 1988.

Chevalier, L. *The Assassination of Paris*, Chicago: University of Chicago Press, 1994.

Christie, C. *Ideology and Revolution in Southeast Asia, 1900–1980: Political Ideas of the Anti-Colonial Era*, London: Routledge, 2001.

The Clarion, 'How I became a socialist', (February, 1896), available at: www.wcml.org.uk/group/scout.htm, accessed 07.09.2006.

Clark, G. and Subhan, N. 'Some definitions', in Ebbutt, K. and Pearce, B. (Eds), *Racism and Schools: Contributions to a Discussion*, London: Communist Party of Great Britain, undated.

Clifford, J. 'Traveling cultures', in Grossberg, L., Nelson, C. and Treichler, P. (Eds), *Cultural Studies*, London: Routledge, 1992.

Cobbett, W. *Rural Rides*, Volume 1, London: J. M. Dent, 1917.

Cobbett, W. 'To the Blanketteers', *Cobbett's Weekly Political Register*, 27 March, 1819, 827–58.

Cohen, M. *Profane Illumination: Walter Benjamin and the Paris of Surrealist Revolution*, Berkeley: University of California Press, 1993.

Colley, L. 'I am the watchman', *London Review of Books*, 20 November, 2003, 16–17.

Collins, M. *The Likes of Us: A Biography of the White Working Class*, London: Granta Books, 2004.

Conflux, available at: www.glowlab.com/christina-ray/conflux-2007/, accessed 09.09.2007 (updated link: http://confluxfestival.org/2009/).

Connerton, P. *How Modernity Forgets*, Cambridge: Cambridge University Press, 2009.

Constant, 'Une autre ville pour une autre vie', *Internationale Situationniste*, 3, 1959, 37–40.

Constant, 'A conversation with Constant', in de Zegher, C. and Wigley, M. (Eds), *The Activist Drawing: Retracing Situationist Architecture from Constant's New Babylon to Beyond*, Cambridge, MA: MIT Press, 2001.

Coutois, S. (Ed.), *The Black Book Of Communism: Crimes, Terror, Repression*, Cambridge: Harvard University Press, 1999.

Coverley, M. *Psychogeography*. Harpenden: Pocket Essentials, 2006.

Crook, S. 'Moving mountains: "shamanic" rock art and the International of Experimental Artists', *Transgressions: A Journal of Urban Exploration*, 4, 1998, 36–48.

Cunningham, H. 'The language of patriotism', in Samuel, R. (Ed.), *Patriotism: The Making and Unmaking of British National Identity: Volume I: History and Politics*, London: Routledge, 1989.

d'Encausse, H. *The Nationality Question in the Soviet Union and Russia*, Oslo: Scandinavian University Press, 1995.

Dabashi, H. *The Theology of Discontent: The Ideological Foundation of the Islamic Revolution in Iran*, New York: New York University Press, 1993.

Davis, F. *Yearning for Yesterday: A Sociology of Nostalgia*, New York: Free Press, 1979.

de Sousa Santos, B. *The Rise of the Global Left*, London: Zed Press, 2006.

de Sousa Santos, B. 'Beyond abyssal thinking: from global lines to ecologies of knowledges', available at: www.eurozine.com, accessed 29.09.2009.

de Zegher, C. and Wigley, M. (Eds) *The Activist Drawing: Retracing Situationist Architecture from Constant's New Babylon to Beyond*, Cambridge, MA: MIT Press, 2001.

Debord, G. 'Sur le passage de quelques personnes a travers une assez courte unite de temps', Dansk-Fransk Experimenatalfilmskompagni (20 minutes), 1959.

Debord, G. 'Critique de la séparartion', Dansk-Fransk Experimenatalfilmskompagni (20 minutes), 1961.

Debord, G. *La société du spectacle*, Paris: Editions Buchet-Chastel, 1967.

Debord, G. 'In girum imus nocte et consumimur igni', Simar Films (80 minutes), 1979.

Debord, G. *Society of the Spectacle*, Detroit: Black and Red, 1983.

Debord, G. 'On wild architecture', in Sussman, E. (Ed.), *On the Passage of a Few People through a Rather Brief Moment of Time: The Situationist International 1957–1972*, Cambridge, MA: MIT Press, 1989.

Debord, G. 'Two accounts of the derive', in Sussman, E. (Ed.), *On the Passage of a Few People through a Rather Brief Moment of Time: The Situationist International 1957–1972*, Cambridge, MA: MIT Press, 1989.

Debord, G. *Comments on the Society of the Spectacle*, London: Verso, 1990.

Debord, G. *Panegyric*, London: Verso, 1991,

Debord, G. *Society of the Spectacle and Other Films*, London: Rebel Press, 1992.

Debord, G. *Panégyrique 2*, Paris: Arthème Fayard, 1997.

Dench, G. and Gavron, K. *The New East End: Kinship, Race and Conflict*, London: Profile Books, 2006.

Debord, G. and Wolman, G. 'Methods of detournement', in Knabb, K. (Ed.), *Situationist International Anthology*, Berkeley: Bureau of Public Secrets, 1981.

Derrida, J. *Spectres of Marx*, London: Routledge, 1994.

Derrida, J. *On Cosmopolitanism and Forgiveness*, London: Routledge, 2001.

Derry, J. *The Radical Tradition: Tom Paine to Lloyd George*, London: Macmillan, 1967.

Deyo, L. and Leibowitz, D. *Invisible Frontier: Exploring the Tunnels, Ruins, and Rooftops of Hidden New York*. New York: Three Rivers Press, 2003.

Dhondy, F. 'Teaching young blacks', in Dhondy, F., Besse, B. and Hassan, L. (Eds), *The Black Explosion in British Schools*, London: Race Today Publications, 1982.

Dirlik, A. *The Postcolonial Aura: Third World Criticism in the Age of Global Capitalism*, Boulder: Westview, 1997.

Doane, J. and Hodges, D. *Nostalgia and Sexual Difference: The Resistance to Contemporary Feminism*, New York: Methuen, 1987.

Dodgson, P. and Stewart, D. 'Multiculturalism or anti-racist teaching: a question of alternatives', *Multiracial Education*, 9, 3, 1981, 41–51.

Driver, C. *Tory Radical: The Life of Richard Oastler*, New York: Oxford University Press, 1946.

Dyck, I. *William Cobbett and Rural Popular Culture*, Cambridge: Cambridge University Press, 1992.

Ebbatson, R. *An Imaginary England: Nation, Landscape and Literature, 1840–1920*, Aldershot: Ashgate, 2005.

Ebbutt, K. and Pearce, B. (Eds) *Racism and Schools: Contributions to a Discussion*, London: Communist Party of Great Britain, undated.

Eisenstadt, S. 'Multiple modernities', *Daedalus*, 129, 1, 2000, 1–29.

el-Ojeili, C. 'Forget Debord?', *Thesis Eleven*, 89, 2007, 115–27.

Engels, F. 'Letter from Frederick Engels to Henry Mayer Hyndman', dated 13 March 1882, in P. Ashraf, *The Life and Times of Thomas Spence*, Newcastle: Frank Graham, 1983.

Evans, B. and Evans, C. *A Dictionary of Contemporary American Usage*, New York: Random House, 1957.

Fanon, F. *The Wretched of the Earth*, Harmondsworth: Penguin, 1967.

Fanon, F. *Black Skin, White Masks*, London: Pluto, 1986.

Fitzgerald, F. *Fire in the Lake*, Boston: Little, Brown and Company, 1972.

Flynn, D. 'Beyond boundaries', *Chartist*, January/February, 2008, 30.

Ford, J. 'Paul Gilroy, *After Empire* (London: Routledge, 2004) and Huey P Newton & V I Lenin (ed. Amy Gdala), *Revolutionary Intercommunalism & the Right of Nations to Self-Determination* (London: Superscript, 2004)'.

Foucault, M. *Language, Counter-Memory, Practice*, Ithaca: Cornell University Press, 1977.

Foucault, M. 'The ethic of care for the self as a practice of freedom', *Philosophy and Social Criticism*, 12, 2/3, 1987, 112–31.

Frisby, D. *Fragments of Modernity*, Cambridge: Polity Press, 1985.

Fritzsche, P. 'How nostalgia narrates modernity', in Fritzsche, P. and Confino, A. (Eds), *The Work of Memory: New Directions in the Study of German Society and Culture*, Champaign, IL: University of Illinois Press, 2002.

Fritzsche, P. *Stranded in the Present: Modern Time and the Melancholy of History*, Cambridge: Harvard University Press, 2004.

Frow, J. 'Tourism and the semiotics of nostalgia', *October*, 57, 1991, 123–51.

Füredi, F. *The Silent War: Imperialism and the Changing Perception of Race*, London: Pluto, 1998.

Gabriel, Y. 'Organizational nostalgia – reflections of "The Golden Age"', in S. Fineman (Ed.), *Emotion in Organisations*, London: Sage, 1993.

Gallop, G. 'Introductory essay: Thomas Spence and the Real Rights of Man', in T. Spence, *Pigs' Meat: Selected Writings of Thomas Spence*, Nottingham: Spokesman, 1982.

Gandhi, *The Collected Works of Mahatma Gandhi: Volume 58*, New Delhi: Ministry of Information and Broadcasting, 1984.

Gandhi, *Gandhi's Experiments with Truth: Essential Writings by and about Mahatma Gandhi*, Lanham: Lexington Books, 2006.

Gaonkar, D. 'On alternative modernities', *Public Culture*, 11, 1, 1999, 245–68.

Gaspar, E. ' Nationalism vs. internationalism: Hungarian history in the re-making', *RFE/RL Collection; Background Reports*, (1969), available at: http://www.osaarchivum.org/files/holdings/3000/8/3text_da/34–4-255.shtml, accessed 29.06.2009.

Geoghegan, V. '"Let the dead bury the dead": Marx, Derrida and Bloch', *Contemporary Political Theory*, 1, 2002, 5–18.

Geschiere, P. *The Perils of Belonging: Autochthony, Citizenship, and Exclusion in Africa and Europe*, Chicago: Chicago University Press, 2009.

Gill, D. 'It's a game of three halves when anarchists hit the soccer pitch', *The Observer* 11 August, 1996.

Gill, H. 'Hegemony and ambiguity: discourses, counter-discourses and hidden meanings in French depictions of the conquest and settlement of Algeria', *Modern and Contemporary France*, 14, 2, 2006, 157–72.

Gilroy, P. *There Ain't No Black in the Union Jack: the Cultural Politics of Race and Nation*, London: Hutchinson, 1987.

Gilroy, P. 'The end of anti-racism', W. Ball and J. Solomos (Eds), *Race and Local Politics,* London: Macmillan, 1990.

Gilroy, P. *The Black Atlantic*, London: Verso, 1993.

Gilroy, P. *Small Acts: Thoughts on the Politics of Black Cultures*, London: Serpent's Tail, 1993.

Gilroy, P. *Against Race: Imagining Political Culture beyond the Color Line*, Cambridge: Harvard University Press, 2000.

Gilroy, P. *After Empire: Melancholia or Convivial Culture?* London: Routledge, 2004.

Gilroy, P. *Postcolonial Melancholia*, New York: Columbia University Press, 2005.

Glasier, J. *William Morris and the Early Days of the Socialist Movement*, London: Longmans, Green and Company, 1921.

Glassman, J. 'U.S. youths turning normal and conservative', available at: findarticles.com/p/articles/mi_qn4188/is_20040706/ai_n11464766, accessed 23.07.2008.

Glazer, P. *Radical Nostalgia: Spanish Civil War Commemoration in America*, Rochester, NY: University of Rochester Press, 2005.

Gold, T. 'After comradeship: personal relations in China since the Cultural Revolution', *The China Quarterly*, 104, 1985, 657–75.

Goodhart, D. *Progressive Nationalism: Citizenship and the Left*, London: Demos, 2006.

Gordon, L. 'Fanon's tragic revolutionary violence', in Gordon, L. Sharpley-Whiting, T. and White, R. (Eds), *Fanon: A Critical Reader*, Oxford: Blackwell, 1996.

Graham, H. 'The radical as the past in the present: how to write histories of the British Women's Liberation Movement', paper presented to Gender and Power in the New Europe: Fifth European Feminist Research Conference, Lund University, (20–24 August, 2003).

Gray, A. *The Socialist Tradition: Moses to Lenin*. London: Longmans, 1947.

Greene, G. 'Feminist fiction and the uses of memory', *Signs: Journal of Women in Culture and Society*, 16, 1991, 290–321.

Gupta, A. *Postcolonial Developments: Agriculture in the Making of Modern India*, Durham, NC: Duke University Press, 1998.

Gupta, D. *Learning to Forget: The Anti-Memoirs of Modernity*, New Delhi: Oxford University Press, 2005.

Halfin, I. *From Darkness to Light: Class, Consciousness, and Salvation in Revolutionary Russia*, Pittsburgh: University of Pittsburgh Press, 2000.

Hall, S., Critcher, C., Jefferson, T., Clarke, J. and Roberts, B. *Policing the Crisis: Mugging, the State and Law and Order*, London: Macmillan, 1978.

Hannerz, U. 'Cosmopolitans and locals in world culture', in Featherstone, M. (Ed.), *World Cultures*, London: Sage, 1990.

Hansen, W. 'Another side to Frantz Fanon: reflections on socialism and democarcy', *New Political Science*, 19, 3, 1997, 89–111.

Hardt, M. and Negri, A. *Empire*, Cambridge: Harvard University Press, 2000.

Harootunian, H. *Overcome by Modernity: History, Culture and Community in Interwar Japan*, Princeton: Princeton University Press, 2000.

Hart, J. 'A new way of walking: artist-explorers called psychogeographers are changing the way we experience the city', available at: www.utne.com/2004–07-01/a-new-way-of-walking.aspx, accessed 07.07.2009.

Hay, S. *Asian Ideas of East and West: Tagore and his Critics in Japan, China, and India*, Cambridge: Harvard University Press, 1970.

Heartfield, J. 'Londonnostalgia', reprinted from *Blueprint*, September, 2004, available at: www.design4design.com/artcules/artcles_story.asp?STORYID=5765, accessed 05/04/2005.

Hegel, G. *The Philosophy of History*, New York: Cosimo, 2007.

Helmer, J. and Malzacher, F. (Eds), *Not Even a Game Anymore, the Theatre of Forced Entertainment*, Berlin: Alexander Verlag, 2004.

Henderson, P. *William Morris: His Life, Work and Friends*, Harmondsworth: Penguin, 1973.

Hewison, R. *The Heritage Industry: Britain in a Climate of Decline*, London: Methuen, 1987.

Hewitt, A. *Fascist Modernism: Aesthetics, Politics, and the Avant-Garde*, Stanford, CA: Stanford University Press, 1996.

Higgens, J. *Raymond Williams: Literature, Marxism and Cultural Materialism*, London: Routledge, 1999.

Hill, C. *Puritanism and Revolution: Studies in Interpretation of the English Revolution of the 17th Century*, London: Pimilco, 2001.

Ho, E. 'Postimperial landscapes: "Psychogeography" and Englishness in Alan Moore's graphic novel *From Hell: A Melodrama in Sixteen Parts*', *Cultural Critique*, 63, 2006, 99–121.

Hobsbawm, E. *Primitive Rebels*, Manchester: Manchester University Press, 1959.

Hobsbawm, E. *The Age of Revolution, 1789–1848*, New York: New American Library, 1962.

Hobsbawm, E. 'Introduction', in Hobsbawm, E. (Ed.), *Labour's Turning Point 1880–1900: Second Edition*, Hassocks: Harvester Press, 1974.

Hodkin, K. and Radstone, S. (Eds) *Contested Pasts: The Politics of Memory*, London: Routledge, 2003.

Hofer, J. 'Medical dissertation on nostalgia by Johannes Hofer, 1688', *Bulletin of the History of Medicine*, 2, 1934, 376–91.

Hofstadter, R. *The American Political Tradition and the Men Who Made It*, New York: Vintage Books, 1989.

Home, S. *The Assault on Culture: Utopian Currents from Lettrisme to Class War*, Stirling: AK Press, 1991.

Home, S. 'The perfection of suicide is in its ambiguity', *Transgressions: A Journal of Urban Exploration*, 1, 1994, 82.

Home, S. (Ed.) *Mind Invaders: A Reader in Psychic Warfare, Cultural Sabotage and Semiotic Terrorism*, London: Serpent's Tail, 1997.

Home, S. 'Introduction – Mondo Mythopoesis', in Home, S. (Ed.), *Mind Invaders: A Reader in Psychic Warfare, Cultural Sabotage and Semiotic Terrorism*, London: Serpent's Tail, 1997.

Home, S. *How I Discovered America: Infopool 6*. London: Infopool, 2002.

Hougan, J. *Decadence: Radical Nostalgia, Narcissism, and Decline in the Seventies*, New York: William Morrow and Company, 1975.

House of Commons. *An Act for the More Effectually Preventing Seditious Meetings and Assemblies*, 17 March, 1817.

Howland, E. 'Nostalgia', *Journal of Existential Psychiatry*, 3, 1962, 197–204.

Hugill, B. 'Cultists go round in circles', *The Observer*, 28 August, 1994.

Hutcheon, L. 'Irony, nostalgia and the postmodern', available at: library.utoronto.ca/utel/criticism/hutchinp.html, accessed 29.08.2005.

Huyssen, A. *Present Pasts: Urban Palimpsests and the Politics of Memory*, Stanford, CA: Stanford University Press, 2003.

Hyams, E. *A Dictionary of Modern Revolution*, London: Allan Lane, 1973.

Hyndman, H. *The Nationalization of the Land in 1775 and 1882: Being a Lecture Delivered at Newcastle-upon-Tyne by Thomas Spence, 1775*, London: E. W. Allen, 1882.

Hyndman, H. *The Historical Basis of Socialism in England*, London: Kegan Paul and Trench, 1883.

Inge, W. *Outspoken Essays: Second Series*, London: Longmans, Green and Company, 1927.

Ivy, M. *Discourses of the Vanishing: Modernity, Phantasm, Japan*, Chicago: University of Chicago Press, 1995.

Iwabuchi, K. 'Nostalgia for a (different) Asian modernity: media consumption of 'Asia' in Japan', *Positions: East Asia Cultures Critique*, 10, 3, 2002, 547–73.

Jackson, K. *The Verbals: Kevin Jackson in Conversation with Iain Sinclair*, Tonbridge: Worple Press, 2003.

Jacoby, M. *The Longing for Paradise*, Boston: Sigo Press, 1985.

Jameson, F. 'Third-World literature in the era of multinational capitalism', *Social Text*, 15, 1986, 65–88.

Jameson, F. *Postmodernism, or the Cultural Logic of Late Capitalism*, Durham, NC: Duke University Press, 1991.

Jay, M. 1982 'Anamnestic totalization: reflections on Marcuse's theory of remembrance', *Theory and Society*, 11, 1, 1982, 1–15.

Johnson, R. '"Really useful knowlegde": radical education and working-class culture', in Clarke, J., Critcher, C. and Johnson, R. (Eds), *Working-Class Culture: Studies in History and Theory*, London: Hutchinson, 1979.

Jones, E. *Notes to the People: Volume I*, London: J. Pavey, 1851.

Jorn, A. 'La fin de l'économie et la réalisation de l'art', *Internationale Situationniste*, 4, 1960, 19–22.

Jorn, A. 'La création ouverte et ses ennemis', *Internationale Situationniste*, 5, 1960, 29–50.

Jorn, A. *Open Creation and Its Enemies*, London: Unpopular Books, 1993.

Kaarsholm, P. 'Pro-Boers', in Samuel, R. (Ed.), *Patriotism: The Making and Unmaking of British National Identity: Volume I: History and Politics*, London: Routledge, 1989.

Kaufman, V. *Guy Debord: Revolution in the Service of Poetry*, Minneapolis: University of Minnesota Press, 2006.

Keiller, P. 'London', Koninck/Channel 4 (82 minutes), 1994.

Keiller, P. 'Robinson in space', BBC/Koninck (78 minutes), 1997.

Khatib, A. 'Essai de description psychogéographique des Halles', *Internationale Situationniste*, 2, 1958, 13–18.

Kidd, B. *Principles of Western Civilisation: Being the First Volume of a System of Evolutionary Philosophy*, London: Macmillan, 1902.

Kierman, B. *The Pol Pot Regime: Race, Power, and Genocide in Cambodia under the Khmer Rouge, 1975–79*, New Haven: Yale University Press, 1996.

Kinna, R. *William Morris: The Art of Socialism*, Cardiff: University of Wales Press, 2000.

Kirk, N. 'History, language, ideas and post-modernism: a materialist view', *Social History*, 19, 2, 1994, 221–40.

Klein, K. 'On the emergence of memory in historical discourse', *Representations*, 69, 2000, 127–50.

Knowles, S. 'Macrocosm-opolitanism? Gilroy, Appiah, and Bhabha: the unsettling generality of cosmopolitan ideas', *Postcolonial Text*, 3, 4, 2007, 1–11.

Knox, T. 'Thomas Spence: the trumpet of jubilee', *Past and Present*, 76, 1977, 75–98.

Kopytoff, I. 'Socialism and traditional African societies', in Frieland, W. and Rosberg, C. (Eds), *African Socialism*, Stanford, CA: Stanford University Press, 1964.

Kothari, U. 'Global peddlers and local networks: migrant cosmopolitanisms', *Society and Space*, 26, 2008, 500–16;

Kracauer, S. *Strassen in Berlin und anderswo*, Frankfurt am Main: Suhrkamp, 1964.

Kristol, I. 'Capitalism, Socialism, and Nihilism', in Kirk, R. (Ed.), *The Portable Conservative Reader*, Harmondsworth: Penguin, 1982.

Kubik, J. 'Historical memory and the end of communism', *Journal of Cold War Studies*, 9, 2, 2007, 127–33.

Kulski, W. 'Soviet colonialism and anti-colonialism', *Russian Review*, 18, 2, 1959, 113–25.

Kundera, M. *The Book of Laughter and Forgetting*, New York: Alfred A. Knopf, 1980.

Kunstler, J. *The Geography of Nowhere*, New York: Simon and Schuster, 1993.

Ladino, J. 'Rediscovering nostalgia: the significance of counter-nostalgia in American literature', paper presented to the Nostalgia and Cultural Memory English Graduate Conference, University of Victoria, 4–5 March 2005.

Ladino, J. 'Longing for wonderland: nostalgia for nature in post-frontier America', *Iowa Journal of Cultural Studies*, 5, 2005, 61–84.

Lasch, C. *The True and Only Heaven: Progress and Its Critics*, New York: W. W. Norton, 1991.

Latour, B. *We Have Never Been Modern*, Cambridge: Harvard University Press, 1993.

Lears, J. 'Looking backward: in defense of nostalgia', *Lingua Franca*, December 1997/January 1998.

Léauthier, A. 'Submission is advancing at a frightful speed', translated from *Libération* (3–4 February, 2001), available at: www.cddc.vt.edu/sionline/postsi/submission.html, accessed 22.04.2005.

Lecky, W. *The Rise and Influence of Rationalism in Europe*, London: Longmans, Green and Company, 1910.

Lefebvre, H. *Position : contre les technocrates*, Paris: Gonthier, 1967.

Legg, S. 'Memory and nostalgia', *Cultural Geographies*, 11, 2004, 99–107.

Legg, S. 'Contesting and surviving memory: space, nation and nostalgia in Les Lieux de Mémoire', *Environment and Planning D: Society and Space*, 23, 2005, 481–504.

Legg, S. 'Sites of counter-memory: the refusal to forget and the Nationalist Struggle in Colonial Delhi, *Historical Geography*, 33, 2005, 180–201.

Lenin, V. *Imperialism: The Highest Stage of Capitalism*, Chippendale: Resistance Books, 1999.

Lerner, L. *The Uses of Nostalgia: Studies in Pastoral Poetry*, London: Chatto and Windus, 1972.

Lettrist International. *Potlatch 1954–1957*, Paris: Editions Gérard Lebovici, 1985.

Logan, P. 'Nostalgia without nostalgia: review of Linda M. Austin, *Nostalgia in Transition: 1780–1917*', *Novel*, 42, 1, 2009, 141–4.

Lowenthal, D. *The Past is a Foreign Country*, Cambridge: Cambridge University Press, 1985.

Lowenthal, D. 'Nostalgia tells it like it wasn't', in Shaw, C. and Chase, M. (Eds), *The Imagined Past: History and Nostalgia*, Manchester: Manchester University Press, 1989.

Löwith, K. *Max Weber and Karl Marx*, London: Routledge, 1993.

Löwy, M. 'Consumed by night's fire: the dark romanticism of Guy Debord', *Radical Philosophy*, 87, 1998, 31–4.

Löwy, M. 'The revolutionary romanticism of May 1968', *Thesis Eleven*, 68, 2002, 95–100.

Löwy, M. and Sayre, R. *Romanticism against the Tide of Modernity*, Durham, NC: Duke University Press, 2001.

London Pyschogeographical Association. *The Great Conjunction: The Symbols of a College, the Death of a King and the Maze on the Hill*, London: Unpopular Books, 1992.

London Psychogeographical Association, 'Oxford triangulation by the night patrol', *London Psychogeographical Association Newsletter*, 2, 1993, 2.

London Psychogeographical Association, 'Cerne Abbas, MayDay 1993', *London Psychogeographical Association Newsletter*, 3, 1993, 3.

London Psychogeographical Association, 'Future trips of the LPA', *London Psychogeographical Association Newsletter*, 8, 1994, 4.

London Psychogeographical Association, 'Run up to ritual murder', *London Psychogeographical Association Newsletter*, 14, 1996, dated Beltaine 397, 1–4.

London Psychogeographical Association, 'Say no to the millennium', *London Psychogeographical Association Newsletter*, 18, 1997, dated Beltaine 398, 1, 4.

Lukács, G. *The Theory of the Novel*, London: Merlin Press, 1971.

Lukács, G. *The Historical Novel*, Lincoln: University of Nebraska Press, 1983.

Lyons, A. *Robert Blatchford: The Sketch of a Personality: An Estimate of Some Achievements*, London: Clarion Press, 1910.

MacCabe, C. 'Paul Gilroy: against the grain', available at: www.opendemocracy.net/globalization-Literature/gilroy_3465.jsp, accessed 20.09.2009.

MacCarthy, F. *William Morris: A Life for Our Time*, London: Faber and Faber, 1994.

McDonough, T. 'The derive and situationist Paris', in Andreotti, L. and Costa, X. (Eds), *Situacionistas: arte, politica, urbanismo/ situationists: art, politics, urbanism*, Barcelona: Museu d'Art Contemporani de Barcelona, 1996.

Macfarlane, R. 'A road of one's own: past and present artists of the randomly motivated walk', *Times Literary Supplement*, 7 October, 2005, 3–4.

MacFarquhar, R. and Schoenhals, M. *Mao's Last Revolution*, Cambridge: Harvard University Press, 2006.

Malthus, T. *Additions to the Fourth and Former Editions of an Essay on the Principle of Population*, London: John Murray, 1817.

Manchester Area Psychogeographic. 'From temple to fairy hill', *Manchester Area Psychogeographic*, 5, 1996, 4.

Manchester Area Psychogeographic. 'An interview with: Manchester Area Psychogeographic', available at: www.uncarved.org/turb/articles/map-int.html, accessed 09.08.2007.

Mandler, P. 'Against "Englishness": English culture and the limits to rural nostalgia, 1859–1940', *Transactions of the Royal Historical Society*, 6th series, 7, 1997, 157–8.

Marc, F. 'The "savages" of Germany', in Harrison, C. and Wood, P. (Eds), *Art in Theory 1900–1990: An Anthology of Changing Ideas*, Oxford: Blackwell, 1992.

Marcus, G. *Lipstick Traces: A Secret History of the Twentieth Century*, London: Secker & Warburg, 1989.

Marcuse, H. *Eros and Civilization*, London: Sphere, 1971.

Marcuse, H. *One-Dimensional Man*, London: Abacus, 1972.

Mariátegui, J. *The Heroic and Creative Meaning of Socialism*, Atlantic Highlands: Humanities Press, 1996.

Marris, P. *Loss and Change*, London: Routledge and Kegan Paul, 1974.

Martin, A. 'Nostalgia', *American Journal of Psychoanalysis*, 14, 1954, 99–100.

Marx, K. *Pre-Capitalist Economic Formations*, New York: International Publishers, 1965.

Marx, K. 'Letters from the Deutsch-Französische Jahrbücher', from *Collected Works of Karl Marx and Friedrich Engels*, Volume 3, New York: International Publishers, 1975.

Marx, K. 'Montesquieu LVI', from *Collected Works of Karl Marx and Friedrich Engels*, Volume 8, New York: International Publishers, 1975.

Marx, K. *Early Writings*, Harmondsworth, Penguin, 1975.

Marx, K. 'The Eighteenth Bumaire of Louis Bonaparte', in *Karl Marx: Surveys from Exile: Political Writings: Volume 2*, Harmondsworth: Penguin, 1992.

Marx, K. *Grundrisse: Foundations of the Critique of Political Economy*, Harmondsworth: Penguin, 1993.

Marx, K. and Engles, F. *Collected Works of Karl Marx and Friedrich Engels*, Volume 42, New York: International Publishers, 1975.

Massey, D. 'A global sense of place', in Barns, T. and Gregory, D. (Eds), *Reading Human Geography*, London: Arnold, 1997.

Massey, D. *World City*, Cambridge: Polity Press, 2006.

Mazlakh, S. and Shakhrai, V. *On the Current Situation in the Ukraine*, Ann Arbor: University of Michigan Press 1970.

Mboya, T. 'African socialism', in Frieland, W. and Rosberg, C. (Eds), *African Socialism*, Stanford, CA: Stanford University Press, 1964.

Meadows, Donella, Meadows, Dennis, Randers, J. and Behrens, W. *The Limits of Growth*, London: Pan Books, 1983.

Meier, P. *William Morris: The Marxist Dreamer*, Brighton: Harvester, 1978.

Melville, K. *Communes in the Counter Culture: Origins, Theories, Styles of Life*, New York: William Morrow and Company, 1972.

Mension, J-M. *The Tribe*, San Francisco: City Lights Books, 2001.

Mignolo, W. *Local Histories/Global Designs*, Princeton: Princeton University Press, 2000.

Mignolo, W. 'The many faces of cosmopolis: border thinking and critical cosmopolitanism', *Public Culture*, 12, 3, 2000, 721–48.

Miliband, R. 'Socialism and the myth of the golden past', *The Socialist Register*, 1964, 92–103.

Mill, J. 'The spirit of the age', *Examiner*, 9 January, 1831, 20–1.

Mill, J. *Socialism*, New York: John B. Alden, 1886.

Mitscherlich, A. and Mitscherlich, M. *The Inability to Mourn: Principles of Collective Behaviour*, New York: Grove Press, 1967.

Mitzman, A. *The Iron Cage: An Historical Interpretation of Max Weber*, New York: Knopf, 1970.

Modood, T. '"Black", racial equality and Asian identity', *New Community*, 14, 3, 1988, 397–404.

Monroe, A. *Interrogation Machine: Laibach and NSK*. Cambridge, MA: MIT Press, 2005.

Moorcock, M. *Mother London*. London: Secker & Warburg, 1988.

Moore, D. 'Is the post- in postcolonial the post- in post-Soviet? Toward a global postcolonial critique', *PMLA*, 116, 1, 2001, 111–28.

Morey, P. and Procter, J. 'Colonial discourse, postcolonial theory', *Year's Work in Critical and Cultural Theory*, 11, 1, 2003, 43–57.

Morris, B. *Ecology and Anarchism*, London: Images Publishing, 1996.

Morris, M. 'At Henry Parkes Motel', *Cultural Studies*, 2, 1988, 1–47.

Morris, W. *The Wood beyond the World*, London: Kelmscott Press, 1894.

Morris, W. *The Well at the World's End*, London: Kelmscott Press, 1896.

Morris, W. *The Water of the Wondrous Isles*, London: Kelmscott Press, 1897.

Morris, W. *The Pilgrims of Hope and Chants for Socialists*. London: Longmans, Green and Company, 1915.

Morris, W. *News from Nowhere; or, an Epoch of Rest* News from Nowhere, London: Routledge, 1972.

Morris, W. *Political Writings: Contributions to 'Justice' and 'Commonweal' 1883–1890*, Bristol: Thoemmes Press, 1994.

Mullard, C. *Race, Power and Resistance*, London: Routledge and Kegan Paul, 1985.

Muro, D. 'Nationalism and nostalgia: the case of radical Basque nationalism', *Nations and Nationalism*, 11, 4, 2005, 571–589.

Mutch, D. 'The *Merrie England* Triptych: Robert Blatchford, Edward Fay and the didactic use of Clarion fiction', *Victorian Periodicals Review*, 38, 1, 2005, 83–103.

Nada, M. 'We are all hybrids now: the dangerous epistemology of post-colonial populism', *Journal of Peasant Studies*, 28, 2, 2001, 162–86.

Nandy, A. *The Intimate Enemy: Loss and Recovery of Self under Colonialism*, Delhi: Oxford University Press, 1983.

Nandy, A. 'Modernity and the sense of loss', *Zeitschrift für Kulturaustausch*, 1, 2005, 40–2.

Naqvi, N. *The Nostalgic Subject. A Genealogy of the 'Critique of Nostalgia'*, Working Paper 23, (University of Messina: Centro Interuniversitario per le ricerche sulla Sociologia del Diritto e delle Istituzioni Giuridiche, undated), available at: www.cirsdig.it/Pubblicazioni/naqvi.pdf, accessed 09.09.2019.

Natali, M. 'History and politics of nostalgia', *Iowa Journal of Cultural Studies*, 5, 2005, available at: www.uiowa.edu/~ijcs/nostalgia/nostfe1.htm, accessed 07.09.2009.

Niezen, R. 'Postcolonialism and the utopian imagination', *Israel Affairs*, 13, 4, 2007, 714–29.

Ninjalicious. *Access All Areas: A User's Guide to the Art of Urban Exploration*, Toronto: Infiltration, 2005.

Noe, E. and Gannon, M. 'Younger voters are more conservative, but less likely to vote on election day', available at: www.siue.edu/ALESTLE/library/FALL2000/november2/yvoters.html, accessed 05.10.2009.

Nora, P. 'Between memory and history: Les Lieux de Mémoire', *Representations*, 26, 1989, 7–24.

Nordau, M. *Degeneration,* Lincoln: University of Nebraska Press, 1993.

North East Essex Psychogeographical Project. *Outer Space Wayz*, Brightlingsea: North East Essex Psychogeographical Project, undated.

Nottingham Psychogeographical Unit. 'An appeal to stop building altogether', *Nottingham Psychogeographical Unit Stories*, 3, 1998, 1–2.

Nottingham Psychogeographical Unit. 'Think of Nottingham: a mental mapping workshop', www.corinna.it/qui/npu/mental/think.htm, now available at: fasica.altervista.org/npu/mental/think.htm, accessed 29.09.2009.

Nyerere, J. *Ujamaa: Essays on Socialism*, Dar es Salaam: Oxford University Press, 1968.

Ollman, B. *Alienation: Marx's Conception of Man in Capitalist Society*, Cambridge: Cambridge University Press, 1971.

Orwell, G. *The Road to Wigan Pier*, London: London: Secker & Warburg, 1973.

Özyürek, E. *Nostalgia for the Modern: State Secularism and Everyday Politics in Turkey*, Durham, NC: Duke University Press, 2006.

Parssinen, T. 'Thomas Spence and the origins of English land nationalisation', *Journal of the History of Ideas*, 34, 1973, 135–41.

Pearson, R. *The Rise and Fall of the Soviet Empire,* London: Palgrave Macmillan, 1998.

Peking Review, 'Red Guards destroy the old and establish the new', *Peking Review*, 2 September, 1966, 17–19.

Penty, A. *Old Worlds for New: A Study of the Post-Industrial State*, London: George Allen and Unwin, 1917.

Pinder, D. ' "Old Paris is no more": geographies of spectacle and anti-spectacle', *Antipode*, 32, 4, 2000, 357–86.

Pinder, D. 'Utopian transfiguration: the other spaces of New Babylon', in Borden, I. and McCreery, S. (Eds), *New Babylonians*, London, Architectural Design, 2001.

Pinder, D. *Visions of the City: Utopianism, Power and Politics in Twentieth-Century Urbanism*, Edinburgh: Edinburgh University Press, 2005.

Pinder, D. 'Arts of urban exploration', *Cultural Geographies*, 12, 2005, 383–411.

Plant, S. *The Most Radical Gesture: The Situationist International in a Postmodern Age*, London: Routledge, 1992.

Plokhy, S. *Unmaking Imperial Russia: Mykhailo Hrushevsky and the Writing of Ukrainian history*, Toronto: University of Toronto Press, 2005.

Pollock, S., Bhabha, H., Breckenridge, C. and Chakrabarty, D. 'Cosmopolitanisms', *Public Culture*, 12, 3, 2000, 577–89.

Poor Man's Guardian, 19 November, 1831.

Proudhon, P. *What is Property?*, Whitefish: Kessinger Publishing, 2004.

Proust, M. *Swann's Way*, Newton Abbot: David and Charles, 2002.

Prym, D. 'The Clarion Clubs, rambling and the Holiday Associations in Britain since the 1890s', *Journal of Contemporary History*, 11, 2/3, 1976, 65–77.

Pye, D. *'Fellowship is Life': The National Clarion Cycling Club 1895–1995*, Halliwell: Clarion Publishing, 1995.

Račevskis, K. 'Toward a postcolonial perspective on the Baltic states', *Journal of Baltic Studies*, 33, 1, 2002, 37–56.

Radstone, S. and Hodkin, K. (Eds) *Regimes of Memory*, London: Routledge, 2003.

Raman, A. 'Teenagers react against "anything goes" society', *The Guardian*, Thursday, 11 March, 2004.

Ribemont-Dessaignes, G. 'History of Dada', in Motherwell, R. (Ed.), *The Dada Painters and Poets: An Anthology*, Cambridge: Harvard University Press, 1981.

Richards, S. 'Polemics on the Irish past: the "return to the source" in Irish literary revivals', *History Workshop Journal*, 31, 1, 1991, 120–35.

Riesel, R. *Remarques sur l'agriculture genetiquement modifiee et la degradation des especes*, Paris: Editions de l'Encyclopedie des nuisances, 1999.

Riesel, R. 'Biotechnology: public and private', available at: www.notbored.org/biotechnology.html, accessed 11.05.2005.

Ritivoi, A. *Yesterday's Self: Nostalgia and the Immigrant Identity*, New York: Rowman and Littlefield, 2002.

Robotham, D. 'Cosmopolitanism and planetary humanism: the strategic essentialism of Paul Gilroy', *The South Atlantic Quarterly*, 104, 3, 2005, 561–82.

Rosemont, F. 'Surrealists on whiteness from 1925 to the present', *Race Traitor*, 9, 1998, 5–18.

Rubenstein, R. *Home Matters: Longing and Belonging, Nostalgia and Mourning in Women's Fiction*, London: Palgrave, 2001.

Rumney, R. *The Consul*, San Francisco: City Lights Books, 2002.

Rushdie, S. *The Ground Beneath Her Feet*, London: Jonathan Cape, 1999.

Sadler, S. *The Situationist City*, Cambridge, MA: MIT Press, 1998.

Said, E. *Culture and Imperialism*, London: Chatto and Windus, 1993.

Samuel, R. 'Faith hope and struggle: the lost world of British communism, part one', *New Left Review*, 154, 1985, 3–53.

Samuel, R. 'Staying power: the lost world of British communism, part two', *New Left Review*, 156, 1986, 63–113.

Samuel, R. 'Class politics: the lost world of British communism, part three', *New Left Review*, 165, 1987, 52–91.

Samuel, R. 'Introduction: exciting to be English', in Samuel, R. (Ed.), *Patriotism: The Making and Unmaking of British National Identity: Volume I: History and Politics*, London: Routledge, 1989.

Samuel, R. *Theatres of Memory*, London: Verso, 1994.

San Juan, E. *Beyond Postcolonial Theory*, New York: St. Martin's Press, 1998.

Sayre, R. and Löwy, M. 'Figures of romantic anti-capitalism', *New German Critique*, 32, 1984, 42–92.

Scanlan, S. 'Introduction: nostalgia', *Iowa Journal of Cultural Studies*, 5, available at: www.uiowa.edu/~ijcs/nostalgia/nostfe1.htm, accessed 07.09.2009.

Scheffler, S. 'Conceptions of cosmopolitanism', *Utilitas*, 11, 3, 1999, 255–76.

Schlicke, P. 'Hazlitt, Horne, and the spirit of the age', *Studies in English Literature*, 45, 4, 2005, 829–51.

Schumacher, F. 'The problem of production', in Dodson, A. (Ed.), *The Green Reader*, London: Andre Deutsch, 1991.

Scott, S. *In Search of the Primitive: A Critique of Civilization*, New Brunswick: Transaction Books, 1974.

Scott, D. *Refashioning Futures: Criticism after Postcoloniality*, Princeton: Princeton University Press, 1999.

Scott, D. *Conscripts of Modernity: The Tragedy of Colonial Enlightenment*, Durham, NC: Duke University Press, 2004.

Seabrook, J. *City Close-Up*, London: Allen Lane, 1971.

Seabrook, J. *What Went Wrong? Working People and the Ideals of the Labour Movement?*, London: Victor Gollancz, 1978.

Seager A. and Balakrishnan, A. 'Young exiles embrace the Anglo model', *The Guardian*, Saturday, 8 April, 2006.

Segal, L. 'Lost worlds: political memoirs of the left in Britain', *Radical Philosophy*, 121, 2003, 6–23.

Segal, L. 'Lost worlds: political memoirs of the left (II)', *Radical Philosophy*, 123, 2004, 8–28.

Sennett, R. *The Fall of the Public Man*, New York: Alfred Knopf, 1977.

Shaw, B. 'Reason, nostalgia, and eschatology in the critical theory of Max Horkheimer', *The Journal of Politics*, 47, 1, 1985, 160–81.

Shaw, C. and Chase, M. 'The dimensions of nostalgia', in Shaw, C. and Chase, M. (Eds), *The Imagined Past: History and Nostalgia*, Manchester: Manchester University Press, 1989.

Shaw, C. and Chase, M. (Eds) *The Imagined Past: History and Nostalgia*, Manchester: Manchester University, 1989.

Shohat, E. 'Notes of the "post-colonial"', *Social Text*, 31/32, 1992, 99–113.

Silver, C. 'Socialism internalised: the last romances of William Morris', in Boos, F. and Silver, C. (Eds), *Socialism and the Literary Artistry of William Morris*, Columbia: University of Missouri Press, 1990.

Sinclair, I. *The Kodak Mantra Diaries*, London: Albion Village Press, 1971.

Sinclair, I. *Muscat's Würm*, London: Albion Village Press, 1972.

Sinclair, I. 'The house in the park: a pyschogeographical response', in Lingwood, J. (Ed.), *House: Rachel Whiteread*, London: Phaidon Press, 1995.

Sinclair, I. *Lud Heat and Suicide Bridge*, London: Vintage, 1995.

Sinclair, I. *Crash: David Cronenberg's Post-Mortem on J. G. Ballard's 'Trajectory of Fate'*, London: British Film Institute, 1999.

Sinclair, I. *London Orbital*, Illuminations Films, 2002.

Sinclair, I. *London Orbital*, London: Penguin, 2003.

Sinclair, I. *Lights Out for the Territory*, London: Penguin, 2003.

Sinclair, I. *Edge of the Orison: In the Traces of John Clare's 'Journey out of Essex'*, London: Penguin, 2005.

Sinclair, I. (Ed.) *London: City of Disappearances*, London: Penguin, 2006.

Sinclair, I. *Hackney, That Rose-Red Empire: A Confidential Report*, London: Penguin, 2009.

Situationist International. 'Les souvenirs au-dessous de tout', *Internationale Situationniste*, 2, 1958, 3–4.

Situationist International. 'Discussion sur un appel aux intellectuels et artistes revolutionnaires', *Internationale Situationniste*, 3, 1959, 22–4.

Situationist International. 'La frontiere situationniste', *Internationale Situationniste*, 5, 1960, 7–9.

Situationist International. 'Critique de l'urbanisme', *Internationale Situationniste*, 6, 1961, 5–11.

Situationist International. 'La technique de l'isolement', *Internationale Situationniste*, 9, 1964, 6.

Situationist International. 'L'élite et le retard', *Internationale Situationniste*, 12, 1969, 93–5.

Situationist International. 'On the poverty of student life', in Knabb, K. (Ed.), *Situationist International Anthology*, Berkeley: Bureau of Public Secrets, 1981.

Sivanandan, A. *Communities of Resistance: Writings on Black Struggles for Socialism*, London: Verso, 1990.

Slater, H. *Divided We Stand: An Outline of Scandinavian Situationism*, London: Infopool, 2001.

Smith, A. *The Ethnic Origins of Nations*, Oxford: Blackwell, 1986.

Smith, A. *Myths and Memories of the Nation*, Oxford: Oxford University Press, 1999.

Smith, K. 'Mere nostalgia: notes of a progressive paratheory', *Rhetoric and Public Affairs*, 3, 4, 2000, 505–27.

Smith, P. 'On the passage of a few people: situationist nostalgia', *Oxford Art Journal*, 14, 1, 1989, 118–25.

Solnit, R. *A Field Guide to Getting Lost*, Edinburgh: Canongate, 2006.

Sonn, R. *Anarchism and Cultural Politics in Fin-De-Siècle France*, Lincoln: University of Nebraska Press, 1989.

Spence, T. *Pigs' Meat: Selected Writings of Thomas Spence*, Nottingham: Spokesman, 1982.

Spencer, L. 'British working class fiction: the sense of loss and the potential for transformation', *Socialist Register*, 24, 1988, 366–86.

The Staff of the 'Clarion', *Contraptions*, London: Walter Scott, undated.

Stafford, W. *Socialism, Radicalism, and Nostalgia: Social Criticism in Britain, 1775–1830*, Cambridge: Cambridge University Press, 1987.

Stauth, G. and Turner, B. 'Nostalgia, postmodernism and the critique of mass culture', *Theory, Culture and Society*, 5, 1988, 509–26.

Steinberg, M. 'Culturally speaking: finding a commons between post-structuralism and the Thompsonian perspective', *Social History*, 21, 2, 1996, 193–214.

Steiner, T. 'Strategic nostalgia, Islam and cultural translation in Leila Aboulela's *The Translator* and *Coloured Lights*', *Current Writing*, 20, 2, 2008, available at: currentwriting.ukzn.ac.za/index.php/archive/10-volume-20-number-2/78-strategic-nostalgia-islam-and-cultural-translation-in-leila-aboulelas-the-translator-and-coloured-lights.html, accessed 30.09.2009.

Strangleman, T. 'The nostalgia of organisations and the organisation of nostalgia: past and present in the contemporary railway industry', *Sociology*, 33, 4, 1999, 725–46.

Tabar, L. 'Memory, agency, counter-narrative: testimonies from Jenin refugee camp', *Critical Arts*, 21, 1, 2007, 6–31.

Taguieff, P-A. *Les contre-réactionnaires: Le progressisme entre illusion et imposture*, Paris: Denoel, 2007.

Taguieff, P-A. 'L'immigrationnisme, ou la dernière utopie des bien-pensants', available at: www.communautarisme.net/L-immigrationnisme,-ou-la-derniere-utopie-des-bien-pensants_a754.html, accessed 28.07.2009.

Taylor, L. 'Low blows of a class warrior', *The Independent*, Friday, 16 July, 2004.

Terdiman, R. 'Deconstructing memory: on representing the past and theorizing culture in France since the Revolution', *Diacritics*, 15, 4, 1985, 13–36.

Thompson, A. 'Preface', in R. Blatchford, *My Eighty Years*, London: Cassell and Company, 1931.

Thompson, C. and Tambyah, S. 'Trying to be cosmopolitan', *Journal of Consumer Research*, 26, 1999, 214–41.

Thompson, E. P. *The Making of the English Working Class*, Harmondsworth: Penguin, 1968.

Thompson, E. P. *William Morris: Romantic to Revolutionary*, New York: Pantheon Books, 1976.

Thompson, E. P. *The Poverty of Theory and Other Essays*, London: Merlin, 1978.

Thompson, E. P. *Witness against the Beast: William Blake and the Moral Law*, Cambridge: Cambridge University Press, 1993.

Thompson, L. *Robert Blatchford: Portrait of an Englishman*, London: Victor Gollancz, 1951.

Thorsen, J., Nash, J. and Strid, H. *CO-RITUS Manifesto*, available at: www.infopool.org.uk/6105.html, accessed 12.09.2009.

Thrift, N. 'Performance and . . .', *Environment and Planning A*, 35, 2003, 2019–2024.

Thrift, N. 'Summoning life', in Cloke, P., Crang, P. and Goodwin, M. (Eds), *Envisioning Human Geography*, London: Arnold, 2004.

Tichelar, M. 'Socialists, Labour and the land: the response of the Labour Party to the Land Campaign of Lloyd George before the First World War', *Twentieth Century British History*, 8, 2, 1997, 127–44.

Till, K. 'Memory studies', *History Workshop Journal*, 62, 2006, 325–41.

Tjivikua, T. 'Fighting on', *Zeitschrift für Kulturaustausch*, 1, 2005, 22–3.

Tolia-Kelly, D. 'Investigations into diasporic "cosmopolitanism": beyond mythologies of the "non-native"', in Wyer, C. and Bressey, C. (Eds), *New Geographies of Race and Racism*, Aldershot: Ashgate, 2008.

Tompsett, F. 'Preface to the English edition', in Jorn, A. *Open Creation and Its Enemies with Originality and Magnitude (On the System of Isou)*, London: Unpopular Books, 1994.

Tompsett, F. 'East London: Portal to the land of unbelief', *Infotainment* 1, 1998, 2.

Tönnies, F. *Community and Association*, London: Routledge, 1955.

Toynbee, P. Interview with Polly Toynbee, available at: www.openleft.co.uk/2009/07/20/polly-toynbee/, accessed 20.09.2009.

Trotsky, L. 'Family relations under the Soviets: fourteen questions answered', *The Class Struggle*, June–July, 1934.

Tzara, T. 'Tristan Tzara: Lecture on Dada', in Motherwell, R. (Ed.), *The Dada Painters and Poets: An Anthology*, Cambridge: Harvard University Press, 1981.

Tzara, T. *Seven Dada Manifestos and Lampisteries*, London: Calder Press, 1992.

Vague, The West Eleven Days of My Life: English Psychogeography, Vague 24, undated.

Vague, Wild West 11: Grove Massive Psychogeography Report, Vague 28, undated.

Vague, Entrance to Hipp: An Historical and Psychogeographical Report on Notting Hill, Vague 29, 1997.

Vague, London Psychogeography: Rachman and Rillington Place, Vague 30, 1998.

Vaneigem, R. 'Commentaires contre l'urbanisme', *Internationale Situationniste*, 6, 1961, 33–7.

Vogel, E. 'From friendship to comradeship', *The China Quarterly*, 21, 1965, 46–60.

Volkan, V. 'Nostalgia as a linking phenomenon', *Journal of Applied Psychoanalytic Studies*, 1, 2, 1999, 169–79.

Wagner, T. *Longing: Narratives of Nostalgia in the British Novel, 1740–1890*, Lewsiburg: Bucknell University Press, 2004.

Walicki, A. *Marxism and the Leap to the Kingdom of Freedom: The Rise and Fall of the Communist Utopia*, Stanford, CA: Stanford University Press, 1997.

Wallis, B. (Ed.) *If You Lived Here: The City in Art, Theory and Social Activism*, Seattle: Bay Press, 1991.

Ward, P. *Red Flag and Union Jack: Englishness, Patriotism and the British, Left, 1881–1924*. Woodbridge: Boydell Press, 1998.

Weber, M. *From Max Weber: Essays in Sociology*, New York: Oxford University Press, 1946.

Weil, S. *L'Enracinement*, Paris: Editions Gallimard, 1949.

Weil, S. *The Need for Roots: Prelude to a Declaration of Duties towards Mankind*, London: Routledge, 2002.

Wenzel, J. 'Remembering the past's future: anti-imperialist nostalgia and some versions of the Third World', *Cultural Critique*, 62, 2006, 1–32.

Werbner, P. 'Global pathways: working class cosmopolitans and the creation of transnational ethnic worlds', *Social Anthropology*, 7, 1, 1999, 17–35.

Wheeler, W. 'Nostalgia isn't nasty: the postmodernising of parliamentary democracy', in Perryman, M. (Ed.), *Altered States: Postmodernism, Politics, Culture*, London: Lawrence & Wishart, 1994.

Widal, V. 'Nostalgie', *Dictionnaire Encyclopédie des Sciences Médicales*, Paris: G. Masson and P. Asselin, 1879.

Williams, R. *Culture and Society, 1790–1950*, Harmondsworth: Penguin, 1971.

Williams, R. *The Country and the City*, Oxford: Oxford University Press, 1975.

Wright, M. 'Robert Blatchford, the Clarion Movement and the crucial years of British socialism, 1891–1900', in Brown, T. (Ed.), *Edward Carpenter and Late Victorian Radicalism*, London: Frank Cass, 1990.

Wright, P. *On Living in an Old Country: The National Past in Contemporary Britain*, London: Verso, 1985.

Yekelchyk, S. *Stalin's Empire of Memory: Russian-Ukrainian Relations in the Soviet Historical Imagination*, Toronto: University of Toronto Press, 2004.

Yeo, S. 'A new life: the religion of socialism in Britain, 1883–1896', *History Workshop Journal*, 4, 1, 1977, 5–56.

Yew, L. *From Third World to First: The Singapore Story, 1965–2000*, New York: HarperCollins, 2000.

Young, J. 'A very English socialism and the Celtic fringe 1880–1991', *History Workshop Journal*, 35, 1993, 136–52.

Young, R. *Postcolonialism: An Historical Introduction*, Oxford: Blackwell, 2001.

Index